D0205858

Urban Fortunes

For Ashby Owens
and Jane Cryer

Historical Urban Studies

Series editors: Richard Rodger and Jean-Luc Pinol

Titles in this series include:

Capital Cities and their Hinterlands in Early Modern Europe
edited by Peter Clark and Bernard Lepetit

*Power, Profit and Urban Land: Landownership in Medieval and
Early Modern Northern European Towns*
edited by Finn-Einar Eliassen and Geir Atle Ersland

Advertising and the European City
edited by Clemens Wischermann and Elliot Shore

*Cathedrals of Urban Modernity:
The First Museums of Contemporary Art, 1800–1930*
J. Pedro Lorente

*Body and City: A Cultural History of
Urban Public Health*
edited by Helen Power and Sally Sheard

The Artisan and the European Town, 1500–1900
edited by Geoffrey Crossick

Urban Governance: Britain and Beyond since 1750
edited by R.J. Morris and R.H. Trainor

Urban Fortunes

Property and Inheritance in the Town, 1700–1900

edited by

Jon Stobart and
Alastair Owens

Ashgate

Aldershot • Burlington USA • Singapore • Sydney

Published by
Ashgate Publishing Limited
Gower House, Croft Road
Aldershot, Hampshire GU11 3HR
England

Ashgate Publishing Company
131 Main Street
Burlington VT 05401
USA

Ashgate website: http://www.ashgate.com

ISBN 0 7546 0081 5

British Library Cataloguing-in-Publication Data
Urban Fortunes: Property and Inheritance in the Town, 1700–1900.
 (Historical Urban Studies)
  1. Inheritance and succession—Social aspects—Great Britain. 2. Cities and towns—Great Britain—History—18th century. 3. Cities and towns—Great Britain—History—19th century. 4. Property—Great Britain—History—18th century. 5. Property—Great Britain—History—19th century.
  I. Stobart, John. II. Owens, Alastair.
  306.3'2'0941'09033

US Library of Congress-in-Publication Data
Urban Fortunes: Property and Inheritance in the Town, 1700–1900 / edited by Jon Stobart and Alastair Owens.
   p.   cm. — (Historical Urban Studies). Includes bibliographical references and index.
   1. Wealth—Great Britain—History. 2. Inheritance—Great Britain—History. 3. Property—Great Britain—History. I. Stobart, Jon, 1966–. II. Owens, Alastair, 1971–. III. Series.
   HC260.W4 U73 2000   00–030577
   305.5'234'0941–dc21   CIP

This volume is printed on acid-free paper.

Printed and bound by Athenaeum Press, Ltd.,
Gateshead, Tyne & Wear.

Contents

Historical Urban Studies
General Editors' Preface

Density and proximity of buildings and people are two of the defining characteristics of the urban dimension. It is these which identify a place as uniquely urban, though the threshold for such pressure points varies from place to place. What is considered an important cluster in one context – may not be considered as urban elsewhere. A third defining characteristic is functionality – the commercial or strategic position of a town or city which conveys an advantage. Over time, these functional advantages may diminish, or the balance of advantage may change within a hierarchy of towns. To understand how the relative importance of towns shifts over time and space is to grasp a set of relationships which is fundamental to the study of urban history.

Towns and cities are products of history, yet have themselves helped to shape history. As the proportion of urban dwellers has increased, so the urban dimension has proved a legitimate unit of analysis through which to understand the spectrum of human experience and to explore the cumulative memory of past generations. Though obscured by layers of economic, social and political change, the study of the urban milieu provides insights into the functioning of human relationships and, if urban historians themselves are not directly concerned with current policy studies, few contemporary concerns can be understood without reference to the historical development of towns and cities.

This longer historical perspective is essential to an understanding of social processes. Crime, housing conditions and property values, health and education, discrimination and deviance, and the formulation of regulations and social policies to deal with them were, and remain, amongst the perennial preoccupations of towns and cities – no historical period has a monopoly of these concerns. They recur in successive generations, albeit in varying mixtures and strengths; the details may differ but the central forces of class, power and authority in the city remain. If this was the case for different periods, so it was for different geographical entities and cultures. Both scientific knowledge and technical information were available across Europe and showed little respect for frontiers. Yet despite common concerns and

access to broadly similar knowledge, different solutions to urban problems
were proposed and adopted by towns and cities in different parts of Europe.
This comparative dimension informs urban historians as to which were
systematic factors and which were of a purely local nature: general and
particular forces can be distinguished.

These analytical frameworks, considered in a comparative context, inform
the books in this series.

Jean-Luc Pinol
Richard Rodger

Centre de Recherches Historique sur la ville, Strasbourg
University of Leicester

List of tables

List of figures and plates

Notes on contributors

Geoffrey Crossick is Professor of History and Pro-Vice-Chancellor (Academic) at the University of Essex. He has published widely on European social and urban history, most notably on the petite bourgeoisie. His books include *The Lower Middle Class in Britain 1870–1914* (ed., 1977); *Shopkeepers and Master Artisans in Nineteenth-Century Europe* (ed., with H.-G. Haupt, 1984); *The Petite Bourgeoisie in Europe 1780–1914: Enterprise, Family and Independence* (with H.-G. Haupt, 1995); *The Artisan and the Town in Europe since 1500* (ed., 1997). A recently written analysis of the organisation of space in modern Europe will appear in a new comparative social and economic history of Europe. He is currently writing a book on *London 1800–1939*.

David R. Green is a Senior Lecturer in Geography at King's College, London and editor of the *London Journal*. His research focuses on a diverse range of topics from poverty and the Poor Law to the London middle class. His publications include *From Artisans to Paupers: Economic Change and Poverty in London, 1790–1870* (1995). Current research focuses on welfare, inheritance and the metropolitan middle class.

Penelope Lane is a Research Associate at the Centre for Urban History, University of Leicester. Her research interests include women's work and wages; property and inheritance; and the formation of business and social networks. She is currently engaged on a Leverhulme Trust funded project 'Urban and Industrial Change in the Midlands, 1700–1840'.

Ann McCrum is a research student in the Department of Economic and Social History at the University of Edinburgh. She is in the final stages of completing a doctoral thesis entitled 'Property and provision: Scottish middle-class inheritance in the nineteenth century'. Other work includes a survey (with R. J. Morris) of computerised-aided analysis of probate documents.

Alastair Owens is an historical geographer whose research interests focus on the social relations of property in nineteenth-century Britain. He has recently completed a doctoral thesis entitled 'Small fortunes: property, inheritance and the middling sort in Stockport, 1800–1857'. Alastair lectures at the University of Luton.

W. D. Rubinstein is Professor of Modern History at the University of Wales, Aberystwyth. He has written widely on wealth holding and elites in modern British history and on other topics, including modern Jewish history. His works include *Men of Property: The Very Wealthy in Britain Since the Industrial Revolution* (1981) and *Capitalism, Culture, and Decline in Britain, 1750–1990* (1993).

Lorna Scammell (formerly Weatherill) has been a database adviser at the University of Newcastle upon Tyne since 1990. Her current interests include attempts to enable people to display research databases on-line on the Internet (see http://seastorm.ncl.ac.uk/). Her publications include *The Pottery Trade and North Staffordshire, 1660–1760*, (1971); *Consumer Behaviour and Material Culture in Britain, 1660–1760* (1988 and 1996); *Richard Latham's Account Book, 1725–1765* (ed., 1990).

Jon Stobart is a Senior Lecturer in Geography at Coventry University. His published work includes a number of studies of regional development in north-west England and the Midlands, and several articles on the changing structure of urban systems during the eighteenth century. Current research focuses on retail and leisure development in the eighteenth and nineteenth centuries, and commercial and social networks in eighteenth-century towns.

Preface

Property is central to historical analyses of production, reproduction and consumption. It lies at the heart of discussions of material culture, class relations and the household economy. In the last few years, however, interest in property has spread beyond the acquisition and possession of goods to examine what the disposal, transmission and gifting of property might tell us about changing society and culture. This collection of articles draws together research from a variety of disciplines and represents a wide range of approaches to and perspectives on the ownership, use and transmission of property in eighteenth- and nineteenth-century towns. They explore the changing meanings of property to households and individuals; the social, economic and geographical contexts of inheritance practices; the geography of wealth; the role of gender in shaping property relations and, perhaps above all, the enduring link between property, the family and the household in urban contexts.

The articles are substantially revised versions of papers first presented at a small colloquium at the Institute of Historical Research, London in January 1999. Discussion at the time and in subsequent correspondence has done much to shape individual chapters and the overall themes of the book. We would like thank our fellow contributors for their helpful comments and suggestions. Finally, we a very grateful to Caroline Cornish, Ruth Peters and, particularly, Cathrin Vaughan at Ashgate for their help in the final production of this book.

Jon Stobart, Coventry
Alastair Owens, Luton

Chapter 1

Introduction

Alastair Owens and Jon Stobart

According to James Penner, the idea of property is, at least in a legal context, undergoing something of a conceptual identity crisis. He claims that if property could talk and were lying on a psychiatrist's couch it would probably be telling the following rather sorry tale:

> Now I am not even my own idea. I am just a bundle of other concepts, a mere chimera of an entity. I am just a quivering, wavering, normative phantasm, without any home, without anything to call my own but an album full of fading and tattered images of vitality and consequence and meaning.[1]

Indeed, it is perhaps something of a paradox that just at the time when some writers are celebrating the 'triumph' of private property within a new world order, others are proclaiming a conceptual identity crisis.[2] We would argue that it is not just in a legal context that property has lost some of its vitality, consequence and meaning. As a category for historical explanation property has also been stripped of some of its former conceptual power. Within the field of social history, for example, the so-called 'linguistic turn' has prompted what some have termed the emergence of a 'post-materialist' history.[3] In evaluating the significance of property in understanding social life, such approaches consciously deny materialist claims about its causative powers. Furthermore, the polemics of scholarly debate have left property a tainted and uncertain idea, recognised at once as a key player in a former conceptual order yet ambiguously positioned in the brave new post-materialist intellectual world. Whilst we would not deny the significance of the complex myriad of 'non-material' sources of social power that constitute identity and experience, this study has been prompted by our belief that, within the field of urban history, property is being unduly neglected. We believe that the study of property still has much to tell us about the nature of urban places, and the individual and

---

[1]   Penner, J. E., *The Idea of Property in Law* (Oxford: Oxford University Press, 1997), p. 1.

[2]   Fukuyama, F., *The End of History and the Last Man* (New York: Free Press, 1992).

[3]   Steinberg, M. W., 'Culturally Speaking: Finding a Commons Between Post-Structuralism and the Thompsonian Perspective', *Social History* 21 (1996), pp. 193–214.

collective lives of urban dwellers in eighteenth- and nineteenth-century Britain. Indeed, we would argue that property needs to be recognised as a fundamental feature of urbanism both past and present.

Part of the reason why property is facing such a crisis stems from the breadth and variety of definitions attached to it and its interpretation within a bewildering number of different theoretical canons. The word 'property' can be called upon to describe just about anything, symbolic, material or theoretical, that is in some way possessed. Different conceptual definitions stress different notions of possession, yet within the dominant liberal western paradigm, property is usually considered as a thing over which an individual exercises exclusive rights.[4] That said, there are many other ways in which property has been conceived.[5] Property has been seen not only as a thing, a right or entitlement, it is also an obligation, a quality, a skill or a characteristic. It can be described as real or personal, fixed, invisible or circulating, public or private, individual or collective. Indeed, this list is almost without limit.

Whilst property can be considered from a variety of perspectives, this book is concerned with grounding our understanding of what it is, and what it does, in the context of the lives of those who owned it. To this end, it concentrates on specific processes associated with inheritance and property transmission. In this way, we see property as both materialistic (wealth and possessions) and symbolic (signalling and reinforcing values and identities). However, our broader concern is with what we might call the social relations of property and the ways in which property helped to reproduce socio-economic structures, especially family and household.[6] As a result, the book is as much concerned – perhaps more so – with the practices and processes connected with the ownership of property, as with the actual things that were possessed. By focusing on these practices and processes we would argue that it is possible to achieve a deeper understanding of both the material and symbolic importance of property within the lives of urban dwellers.

This collection of essays concentrates on property and inheritance in urban settings, mostly in Britain, during the eighteenth and nineteenth centuries. One of the most conspicuous social changes that accompanied the growing industrial and commercial development of Britain during this period was the significant increase in the number of people who owned private property. This

---

[4] Hann, C. M., 'Introduction: The Embeddedness of Property', in C. M. Hann (ed.) *Property Relations: Renewing the Anthropological Tradition* (Cambridge: Cambridge University Press, 1998), p. 6.

[5] See the essays in Macpherson, C. (ed.) *Property: Mainstream and Critical Positions* (Toronto: University of Toronto Press, 1978)

[6] For a more detailed consideration of social reproduction see the essays in Dickinson, J. and Russell, R. (eds) *Family, Economy and State: The Social Reproduction Process Under Capitalism* (London: Croom Helm, 1986).

accumulation of property was concentrated in towns and cities. Indeed, the physical fabric of these places – the streets, houses, workshops, mills, machinery and so on – formed much of that property. Moreover, urban places were also a focus for the acquisition, sale and exchange of material goods. Yet much of the work that has concentrated directly on the question of property ownership in this period has looked at rural contexts rather than urban ones.

Over the period covered by this book, two distinct paradigms have shaped the way in which the social relations of property have been considered by historians. The distinctiveness of each approach owes much to the conventional centennial periodisation of historical enquiry. Historians of the nineteenth century have primarily, though not exclusively, considered the social relations of property through the concept of class. The treatment of property is very much tied to the industrial transformations that were reshaping economies and societies throughout Western Europe. As a result, the social relations of property have become absorbed in narratives of class formation and class conflict which dominate the historiography of the 'age of industry'. Historians of the eighteenth century, on the other hand, have largely approached the study of property and its significance in understanding social relations and identities through the idea of consumption. This perspective frequently takes as its co-ordinates an historical narrative that stresses the growing consumerism of British society which is viewed as a prelude to the so-called 'industrial revolution'.[7] Our aim in this chapter is to survey the way in which these important historical narratives have both opened up and restricted discussions of property. We then turn to considering what the study of inheritance can offer us in trying to uncover the significance of property amongst urban communities of eighteenth- and nineteenth-century Britain.

Property and class

For the nineteenth century, the concept of class remains one of the most important ways in which the social relations of property have been explored by historians. Indeed, according to Patrick Joyce, 'class has become the unacknowledged leading player around which the drama of history ... is written'.[8] During the 1960s and 1970s these dramas focused particularly on the

---

[7] McKendrick, N., Brewer, J. and Plumb, J., *The Birth of a Consumer Society: The Commercialization of Eighteenth-Century England* (London: Hutchinson, 1982). See also critiques in Hudson, P., *The Industrial Revolution* (London: Edward Arnold, 1992), pp. 175–80; Thrift, N. and Glennie, P., 'Historical Geographies of Urban Life and Modern Consumption', in G. Kearns and C. Philo (eds), *Selling Places: The City as Cultural Capital, Past and Present* (Oxford: Pergamon Press, 1993), pp. 33–48.

[8] Joyce, P., *Democratic Subjects: The Self and the Social in Nineteenth-Century*

histories of the labouring classes and it is only comparatively recently that attention has turned to the middle and upper classes.[9] Nevertheless, property has been at the conceptual heart of most theories of class formation. Within the Marxist tradition, for example, the unequal ownership of property forms the main axis of differentiation between the working class and the bourgeoisie. More particularly, Marxists ground the concept of class within the relations of production, whereby the separation of the ownership of the means of production from labour power becomes the central motor of class formation. Indeed, it is the insistence of the primacy of these social relations of property that has proved to be Marxism's most controversial theoretical proposition. Weberian theories of class also put property at the centre of their conceptual apparatus. According to Weber '"property" and the "lack of property" ... are the basic categories of all class situations'. He also maintained that the ownership of different sorts of property 'differentiated the class situations of the propertied', distinguishing, for example, a class of rentiers from a class of entrepreneurs.[10] With varying degrees of consciousness and commitment, a wide range of historical studies of class in industrialising Britain have implicitly adopted these theoretical frameworks which emphasise the importance of property in constituting social relations.[11]

In spite of the central role property plays in theories of class formation, very few studies have actually given much explicit attention to the way in which property was implicated in the construction of classes and the relations within and between them. Frequently, property is reduced to a 'structural mechanism' and confined to a passive role in the formation of social relations. Only rarely have historians explored the meanings and social practices connected with property ownership and the way in which they shaped social relations.[12] Furthermore, as Michael Winstanley has recently observed, there has been surprisingly little empirical investigation of property ownership among the industrial communities where class divisions were supposedly most sharply

---

England (Cambridge: Cambridge University Press, 1994), p. 4.

[9] For the increasing academic interest in the middle classes see Rogers's short, but critical, introduction to a *Journal of British Studies* special edition on the middle class: Rogers, N., 'Introduction – Making the English Middle Class, ca. 1700–1850', *Journal of British Studies* 32 (1993), pp. 299–304. A more thorough survey can be found in Crossick, G., 'La bourgeoisie britannique au 19e siècle: recherches, approches, problematiques', *Annales. Histoire, Sciences Sociales*, 6 (1998), pp. 1089–130.

[10] Weber, M., 'Class, Status and Power', in H. Gerth and C. W. Mills (eds), *From Max Weber: Essays in Sociology* (London: Routledge, 1991), p. 182.

[11] See, for example, Thompson, E. P., *The Making of the English Working Class* (Harmondsworth: Penguin, 1963) and Morris, R. J., *Class, Sect and Party: The Making of the British Middle Class, Leeds, 1820–50* (Manchester: Manchester University Press, 1990).

[12] See, for example, Davidoff, L. and Hall, C., *Family Fortunes: Men and Women of the English Middle Class, 1780–1850* (London: Routledge, 1987), esp. pp. 197–315.

drawn.[13] Part of the reason for this might be that, until recently, historians have tended to concentrate on studying those social classes that did not possess much property rather than those that did. Thus, ten years ago, the Marxist social historian Theodore Koditscheck was able to observe that 'in contrast to the veritable cottage industry which has developed around the making of the English working class, contemporary scholarship has ... produced virtually nothing on the class formation of the bourgeoisie'.[14]

Yet, whilst there has been an outpouring of studies of the English 'middle class' in the eighteenth and nineteenth centuries, the last ten years has also witnessed a profound rethinking of the nature of class history.[15] This rethinking echoes a wider loss of confidence in some of the traditional theoretical tools of social history. Prominent in the resulting conceptual clearout has been the rejection of certain theoretical narratives of class formation. Whilst some historians have preferred a wholesale abandonment of class, identifying broader historical projects like studying the history of 'the social', others have attempted to rework its definitions and de-centre its role as a category for historical explanation.[16] All this has had important implications for the study of the social relations of property. One effect is that the social significance of property has been marginalised. Property's passive, yet fundamental, implication in materialist conceptions of class formation seems to have deflected some historians from continuing to consider it. The result has been that the emphasis of more recent theoretically informed studies of class (and other forms of collective social identity) has been on cultural and political discourses rather than social and economic relationships.[17] Consequently,

---

[13] Winstanley, M., 'Owners and Occupiers: Property, Politics and Middle-Class Formation in Early Industrial Lancashire', in A. Kidd and D. Nicholls (eds), *The Making of the Middle Class? Studies in Regional and Cultural Diversity Since the Eighteenth Century* (Stroud: Alan Sutton, 1998), p. 93.

[14] Koditscheck, T., *Class Formation and Urban Industrial Society: Bradford, 1750–1850* (Cambridge: Cambridge University Press, 1990) p. 30.

[15] See, inter alia, Davidoff and Hall, *Family Fortunes*; Kidd and Nicholls, *The Making of the Middle Class*; Morris, R. J., *Class, Sect and Party*; Wahrman, D., *Imagining the Middle Class: The Political Representation of Class in England, 1780–1840* (Cambridge: Cambridge University Press, 1995).

[16] Patrick Joyce has perhaps been the most vocal critic of certain theoretical understandings of class. See Joyce, P., *Visions of the People: Industrial England and the Question of Class, 1848–1914* (Cambridge: Cambridge University Press, 1991); Joyce, *Democratic Subjects*; Joyce, P., 'The End of Social History?', *Social History* 20 (1995), pp. 73–92. The 'rise' and 'fall' of class is mapped out more generally in Joyce, P., *Class: A Reader* (Oxford, Oxford University Press, 1995). Defences and modest reformulations of the concept of class can be found in Kirk, N., (ed..) *Social Class and Marxism: Defences and Challenges* (Aldershot: Scolar Press, 1996).

[17] For a discussion of this theme in relation to the 'middle class' see Kidd, A. and Nicholls, D., 'Introduction: The Making of the British Middle Class', in Kidd and Nichols *The*

property has been sidelined as a concept worthy of theoretical reflection and empirical study. Yet to forget about property would seem unwise. Not only does its neglect result in an obscuring of the economic bases to social identity, it also sustains the false assumption that economic processes are somehow separate from political and cultural ones. Property itself is not beyond the kind of critical deconstruction that social historians of class have applied to political texts or literary representations. Simon Gunn, in a critique of empirical studies of wealth holding, has recently argued that, within nineteenth-century society, 'wealth itself was not a simple category invariant in its form or social meanings'. He urges scholars to examine 'questions about how wealth was discursively constructed and represented in middle-class culture'.[18] Similar issues are explored by some of the contributors to this book. In chapter 3 for example, Geoffrey Crossick traces some of the shifting meanings of property among the petite bourgeoisie of European towns.

However, we would argue that there are other questions relating to the ownership of property, beyond the meanings attached to wealth, that are posed by the concept of class and its critical deconstruction. Various essays in this book examine the way in which property transmission activities helped to create, nurture and recreate collective social relations. In our own chapters, for example, we explore how the processes of will making and estate disposal drew upon networks of professionals, friends and kin both within and between towns. Elsewhere, contributions by Penelope Lane and David R. Green examine the way in which property transmission was an arena within which gender identities and experiences were shaped – a theme that has recently been integrated into historical studies of class formation.[19] This collection of essays is, therefore, prompted in part by the restricted theorisation and often superficial treatment of property within studies of class formation, and also by the lack of consideration given to property by more recent critiques of class.

Property and consumption

Class-based perspectives on property frequently emphasise production and especially relationships to the means of production; but our social identities, social interaction, and economic, social and psychological attitudes towards material goods are also structured by consumption. Indeed, some of the most interesting and innovative research on property in recent years has stemmed from historical studies of consumption. Class and consumption are not, of

---

Making of the British Middle Class, pp. xv–xxiii. See also Steinberg, 'Culturally Speaking'.

[18] Gunn, S., 'The Manchester Middle Class 1850–80', unpublished University of Manchester PhD thesis (1992), pp. 144 and 160.

[19] See, for example, Davidoff and Hall, *Family Fortunes*.

course, mutually exclusive analytical categories, and the two are frequently combined in studies of the social relations of property. Within certain neo-Weberian theories of class formation, for example, consumption plays an important conceptual role.[20] Indeed, Weber's insistence on the importance of different kinds of property in determining an individual's 'class situation' has been important in stimulating scholars to explore some of the ways in which the acquisition and ownership of certain kinds of property moulded individual and collective social identities. Whilst not all historians have adopted a Weberian theoretical perspective, there has been a prolific outpouring of historical studies of consumption in recent years. Although often focusing on the early modern period, much of this work offers a more tangible insight to the way in which property shaped social relations and identities. For this reason we will explore in greater detail some of the key themes of consumption studies which have a direct bearing upon what is discussed in later chapters.

In the late twentieth century it is a commonplace that people relate to each other and shape their own identities through the buying and selling, and the owning and displaying of goods, as much as, and probably more than, through their manufacture. At their heart, historical studies of consumption are concerned with the availability, acquisition and use of a growing number and range of goods. Property ownership, in this context, is often seen as a signifier of growing consumerism and emerging material culture. Yet the range of property considered within consumption studies is frequently rather narrow. In contrast to the broad conceptions of property as 'capital' or 'productive instruments' favoured by materialist theories of class, consumption studies tend to focus on property in the form of very specific, personal and historically durable possessions. That said, recent studies of consumption have sought to emphasise the deep-seated nature of many of the social, cultural and economic practices and meanings attached to property and consumption.[21] Nevertheless, this core interest is often lost amongst the mélange of theorising that has grown around consumption. Economics, anthropology, psychology, sociology, history and geography (amongst others) all have their own theories, models and explanations of consumption. But these not only fail to talk to each other, they all too frequently lose sight of the materiality of consumption: the money and goods which form its essence.[22]

---

[20] See, for example, Savage, M., Barlow, J., Dickens, P., and Fielding, T., *Property, Bureaucracy and Culture: Middle Class Formation in Contemporary Britain* (London: Routledge, 1992), ch. 6.

[21] For a useful summary of these arguments, see Thrift and Glennie, 'Urban Life and Modern Consumption'.

[22] Fine, B. and Leopold, E. *The World of Consumption* (London: Routledge, 1993), pp. 3–8. For further discussion, see Glennie, P. and Thrift, N. 'Modern Consumption: Theorising Commodities and Consumers', *Environment and Planning D* 11 (1993), pp. 603–6; Miller, D.

Some studies of consumption do cover a broader area than just material property. They incorporate literary and intellectual property, for instance, as well as product-marketing and advertising, the spaces of consumption and its relationship with production systems.[23] However, most historical theories of consumption revolve around attempts to define, identify and explain the emergence of a consumer society.[24] In an influential study, McKendrick emphasised the emulative nature of consumption, but, more recently, such explanations have been seen as too mechanistic and often at variance with the historical record.[25] In their place, two sets of ideas have been formulated. In the first, the growing importance of novelty in society and in the consumption of goods is linked to notions of sociability and exclusion. Material property was an important source of social identity, providing cultural orientation to new and established social groupings. Property and consumption could be used to display status or selfhood to others, or to shape and confirm image and identity to one's self.[26] As such, it was linked to the new sensibilities of polite and refined society.[27] Much has been made of the importance of appearance, speech

'Consumption as the Vanguard of History', in *idem* (ed.), *Acknowledging Consumption: A Review of New Studies* (London: Routledge, 1995), pp. 1–40; Bocock, R. *Consumption* (London: Routledge, 1993), pp. 1–9.

[23] See Brewer, J. and Porter, R. (eds), *Consumption and the World of Goods* (London: Routledge, 1993); Brewer, J. and Staves, S. (eds), *Early Modern Conceptions of Property* (London: Routledge, 1995); Fine and Leopold, *The World of Consumption*; McCracken, G., *Culture and Consumption: New Approaches to the Symbolic Character of Consumer Goods and Activities* (Bloomington: Indiana University Press, 1988); Glennie, P. and Thrift, N., 'Consumers, Identities, and Consumption Spaces in Early-Modern England', *Environment and Planning A* 28 (1996), pp. 25–45; Crossick, G. and Jaumain, S. (eds), *Cathedrals of Consumption: The European Department Store, 1850–1939* (Aldershot: Ashgate, 1999).

[24] For useful summaries, see: McCracken, *Culture and Consumption*, pp. 3–30; Glennie, P., 'Consumption within Historical Studies', in Miller *Acknowledging Consumption*, pp. 164–203; Thrift and Glennie, 'Urban Life and Modern Consumption', pp. 34–9.

[25] McCracken, *Culture and Consumption*, p. 6; Hudson, *The Industrial Revolution*, pp. 175–180; Campbell, C., 'Understanding Traditional and Modern Patterns of Consumption in Eighteenth-Century England: A Character-Action Approach', in Brewer and Porter, *Consumption and the World of Goods*, pp. 40–57; Glennie, 'Consumption within Historical Studies', pp. 178–181; Hunt, M., *The Middling Sort: Commerce, Gender and the Family in England, 1680–1780* (Berkeley: University of California Press, 1996), ch. 1; Williams, R., *Dream Worlds: Mass Consumption in Late Nineteenth-Century France* (Berkeley: University of California Press, 1982).

[26] See Campbell, C., *The Romantic Ethic and the Spirit of Modern Consumption* (Oxford: Blackwell, 1987); Earle, P., *The Making of the English Middle Class: Business, Society and Family Life in London, 1660–1730* (London: Methuen, 1989); Campbell, 'Traditional and modern patterns of consumption'.

[27] These issues are discussed in rather different contexts by: Barker-Benfield, G., *The Culture of Sensibility: Sex and Society in Eighteenth-Century England* (Chicago: Chicago University Press, 1992); Borsay, P., *The English Urban Renaissance: Culture and Society in the Provincial Town, 1660–1770* (Oxford: Clarendon, 1989), pp. 267–83; Bushman, R., *The*

and deportment in eighteenth-century polite society, but property – in terms of both material goods and the wherewithal to acquire them – was vital in distinguishing the middling sorts from their poorer neighbours, and in keeping them from the material and social hardships which they endured.[28] In chapter 3 of this volume, Geoffrey Crossick discusses the importance of property to the nineteenth-century petite bourgeoisie, but many of their concerns about ownership, financial security and social status had been equally felt by their predecessors in the eighteenth century. Peter Borsay, for example, has argued that the goal of preserving exclusivity in the early modern period was pursued through, *inter alia*, architecture, leisure practices and consumption.[29]

Novelty played an important role in this process of social differentiation and cultural orientation. Glen McCracken suggests that, from Elizabethan times, social status was to be found less in the goods which a family accumulated over the generations – the 'patina system' – and more in the consumption of new and fashionable items.[30] Through the seventeenth and eighteenth centuries, consumer goods were seen less as articles of saving and more as items to be used and enjoyed. This was a response both to novelty and fashion, and also to the increased availability of alternative investments, such as government stocks, turnpike and navigation shares.[31] 'Novel goods by virtue of their unfamiliarity offered consumers a lot of interpretative scope' – they could and were used to mould new identities for individuals and groups.[32] At least from the late seventeenth century, the constant demand for new or unfamiliar goods did much to impel fashion changes and encourage a more general growth in consumption.[33] Novelty thus provided a powerful incentive to consume, and novel goods formed important and fundamental 'co-ordinates of meaning'

Refinement of America: People, Houses, Cities (New York: Knopf, 1992).

[28] Barker-Benfield, *Culture of Sensibility*; Earle, *Making of the English Middle Class*; Borsay, *English Urban Renaissance*, pp. 225–41.

[29] Borsay, *English Urban Renaissance*, pp. 284–308. See also Thrift and Glennie, 'Historical Geographies of Urban Life and Modern Consumption, pp. 36–9; Corfield, P., 'Walking the City Streets: Social Role and Social Identification in the Towns of Eighteenth-Century England', *Journal of Urban History* 16 (1990), pp. 132–74.

[30] McCracken, *Culture and Consumption*, esp. ch. 2. This links to Lorna Scammell's discussion, in chapter 2, of 'novel' consumer items in the late seventeenth and early eighteenth centuries, and Geoffrey Crossick's analysis of the investment strategies of the nineteenth-century petite bourgeoisie.

[31] Shammas, C. *The Pre-industrial Consumer in England and America* (Oxford: Clarendon Press, 1990), p. 187.

[32] Glennie, 'Consumption within Historical Studies', p. 180.

[33] Kusamitsu, T. 'Novelty, Give us Novelty: London Agents and Northern Manufacturers', in M. Berg (ed.), *Markets and Manufacturers in Early Industrial Europe* (London: Routledge, 1991), pp. 114–37; Styles, J., 'Manufacture, Consumption and Design in Eighteenth-Century England, in Brewer and Porter, *Consumption and the World of Goods*, pp. 527–54.

which substantiated new cultural categories established during the early modern period.[34]

Whilst this approach looks at changes in society as a whole and views consumption and property ownership in terms of broadly conceived social and cultural transformations, the second set of ideas focuses on individual households, and their ability and willingness to engage with the market. In doing so, it not only takes us to the scale at which decisions about property acquisition, ownership and disposal were actually made, but also reintroduces an important economic dimension to the discussion. According to Jan de Vries, consumer demand grew because of reallocations of the productive resources of households. A series of household-level decisions altered both the supply of marketed goods and labour and the demand for market-bought products. This complex of changes in household behaviour constitutes an 'industrious revolution'.[35] As consumer industries penetrated hitherto underused labour in both town and country (much of it female), cash wages were dispensed amongst a growing number of households. In turn, these wages were used to substitute home-produced goods with novel, fashionable or otherwise desirable market-goods. Thus, whilst real wages might remain steady, consumption could still rise as ever more households were able and willing to orientate themselves towards the market.

The household and its ownership of property has also formed the focus of considerable anthropological interest in consumption. Such studies seek to gain understanding of the motivations to consume; the ways in which households use and value material goods, and the ways in which goods acquire, carry and communicate meaning.[36] Much attention has focused on establishing the (changing) consumption patterns of households in the early modern period especially. In the past, the main concern has been to trace and explain the appearance of novel or luxury items such as bed-linen and pewterware in the sixteenth century, or earthenware and clocks in the late seventeenth and

---

[34] McCracken, *Culture and Consumption*, pp. 73–4.

[35] De Vries, J., 'Between Purchasing Power and the World of Goods: Understanding the Household Economy in Early Modern Europe', in Brewer and Porter, *Consumption and the World of Goods*, p. 113. For a fuller outline of the concept of the 'industrious revolution' see De Vries, J., 'The Industrial Revolution and the Industrious Revolution', *Journal of Economic History*, 54 (1994), pp. 249–71.

[36] The classic study is Douglas, M. and Isherwood, B., *The World of Goods: Towards an Anthropology of Consumption*, second edition (London: Routledge, 1996). See also Weatherill, L., *Consumer Behaviour and Material Culture in Britain 1660–1760* (London: Routledge, 1988); Shammas, *The Pre-industrial Consumer*; Weatherill, L., 'The Meaning of Consumer Behaviour in Late Seventeenth- and Early Eighteenth-Century England', in Brewer and Porter, *Consumption and the World of Goods*, pp. 206–27; Nenadic, S., 'Middle-Rank Consumers and Domestic Culture in Edinburgh and Glasgow 1720–1840', *Past and Present* 145 (1994), pp. 122–56.

eighteenth centuries. Quantitative analyses have attempted to gauge the relative importance of wealth, household size, urbanism, education and other factors in determining ownership patterns. What is often forgotten, though, is the importance of a good's value (be it emotional, social or economic) and its use within the household and its daily routines. In response to this omission, chapter 2 by Lorna Scammell attempts to examine how changing household rituals and standards around the turn of the eighteenth century were affected by, and reflected in, their possession of novel goods. In chapter 3, meanwhile, Geoffrey Crossick assesses the economic and symbolic significance of property to the nineteenth-century petite bourgeoisie of Britain and France.

  The new consumption practices which emerged during the long eighteenth century were closely linked to towns and especially to the new urban settings of Borsay's urban renaissance. At the household level, the growing scale of urban development and closeness of urban living, coupled with the emergence of notions of private space, encouraged an inward focus to urban life. The home became not just (or not even) a place of work and rest, but also one of entertainment. At the same time, it formed an important escape from the public gaze, creating important distinctions between 'front' and 'back' rooms and activities.[37] Accordingly, the decoration, furnishing and ornamentation of the home became an important aspect of the houses of the urban middle ranks. Studies by Lorna Weatherill and Carole Shammas have suggested that urban residence played an increasingly important part in determining ownership of novel goods. Whilst wealth was the most significant factor, urban residents of the eighteenth century were much more likely to own a range of personal consumer goods and household items (including mirrors, pictures and china) than their country cousins.[38] In part, this reflected the accessibility of such items in towns, but, as Lorna Scammell shows in chapter 2, it was also linked to changing behaviour within urban households, especially with regard to meal-taking. As well as being more modern in their consumption patterns, urban households also tended to own greater quantities of such items. As David Green suggests in chapter 9, material property frequently formed the largest proportion of an estate, making its disposal of considerable financial as well as emotional significance.

The growing ability and willingness to consume market goods had a strong gender dimension. Much of the labour drawn into commercial production through the industrious revolution was female, whilst market-oriented

---

[37] This draws on ideas in Goffman, E., *The Presentation of Self in Everyday Life* (Harmondsworth: Penguin, 1969). See also, Weatherill, *Consumer Behaviour and Material Culture*, pp. 137–65; Weatherill, L., 'Consumer Behaviour and Social Status in England 1660–1750, *Continuity and Change* 1 (1986), pp. 191–209.

[38] Shammas, *The Pre-industrial Consumer*, pp. 173–81; Weatherill, *Consumer Behaviour and Material Culture*, pp. 71–90.

consumption frequently involved a reduction of home- and often female-produced goods and their replacement by commercially supplied goods.[39] In other words, women were increasingly buying-in household and personal goods which they had previously produced themselves. This put them in a strategic position in terms of household consumption of material goods. Women – and especially middle-class women – as consumers have received considerable attention in the last few years, both in terms of their seventeenth- and eighteenth-century role within the household and, more specifically, their relationship with late nineteenth-century department stores.[40] So, too, has the position of middle-class women as the home-makers of Victorian Britain, increasingly concerned with family and household as their opportunities in the wider world of work became ever more circumscribed.[41] However, as consumers and especially as controllers of household property, women are too often portrayed as merely responsive to wider economic, social or cultural forces: they are robbed of their independence of thought and action. As Penelope Lane and David Green demonstrate in chapters 8 and 9 respectively, middle-class women were often very actively involved in business and investment. They generated income for their households as well as spending it. Moreover, they did not always have to wait until their husbands were dead (or avoid having one in the first place) to become active in the management of both household and business property. This positive picture of women's control over their own and their household's property forms a useful counter-balance to the image given by Davidoff and Hall of women as marginalised from property and from decisions regarding the inter-generational transfer of that property.[42] Whilst many were relatively powerless in the face of men's property rights, the analyses offered by Ann McCrum, David Green and Penelope Lane show that, if and when they were able to make such decisions, they frequently adopted considerably different bequesting strategies.

---

[39] De Vries, 'Purchasing Power and the World of Goods', p. 119.

[40] See, for example, Weatherill, L., 'A Possession of One's Own: Women and Consumer Behaviour 1660–1740', *Journal of British Studies* 25 (1986), pp. 132–56; Leach, W., 'Transformations in a Culture of Consumption: Women and Department Stores, 1890–1925', *Journal of American History* 71 (1984), pp. 319–42; Walkowitz, J., *City of Dreadful Delight* (London: Virago Press, 1992); de Grazia, V. and Furlough, E. (eds), *The Sex of Things. Gender and Consumption in Historical Perspective* (Berkeley: University of California Press, 1996); Rappaport, E., *Shopping for Pleasure: Gender, Commerce and Public Life in London's West End, 1860–1914* (Princeton: Princeton University Press, 1999).

[41] For a good summary of these arguments, see Williams, P., 'Constituting Class and Gender: A Social History of the Home, 1700–1901', in N. Thrift and P. Williams (eds), *Class and Space: The Making of Urban Society* (London: Routledge and Keegan Paul, 1987), pp. 166–76.

[42] Davidoff and Hall, *Family Fortunes*.

As this brief survey has demonstrated, in understanding the social relations of property, the study of consumption has arguably provided a more fertile perspective than that of class. However, the consumption paradigm is not without its limits.[43] Firstly, as we suggested earlier, the emphasis frequently put on theoretical matters means that scholars often lose sight of the way in which the acquisition and use of goods was grounded in the everyday lives of property owners. Whilst this interest in theory may be seen as a reaction to the very empirical nature of early studies of consumption, the need for a reintegration of these two approaches is pressing. A further limiting feature of the consumption paradigm is its preoccupation with novelty. Such a focus directs attention towards unusual and luxury items, and the conspicuous nature of consumption. This runs the risk of trivialising consumption by suggesting that relationships between ownership and social identity rested upon an almost crass form of materialism. Whilst the acquisition of novel goods was clearly important amongst households and individuals keen to identify themselves with particular social and cultural trends, the rather more mundane consumption patterns of everyday life – the acquisition and use of those goods that were essential for material survival – are all too often hidden from our view. Likewise, those larger items of property that formed the very fabric of towns and cities – factories, workshops, mills, houses, farms and estates – feature in consumption studies only as contexts for property acquisition and ownership rather than as property in their own right. The novelty approach also tends to overemphasise the individualistic nature of consumption. Again, the focus on the way in which people defined themselves through the use of specific goods obscures the ways in which consumption was a collective social project linking individuals and households to the complex social relations of urban communities. Finally, such a perspective overlooks the importance of inheritance as a means of obtaining both specific material goods and the financial wherewithal to acquire other such items.

Ultimately, however, this is not a book about consumption or class, even if our contributors draw upon some of the insights and findings that have been generated from such studies. Rather, it focuses on the social relations of urban property through the lens of inheritance. It is our belief that the study of inheritance, and property transmission more broadly, can provide fresh insights to the significance of property in urban settings, overcoming some of the problems associated with class- and consumption-based studies. At the same time, as the various contributions reveal, the study of inheritance poses fresh questions which are central to analyses of class and consumption. We are not, therefore, claiming that the study of inheritance could or should replace class and consumption perspectives. Instead, we wish to demonstrate how it can

---

[43] For a general critique, see Hudson, *The Industrial Revolution*, pp. 175–80.

enrich our understanding of the social relations of property. It is to this issue that we now turn, in order to consider how inheritance can help provide and understanding of the social and economic importance of property in eighteenth- and nineteenth-century towns and cities.

Inheritance and the social relations of property

The attraction of inheritance stems from the unique and tangible insight that it provides into the social relations of private property within urban capitalist societies like that of eighteenth- and nineteenth-century Britain. It offers a window onto the mechanisms of social and economic reproduction. As Jeffrey Longhofer has remarked, inheritance is a process that 'reproduces or contradicts the economic, political and social relations of specific social formations'.[44] At one level, it reveals the intimate social relationships between property owners and their family, kin and friends. At the same time, an aggregate view of property transmission also reveals the importance of inheritance in 'sustaining and entrenching material inequalities in society'.[45] Inheritance is thus a process which provides a glimpse of the material goods that people possessed, whilst simultaneously disclosing something of the significance of these possessions to their owners and kin. As a result, it links closely with studies of consumption.

In short, inheritance provides detailed evidence of the ways in which some of the most important social and economic features of property-owning societies – the family, inequality, social class and private property – have been sustained. Not surprisingly, perhaps, a recent study of property transmission in contemporary Britain has claimed that 'in a society based upon the ownership of private property ... it is difficult to overestimate the importance of in-heritance'.[46] At a more pragmatic level, inheritance is also an unusually well-documented process in the life course of property owners and part of its attraction to researchers undoubtedly lies in this documentary accessibility. That said, the value of inheritance to researchers in understanding these issues does, in part, hinge upon the legal constraints that testators faced when disposing of their property under different political regimes. In many countries, particularly those whose legal systems were based on the Roman tradition (including Scotland, and many continental European countries and their

---

[44] Longhofer, J., 'Toward a Political Economy of Inheritance: Community and Household among the Mennonites', *Theory and Society* 22 (1993), p. 340.

[45] Hamnett, C., Harmer, M. and Williams, P., *Safe as Houses: Housing Inheritance in Britain* (London: Paul Chapman Publishing, 1991), p. 76.

[46] Finch, J., Mason, J., Masson, J., Wallis, L., and Hayes, L., *Wills, Inheritance and Families* (Oxford: Clarendon Press, 1996), p. 3.

colonies), testamentary freedom was restricted so that property owners could not transmit their entire estate to a single heir at the expense of other family members. France is perhaps the best documented case. There, the civil codes of the post-revolutionary era placed further restraints on an already restricted testamentary regime and abolished primogeniture (the transmission of family estate to the eldest male descendant) in favour of a more 'egalitarian' inheritance system founded upon the partible, or equal, treatment of family heirs.[47] In contrast, English law placed very few restrictions on the disposal of property, so long as the testator was a male or unmarried female. The state regarded property transmission as a private, family affair in which they were reluctant to intervene. As a result, in relation to property transmission, English inheritance practices potentially tell us more about individual decision-making than those elsewhere.

Indeed, both historical and contemporary Western thinkers have regarded inheritance and testamentary disposition (the disposal of property by will) as being key features of private property. John Locke, for example, argued that 'every man is born with … a right … to inherit with his brethren, his father's goods'.[48] William Blackstone went even further, by using inheritance as an important justification for considering private property as a worthy basis for exercising the rights of citizenship. He claimed that 'the transmission of one's possessions to posterity has an evident tendency to make man a good citizen and a useful member of society'.[49] Although more inclined to question the moral legitimacy of inheritance, John Stuart Mill also regarded the disposal of property by a will or other means as an intrinsic feature of private property. He argued that 'a bequest is one of the attributes of property: the ownership of a thing cannot be looked upon as complete without the power of bestowing it, at death or during life, at the owner's pleasure'.[50] More recently, Ronald Chester,

---

[47] On the French system see Darrow, M., *Revolution in the House: Family, Class and Inheritance in Southern France, 1775–1825* (Princeton: Princeton University Press, 1989). For the similarly restrictive situation in pre-Revolutionary France, see Diefendorf, B. B., 'Women and Property in *Ancien Regime* France: Theory and Practice in Dauphine and Paris', in Brewer and Staves *Early Modern Conceptions of Property*, pp. 170–93. The scope for unequal treatment of heirs under French law is explored in La Ferrère, A. 'Inheritances and Gifts *Inter Vivos*: The Use of the Disposable Portion for the Purpose of Unequal Division Between Siblings in France', *Continuity and Change* 7 (1992), pp. 377–404. Similar restrictions on testamentary freedom existed elsewhere. See the example of Scotland outlined by Ann McCrum in her contribution to this volume and the case of Chile in Lamar, M., '"Choosing" Partible Inheritance Strategies: Chilean Merchant Families, 1795–1825', *Journal of Social History* 28 (1994), pp. 125–46.

[48] Quoted in Chester, *Inheritance, Wealth and Society*, p. 14.

[49] Blackstone, W., *Commentaries on the Laws of England*, vol. 2, ed.. A. W. B. Simpson (London: University of Chicago Press, 1979), p. 11.

[50] Mill, J. S., *Principles of Political Economy with Some of Their Applications to Social Philosophy*, book 2 (London: George Routledge and Sons, 1891), p. 160.

echoing John Locke, has suggested that 'inheritance must be seen as ancillary to property'.[51] Indeed, the ability to transmit property can be thought of as corollary to the idea of 'exclusive ownership' which has come to dominate theoretical understandings of property in Britain.[52] To dispose of property is, perhaps more than any other act of appropriation or alienation, to claim exclusive rights to its ownership

In contrast to this Western liberal conception of property which tends to view it as a 'thing' over which individuals exercise exclusive rights, anthropological definitions of property frequently emphasise the social and relational context of its existence.[53] Property, it has been argued, is 'conceivable only in the context of communities of people'.[54] Inheritance, by its very nature, emphasises these social aspects of ownership. It exposes the social networks within which property as a 'thing' took on meaning and significance. As Finch, et al. have convincingly demonstrated, inheritance reveals the way in which property figures in 'how people might conceptualise the claims of others upon them, in the context of their own family circumstances and in light of public expectations about such claims'.[55] To use a concept that Chris Hann has recently resurrected from the work of Karl Polanyi, inheritance demonstrates the social 'embeddedness' of property.[56] Thus, there are good reasons why the study of inheritance can be a rewarding way of exploring the social relations of property. Not only is inheritance central to the very notion of property as a theoretical entity, it also directs attention to many of the social aspects of ownership which this book is concerned with investigating.

Studies of inheritance and property transmission in British contexts have generally focused on the early modern period and have largely concentrated on rural rather than urban contexts. There have been two major strands to this work. The first has been concerned with the role of inheritance – particularly the 'strict settlement' of landed property – in the rise of aristocratic estates. It owes much to the pioneering work of Sir John Habakkuk, whose studies have

---

[51] Chester, *Inheritance, Wealth and Society*, p.12.

[52] On the development of the idea of property as a form of exclusive ownership or title (alternatively referred to as the rise of 'possessive individualism') see, *inter alia*, Macpherson, C. B., *The Political Theory of Possessive Individualism: Hobbes to Locke* (Oxford: Clarendon Press, 1962); and MacFarlane, A., *The Origins of English Individualism. The Family, Property and Social Transition* (Oxford: Blackwell, 1978), pp. 80–101.

[53] Hann, 'The embeddedness of property', pp. 4–5.

[54] Brewer, J. and Staves, S., 'Introduction', in *idem, Early Modern Conceptions of Property*, p. 3.

[55] Finch, et. al., *Wills, Inheritance and Families*, p. 7.

[56] Hann, 'The embeddedness of property', pp. 9–10.

opened up a number of important debates in socio-legal history.[57] Various researchers have demonstrated how inheritance strategies were used to create a complex assemblage of rights and restrictions that sought to preserve family property over future generations.[58] Not only did this preserve patrimony, it also helped to secure family identity and status. However, many of the pioneering studies of landed inheritance have been criticised for their legalistic perspective and their tendency to treat families as economic rather than social units. More recent studies of landed inheritance have addressed these deficiencies and, in particular, have tried to uncover the role of women in the property transmission process.[59] However, whilst such studies have provided much insight to aristocratic life, their focus has been largely limited to the transmission of landed property as opposed to other forms of real and personal estate. As a result, scholars have rarely strayed from the countryside to the town or from studying the wealthy as opposed to those of more modest means.

The second strand of research focuses less on the question of inheritance itself than on the use of a documentary by-product of the property transmission process – the probate inventory – which provides detailed information on individual property holding.[60] Early studies tended to focus on the use of small numbers of inventories to explore, *inter alia*, the living environments, stock-in-trade or farming practices.[61] More recently, the use of computers has

---

[57] Habakkuk, J., 'English Land Ownership, 1680–1740', *Economic History Review* 10 (1939–40), pp. 2–17; Habakkuk, J., 'Marriage Settlements in the eighteenth century', *Transactions of the Royal Historical Society* 4th series, 32 (1950), pp. 15–30; Habakkuk, J., 'The Rise and Fall of English Landed Families, 1600–1800', *Transactions of the Royal Historical Society* 5th series, 29 (1979), pp. 187–207; Habakkuk, J., *Marriage, Debt and the Estates System: English Landownership* (Oxford: Clarendon Press, 1994). Other important works in this field include: Bonfield, L., *Marriage Settlements, 1601–1740: The Adoption of the Strict Settlement* (Cambridge: Cambridge University Press 1983); Spring, E., *Law, Land and Family: Aristocratic Inheritance in England 1300–1800* (Chapel Hill: The University of North Carolina Press, 1990); Staves, S., *Married Women's Separate Property in England, 1660–1833* (Cambridge Mass.: Harvard University Press, 1990); Stone, L. and Stone, J. C., *An Open Elite?* (Oxford: Clarendon Press, 1984); Thompson, F. M. L., (ed.), *Landowners, Capitalists and Entrepreneurs: Essays for Sir John Habakkuk* (Oxford: Clarendon Press, 1994).

[58] Cooper, J. C., 'Patterns of Inheritance and Settlement by Great Landowners from the Fifteenth to the Eighteenth Centuries', in J. Goody, E. P. Thompson and J. Thirsk (eds), *Family and Inheritance in Western Europe, 1200–1800* (Cambridge: Cambridge University Press, 1976), pp. 192–327; Staves, *Married Women's Separate Property*, pp. 199–201.

[59] For critiques and new approaches see: Spring, *Law, Land and Family*; and Staves, *Married Women's Separate Property*.

[60] For a picture of the range of work undertaken, see Overton, M., *A Bibliography of British Probate Inventories* (Newcastle upon Tyne: University of Newcastle upon Tyne, Department of Geography, Occasional Paper, 1983).

[61] See, for example, Bagley, J. J., 'Matthew Markland, a Wigan Mercer', *Transactions, Lancashire and Cheshire Antiquarian Society* 68 (1959), pp. 45–68; Curle, A. O., 'A

considerably increased the scale and scope of such analysis, and historians have drawn on probate inventories to study a number of issues relating to material culture, consumer behaviour and the temporal, spatial and social diffusion of goods, techniques and expertise.[62] Attempts have also been made to utilise data on non-material items, and to reproduce networks of credit and debt, and changing levels of wealth.[63]

Such analyses can tell us much about the changing nature of society and economy. However, in England and Wales inventories effectively cease to exist from the late eighteenth century. For the nineteenth century, other forms of inheritance documents have been most commonly used in studies of wealth holding. Drawing upon estate valuations made for the purposes of probate, several historians have explored the structure and distribution of wealth in Victorian Britain. W. D. Rubinstein has made the most extensive use of probate records and his research has raised some important questions about the geography and sources of middle-class wealth holding in the industrial revolution period.[64] His claim, recently challenged, that commercial and financial wealth was pre-eminent over industrial wealth has allowed him to identify important regional differences in the nature of property ownership.[65] His controversial suggestion – for which he provides more evidence in chapter 6 of this volume – that London, rather than the industrial North, was the centre of wealth making in nineteenth-century Britain, has been connected to wider debates concerning the so-called 'failure' of the British middle class.[66] This

Roxburghshire House and its Contents in 1729', *Scottish Historical Review* 5 (1968), pp. 265–72; Bettey, J. H. and Wilde, D. S., 'The Probate Inventories of Dorset Farmers', *Local Historian* 12 (1977), pp. 228–34.

   [62] See, Weatherill, *Consumer Behaviour and Material Culture*; Shammas, *The Pre-industrial Consumer*; Overton, M., *The Agricultural Revolution* (Cambridge: Cambridge University Press, 1996). For the impact of computerised analysis, see the contributions to Morris, R. J. and McCrum, A., 'Wills, inventories and the computer', *History and Computing*, 7 (1995), Special Issue.

   [63] Holderness, B. A., 'Credit in a Rural Community, 1660–1800: Some Neglected Aspects of Probate Inventories', *Midland History* 3 (1975), pp. 94–115; Riley, D. 'Wealth and Social Structure in North-Western Lancashire in the Later Seventeenth Century: A New Use for Probate Inventories', *Transactions, Historic Society of Lancashire and Cheshire* 141 (1992), pp. 77–100.

   [64] See, among his many publications on wealth holding, Rubinstein, W. D., *Men of Property: The Very Wealthy in Britain Since the Industrial Revolution* (London: Croom Helm, 1981) and Rubinstein, W. D. 'The Victorian Middle Classes: Wealth, Occupation and Geography', *Economic History Review* 30 (1988), pp. 602–23.

   [65] See Rubinstein, W. D., *Men of Property: The Very Wealthy in Britain Since the Industrial Revolution* (London: Croom Helm, 1981). A recent challenge to Rubinstein's thesis has come from Nicholas, T., 'Wealth Making in Nineteenth- and Early Twentieth-Century Britain: Industry v. Commerce and Finance', *Business History,* 41 (1999), pp. 16–36.

   [66] Evidence for the pre-eminence of London is provided in Rubinstein, *Men of Property*; Rubinstein, 'The Victorian Middle Classes', and his essay published in this book.

theme has in itself been an enduring axis of scholarly attention and an important historical narrative for understanding the social relations of property.[67]

This analysis has been invaluable in fuelling debate on the nature and geography of economic activity in the nineteenth century. However, it is not just at the national scale that studies of probate valuations have provided some interesting insights to nineteenth-century society. Probate valuations have also been used by urban historians to examine the internal social and geographical distribution of wealth in towns.[68] However, whilst probate studies provide a useful indication of patterns of property ownership they are not without their problems. Critiques tend to focus on a rather narrow set of issues concerning the accuracy and reliability of the sources, yet there are perhaps more significant criticisms that might usefully be raised here.[69] Whilst studies of wealth holding may suggest social stratification they disclose little about the social meanings of wealth itself. The difference revealed by analysing probate values undoubtedly reveal something of the inequalities and social cleavages that marked nineteenth-century England, and its towns and cities in particular. However, these differences did not simply exist, they had to be produced through the use of property in a variety of ways that made it socially significant and meaningful. One way in which this occurred was through inheritance. Somewhat strangely, however, studies of inheritance in nineteenth-century Britain are few and far between. In this respect, it is ironic that some of the criticisms made of probate valuation studies could be addressed by paying greater attention to the sources of which they were a part.

The lack of attention paid to inheritance within the context of eighteenth-and nineteenth-century Britain, and especially its towns and cities, is particularly surprising given its importance to the middling sort – a group often seen as central to analyses of property. In an attempt to awaken interest in issues of inheritance and property transmission, R. J. Morris has recently

---

[67] Summaries are provided by Gunn, S., 'The Failure of the Victorian Middle Class: A Critique', in J. Seed and J. Wolff (eds), *The Culture of Capital: Art, Power and the Nineteenth-Century Middle Class* (Manchester: Manchester University Press, 1988), pp. 17–44, and Hickox, M. S. 'The English Middle-Class Debate', *British Journal of Sociology* 45 (1995), pp. 311–423.

[68] These include Green, D. R. and Owens, A., 'Metropolitan Estates of the Middle Class, 1800–50: Probates and Death Duties Revisited', *Historical Research* 70 (1997), pp. 294–311; Field, J., 'Wealth, Styles of Life and Social Tone amongst Portsmouth's Middle Class', in R. J. Morris (ed.), *Class, Power and the Social Structure of British Nineteenth-Century Towns* (Leicester: Leicester University Press, 1986), pp. 67–106; Gunn, 'The Manchester Middle Class', pp. 143–55, and Foster, J., *Class Struggle and the Industrial Revolution: Early Industrial Capitalism in Three English Towns* (London: Methuen, 1973).

[69] Gunn 'Failure of the Victorian Middle Class'; Green and Owens 'Metropolitan Estates of the Middle Class'.

claimed that the disposal of property by will was a process that was crucial to the 'making and remaking of the middle classes'.[70] Bequeathing and inheriting were activities that touched the lives of large numbers of middling folk at different stages throughout their life course. Research suggests that between 5 and 10 per cent of people left wills in the early part of the nineteenth century.[71] Moreover, succession could have profound economic and social implications for propertied families. As a result, Morris argues that the study of inheritance can provide a window onto the social relationships of property, family, friendship, gender and status that are 'central to accounts of the middle classes'. Certainly, inheritance is prominent theme in literary representations of middle-class life during the period.[72] Yet, as we have argued above, social and economic historians have been much more interested in the production and consumption of wealth among the middling sort than they have been in its disposal and transmission.

In trying to understand the social and economic importance of property, the study of inheritance does, of course, have its drawbacks, as Geoffrey Crossick observes in chapter 3. It is centred on a particular point in the life course which, although very significant to overall patterns of property ownership, is necessarily only a 'snapshot' of a longer and more complex process of the accumulation and transmission of property. An obvious effect of this concentration of attention upon death is that its significance in understanding the patterns and processes of property transmission is easily overstated. Indeed, although often assumed as such, death may not have been the most important 'occasion' of property transmission over the life course. Indeed, sensitive to this point, Crossick argues that among nineteenth-century European petit-bourgeois owners of small enterprises it 'was at marriage rather than at death that the most significant property transfers ... took place'.[73] Moreover, death was quite obviously an extraordinary moment in the lives of property owners and their immediate kin and acquaintances. The sorts of proprietorial upheavals experienced at death, and the events and processes set in motion by its

---

[70] Morris, R. J., 'Reading the Will: Cash Economy Capitalists and Urban Peasants in the 1830s', in Kidd and Nicholls, *The Making of the Middle Class*, p. 114. On the importance of inheritance to the middle class see also Davidoff and Hall, *Family Fortunes*, pp. 193–317.

[71] Camp, A. J., *Wills and Their Whereabouts* (London: Published by the Author, 1974), p. xxxviii; Cox, J., Wills, *Inventories and Death Duties* (London: Public Record Office, 1988), p.1; Green and Owens, 'Metropolitan Estates of the Middle Class', p. 296–7. For further discussion of the number of people who made wills see the chapter by Alastair Owens in this volume.

[72] This is also a curiously under-researched issue. An important exception is Sadrin, A., *Parentage and Inheritance in the Novels of Charles Dickens* (Cambridge: Cambridge University Press, 1994). However, Sadrin's study focuses on a broader conception of inheritance than the legal form principally discussed in this volume.

[73] See below, p. 70.

occurrence, may have contrasted sharply with the more mundane social relations of property that characterised the rest of the life course. Studies of inheritance often fail to appreciate this important point. Whilst it is beyond the scope of this book to investigate the transfer and disposal of property at other stages in the life-course, a key concern is to set inheritance within the wider economic and social strategies of the middling sort.

Indeed, decisions made upon death about what to do with property often hinged upon what had been done in the past and upon expectations for the future use of property. It would be entirely wrong to suggest that inheritance offers the possibility of uncovering all the manifold and complex ways in which property figured in the life-worlds of its owners. Clearly, therefore, the study of the social relations of property through inheritance has to be approached with caution. Nevertheless, used with care, studies of inheritance can provide rich rewards for historians interested in the social relations of property.

The collection of essays in this volume examines inheritance and property transmission activities from a variety of perspectives. In particular, it emphasises the importance of class, gender, kin and geography in shaping attitudes to, and experiences of, property and its transmission. The book's overall focus on inheritance shows how such processes and practices were shaped by and, in turn, helped to mould the meanings of property, and the roles which it might play in the economic, social and cultural lives of town-dwellers. These considerations provide a much fuller picture of economic and social reproduction which takes us beyond the narrow materiality of property into broader notions and structures of urbanism.[74]

To emphasise these various approaches and emphases, the book is loosely structured in three sections covering the meanings of property ownership (chapters 2 and 3); the processes and patterns of property ownership and transmission (chapters 4, 5 and 6), and property transmission and social reproduction (chapters 7, 8 and 9). In the first of these chapters, Lorna Scammell argues that probate inventories provide reliable evidence about the ownership of property in the late seventeenth and early eighteenth centuries. She goes on to use such evidence to explore the urban dimension of property ownership, initially through detailed quantitative analysis of the data and then in terms of a more nuanced assessment of domestic behaviour and material culture. Her multivariate analysis suggests that living in a town appears to have been closely associated with higher rates of ownership of certain goods, but that wealth and occupational status were also important and sometimes critical

---

[74] For discussion of the significance to urbanism and urbanisation of property transmission and exchange, see Harvey, D., *Social Justice and the City* (London: Edward Arnold, 1973), esp. chs 2 and 6.

in shaping ownership patterns. Being able to afford certain goods was clearly the bottom line in determining who might own what, but Scammell argues that the goods chosen closely reflected the changing needs and lifestyles of the middling sorts. To own material property, households had to know about it, have some material, social or emotional purpose for it, and be able to access and purchase it. That novel goods such as saucepans, table cutlery and china were, in the first instance, urban, indicates both the position of towns in the vanguard of emerging domestic fashions, and the fact that most information and supply networks were urban-centred.

In contrast to this anthropological approach (albeit one which is unusually grounded in quantitative analysis), Geoffrey Crossick explores the social, cultural and political meanings of property to the nineteenth-century petite bourgeoisie. Contrary to general trends towards growing anonymity of investment and an increasing investor passivity, he argues that petits bourgeois sought to maintain a more personal vision of wealth. Drawing on evidence from across Western Europe, he shows a continuing preference for ownership of and investment in real property rather than stocks and shares, and the genuinely personal and very local nature of their loans and investments. As well as being essential for economic assurance, property also held particular cultural and political meanings for petits bourgeois. It represented independence, autonomy and security, and was increasingly important in distinguishing petits bourgeois from large capital and from the working classes in cultural if not yet in political terms. Despite attempts in certain quarters to establish an ideology of patrimony as central to petit bourgeois identity, transmitting the status of property became more important than the inheritance of business-related property *per se*. We thus see the expansion of a more broadly-defined middle class and the absence, in Britain at least, of small enterprise as an issue within wider political debate.

In chapter 4, Alastair Owens focuses attention on the actual processes and practices of will making, and the ways in which these were embedded in the social fabric of towns. Property transmission, he argues, needs to be seen as a social as much as an economic activity; one that drew on specific forms of knowledge and expertise, but also much broader networks of family, friends and professionals. Detailed analysis of early nineteenth-century Stockport reveals a familiar picture of will-makers: predominantly male and mostly, but not exclusively, drawn from the town's middling ranks. These people were careful to make inheritance as secure as possible and so generally called on solicitors to assist in drawing up their wills. This provided legal security and gave the will additional authority, but it did so within a distinctly local context. Local ties were further strengthened by the appointment of family and fellow townspeople to act as executors and trustees, and the general practice of probate being granted by Stockport clergy. The disposal of material property was also localised, most frequently achieved via the advertisements of auctioneers in the town's newspaper. Both will making and property transmission were thus part of a complex set of social networks rooted in a specific place.

These social and geographical contexts of property transmission are further explored by Jon Stobart, but his focus is broadened from a single town to encompass an entire region. His chapter draws on information about executors to wills and administrators of intestate estates to reproduce early eighteenth-century social networks in north-west England. It reveals patterns of social linkages based on kinship, neighbourhood and trade, and confirms the importance of the nuclear family and local communities in shaping individual and group networks of interaction. However, the analysis also emphasises the ways in which the local nexus of social interaction and property ownership were linked to broader social and economic influences through a significant amount of long-distance interaction. People were, in effect, bound into family, neighbourhood and town, but were also linked to much broader networks of interaction which covered the whole country. It was within these complex layers of social relationships that inheritance and property transmission took place. As elsewhere, inheritance practices in the North West were dominated by provision for kin. This meant the wives and children in the first instance, but, in their absence, could spread to a broadly defined family. Importantly, though, it could also encompass a wide variety of (mostly local) friends, charities and organisations.

In the following chapter, attention switches from the geography of property transmission to the geography of property ownership, at least amongst the wealthy. W. D. Rubinstein uses probate records and detailed biographical material to chart the growth and distribution of those dying during the nineteenth century leaving more than £100,000 in personal property. He shows that the number of wealthy individuals grew across the country, with London remaining by far the most important centre of wealth holding. Its share of the these wealthy testators fell steadily after 1840 as the number of rich industrialists and businessmen in the Midlands and the North grew rapidly. Nonetheless, London's importance, especially for the very wealthy, remained unchallenged, not least as it became a favoured investment location for fortunes generated abroad. Some of these wealthy individuals were British merchants or planters retiring to their homeland, but many were genuine foreigners using London as a secure investment centre for what were often vast fortunes. Finally, Rubinstein also notes the way in which inheritance strategies themselves could shape wealth distribution. Many wills contained clauses allowing the sale of estates and this often resulted in disinvestment from industry and business and reinvestment of capital in London-based government stocks and bonds.

Ann McCrum's chapter focuses on the strategies of inheritance and is particularly concerned with the relationship between family and the post-mortem transfer of property. As her study centres on Glasgow and Edinburgh, these matters were shaped in part by the distinctive Scottish legal system (which allowed far less freedom to the testator than English law), but the primary social and economic concerns remained the same. Whilst the family was of paramount importance to all testators, the strategies pursued by men and women were significantly different. Whereas fathers almost invariably aimed at an equal distribution, mothers, generally with much smaller estates, frequently chose to target their bequests and gave unequal shares, favouring their daughters over their sons. A similar pattern is revealed for childless testators: both men and women bequeathed property primarily to family members, but again women favoured female relatives and often engaged in reciprocal inheritance strategies with female siblings. In all arrangements, though, the aim was to reproduce the middle-class family by placing sons in suitable positions, providing marriage portions to daughters and supporting unmarried women within the home.

Women's distinctive position in relationships of property and inheritance is considered in greater detail by Penelope Lane in chapter 8. Using probate data from two Leicestershire towns, she shows that women's ownership and control of property was much greater in the late eighteenth and early nineteenth centuries than is often portrayed. Lane's analysis reveals that, whilst many experienced some a downturn in their economic fortunes when their husbands' died, most engaged actively in pursuing one of a range of opportunities for income generation. Some women were given the power to continue in or liquidate their husband's business – a freedom which suggests that they had considerable skill in the business and sufficient experience to make important commercial decisions. If the latter course was taken, then the resulting money could be lent at interest – traditionally seen as the main income for widows – but it could also be invested more actively by these women: in real estate, local infrastructure or industrial capital, most notably stocking frames. The provision made by men did not mean that their widows would become economically inactive; rather, local economic and especially industrial development created new opportunities for women's property holding and wealth creation.

Female wealth holding is also the subject of David R. Green's chapter on independent women in early nineteenth-century London. Drawing on census and probate data, he shows that widows and spinsters were especially numerous in London, and accounted for an unusually high proportion of those making wills. However, despite the apparently abundant opportunities for establishing small businesses in the capital, women's economic position appears to have declined during this period relative to that of men. Middle-class women were, it seems, being squeezed out of business and channelled into the domestic sphere, in line with the cultural norms of the day. Evidence from wills – despite their short-comings in terms of freehold property, debts and *inter vivos* gifts – reinforces this impression. Women held large proportions of their wealth in personal property, but also had significant amounts of cash, and stocks and shares. Unlike their counterparts in Leicestershire, the majority of London women were clearly generating incomes from secure investments, particularly government stocks. This may reflect the provisions made in their husband's or father's wills, or might arise from positive investment decisions of their own. These independent women generally chose to leave their wealth to a number of beneficiaries, but – as in Scotland – they tended to favour female relatives, especially when naming their residual legatee.

Each chapter thus offers its own perspective on, and insight to, property and inheritance in eighteenth- and nineteenth-century towns. Overall, it is our hope that this book will make a useful contribution to the understanding of the economic and material, as well as the social, political and cultural, significance of property. Property was very real to individuals and families, as well as being important in the shaping of broader group identities. In particular, we would seek to emphasise the significance of the social relations of property as they were constructed and reconstructed through processes of inheritance and property transmission. Intergenerational transfers of property not only structured processes of social and economic reproduction, they also reflected broader socio-economic relations within and beyond the town. Thus, we hope that these essays provide some further insights to the developing nature of urbanism during a period of prolonged urban growth. Finally, it is our hope that this book will open up discussion of these and other issues relating to property, inheritance and the town. If these various contributions do no more than provoke further work, analysis and debate then they will have been worthwhile.

Chapter 2

Town versus country: the property of everyday consumption in the late seventeenth and early eighteenth centuries

*Lorna Scammell**

Was urban life an important focus for the ownership of domestic goods in the pre-industrial era? This chapter reviews the influence of towns by making use of evidence from probate inventories to show distinctions between town and country in the patterns of ownership of key goods between 1675 and 1725.[1] The chapter argues that mechanisms influencing ownership of movable property in both town and country were complex, but were not as different in town and country (at least for many items) as might be expected. It begins with a broad outline of the differences between town and country using fourteen 'key' items and argues that inventories do give reliable evidence about ownership. Perspectives on similarities and differences are then viewed from three separate points of view; firstly, the other variables determining ownership are examined so that the influence of towns is placed in context. Secondly, domestic behaviour and material culture are described to show what people actually did with their possessions. Thirdly, variation in supply shows that ownership could, in some cases, be closely tied to national trading networks. Finally, the obvious conclusion is that a simple dichotomy between town and country does not adequately explain consumer behaviour.

Urban history has repeatedly emphasised that life in towns resulted in different economic and social behaviour on the part of the inhabitants. Town life was even seen at the time as intrinsically different from life in the country

---

* Lorna Scammell was formerly known as Lorna Weatherill.

[1] This chapter is based on research published in Weatherill, L., *Consumer Behaviour and Material Culture, 1660–1760* (London: Routledge, 1988 and 1996). The original data can be roughly searched on the World Wide Web at http://seastorm.ncl.ac.uk/invs/. For further background see Brewer, J. and Porter, R. (eds), *Consumption and the World of Goods* (London: Routledge, 1993); Shammas, C., *The Pre-industrial Consumer in England and America* (Oxford: Oxford University Press, 1990); Levine D. and Wrightson, K., *The Making of an Industrial Society* (Oxford: Oxford University Press, 1991).

and the overall impression given by observers like Defoe and Fiennes is that towns were worth visiting and that something interesting would be found there. The plays and poetry of the period give an impression of the sophistication of town-dwellers; towns have been seen as a vital force in breaking down traditional patterns of consumption and especially as the places where new ideas are first introduced.[2] This kind of evidence has led historians to expect differences between the material life of people in towns and in the country.[3] Yet even as simple a listing as Table 1.1 does not support the view that there was a straightforward dichotomy between town and country in the ownership of movable property.[4]

Does this sample of inventories fairly represent towns, so that we can have faith in the similarities and differences outlined in the tables? In summary, and at a high level of generalisation, they do give a fair comparison of domestic material culture in provincial towns and rural areas. The whole sample was taken from seven dioceses in England at ten-year intervals between 1675 and 1725. The sample was not deliberately stratified to include a sample of urban inventories but the urban ones were identified from the main sample. The advantage of this was that the sample was taken of estates where urban and rural probate practices were sufficiently similar for valid comparisons. Furthermore, the urban inventories cover both major and smaller towns. By the late seventeenth century there was considerable diversity in town life, most notably between small market towns and the great cities. Urban networks were becoming increasingly complex with provincial capitals, market towns, small towns, industrial centres and resort towns. Small towns and large villages were not clearly distinct, although a higher density of dwellings and a mixed occupational structure usually distinguished a small town from a large village.

There is no absolute agreement about the minimum population necessary for urban functions and status. Gregory King included small settlements and assumed that the smallest size for market towns was about 500 people. There is much to be said for taking this contemporary and informed view into account.

---

    [2] Defoe, D., *A Tour Through the Whole Island of Great Britain* (London: Everyman, 1962); Morris, C. (ed.), *The Journeys of Celia Fiennes* (London: Futura, 1983); William Wycherley, *The Country Wife*, first performed in 1675.
    [3] Chalklin, C. W., *The Provincial Towns of Georgian England: A Study in the Building Process, 1740–1820* (London: Edward Arnold, 1974); Clark, P. and Slack, P., *English Towns in Transition* (Oxford: Oxford University Press, 1976); Corfield, P., *The Impact of English Towns, 1700–1800* (Oxford: Oxford University Press, 1982); P. Clark (ed.), *The Transformation of English Provincial Towns, 1600–1800* (London: Hutchinson, 1984); Borsay, P., *The English Urban Renaissance: Culture and Society in the Provincial Town, 1660–1770* (Oxford: Clarendon Press, 1989).
    [4] Details about the sample are fully described in Weatherill, *Consumer Behaviour*, pp. 201–7. In this chapter, I focus on provincial towns and so have excluded those from London.

Table 2.1

**Town versus country: ownership of household goods in a sample of
inventories from seven dioceses in England, 1675–1725**

n = 2535	Country (n = 2034) % with	All towns (n = 501) % with	Large town (n = 216) % with	Small town (n = 285) % with
Tables	88	92	91	93
Cooking pots	69	71	72	70
Pewter	93	94	93	94
Books	17	22	21	23
Clocks	18	20	18	20
* Earthenware	35	42	45	39
* Table linen	35	55	54	55
* China	1	8	8	7
* Curtains	6	20	27	14
* Glasses	21	53	57	50
* Knives / forks	2	5	7	5
* Pictures	5	31	41	22
* Saucepans	5	11	11	9
* Utensils for hot drinks	2	5	6	3

Notes: See note 6 for details about the tables. An asterisk marks those items where the
         difference between all towns and the country are significant. The p-value for chi-
         square in less than 0.005.

Source: A sample of probate inventories from seven dioceses in England: for details see the
         text and Weatherill, *Consumer Behaviour*, pp. 201–7. I have excluded those from
         London in order to concentrate on provincial towns. The major towns include
         Durham, Newcastle, Berwick, Carlisle, Southampton, Winchester, Canterbury,
         Cambridge, Shrewsbury, Liverpool and Manchester. The others are the smaller
         market towns ubiquitous in England – for details see the text and Weatherill,
         Consumer Behaviour, pp. 74–6.

There were around 500 market centres with populations of 500 to 1500 which
had with spheres of influence of only a few miles. These small places were
local centres with craft and other trades people serving a restricted population.
Their function was to provide services for the local population and to process
and market agricultural products. They were distinct from the dispersed population of the countryside because the majority of people who lived in them did
not farm the land, although some did. On the other hand, the more
sophisticated characteristics of towns were not fully developed in small places.
There were only forty or fifty towns with populations between 2000 and 5000;
only twenty-four had populations over 5000; seven towns had populations over
10,000. The proportion of the population living in towns depends on whether
the smaller places are included; in 1700 about 11 per cent of the population of

England lived in towns with more than 5000 inhabitants outside London and a further 7 per cent in smaller towns.

From the point of view of this chapter, there is an advantage in taking as towns any settlements with a mixed economy and over 500 inhabitants, although it has the disadvantage of including diverse places. The proportions of urban inventories is in keeping with the proportion of urban-dwellers in the country, although in one diocese (Durham) the proportion was rather higher. Some recognition of the urban hierarchy is possible by dividing the provincial towns according to whether they were regional centres or small local towns (see Table 2.1) although this is not done for most of the tables here in order to retain two way contingency tables for multi-variate analysis as outlined below. The distinctions made here between rural and urban are rather generalised, as is the identification of major urban centres. For example, Carlisle was quite small, with about 3000 to 4000 people, but it was an economic and political centre for an extensive hinterland in the North West and Cumbria. The other towns include small to medium market towns and other small places with a variety of functions but there are no inventories from the developing spas or leisure centres. There were only a few inventories for each settlement so a few errors of definition will not have made a great difference to the overall results. The sample thus gives expression to experiences in many towns in many areas. The strength of the conclusions is that they are based on evidence from ordinary towns, using documents that were made in similar ways in town and country. This is important because much of the discussion about urban consumption is based on observations and commentary about the behaviour of gentry, and aspiring gentry, on holiday in the rising spa centres of Bath, Tunbridge and elsewhere. Such commentary refers to public occasions rather than to household behaviour, but there was more to town life than leisure and luxury and the evidence from inventories has the advantage of drawing attention to this. The tables can thus be looked at with some confidence that they provide an outline for comparing town and country.

There were some items that appear equally in town and country, including well-established articles like pewter and ubiquitous furniture like tables; nor were there changes in these established goods over the decades covered by this survey (Table 2.2). At the other extreme were items where the differences were so marked that they seem to have been urban phenomena, notably window curtains and pictures, which were already recorded in inventories in 1675 but became more common in both town and country by 1725. Utensils for hot drinks, and china, were also concentrated in towns but they were newly available in the 1680s and ownership expanded in the last few decades of this survey; ownership of these, too, was concentrated in towns. There was other property which was more common in towns but the differences were less marked or they were rare everywhere. The listings in Tables 2.1 and 2.2 show patterns in the ownership of key items which suggest that there were varied mechanisms at work. One way to explore these further is to look at other variables that influenced ownership in the whole sample of inventories, specifically wealth, social position, region and gender.[5]

Table 2.2

Town versus country: changes in ownership of some household goods, 1675–1725 (percentage of inventories with each item)

	1675		1685		1695		1705		1715		1725	
	Per cent		Per cent		Per cent		Per cent		Per cent		Per cent	
	c	t	c	t	c	t	c	t	c	t	c	t
Tables	86	89	87	91	88	91	90	95	89	94	90	88
Cooking pots	63	73	67	67	68	73	70	74	73	68	75	74
Pewter	94	94	94	93	93	95	94	91	93	97	90	88
Books	18	20	18	22	16	21	16	18	17	23	13	36
Clocks	8	14	8	11	13	15	19	21	29	32	31	33
Earthenware	26	37	26	33	34	37	34	34	43	54	51	74
Table linen	35	62	41	52	36	53	34	53	33	59	31	50
China	0	0	1	4	1	9	2	10	2	15	4	10
Curtains	4	10	5	16	5	16	6	20	7	31	10	40
Glasses	11	41	16	50	20	49	25	58	30	64	28	67
Knives / forks	0	2	0	2	3	3	3	5	2	12	5	12
Pictures	3	24	3	22	3	25	5	24	9	53	10	48
Saucepans	1	2	2	6	5	6	5	9	9	21	12	36
Utensils for hot drinks	0	0	0	0	0	2	1	1	3	14	6	19

Notes: c = country; t = town.
Source: See text and Table 2.1.

Other influences: a multi-variate approach

Attention is focused here on a few goods with varying characteristics, namely books, clocks, earthenware, curtains and china. These represent different usage and supply conditions and are therefore revealing of different influences over ownership. Books were associated with literacy and a wider culture. Clocks were associated with keeping time and they also had a high intrinsic value. China was a new, decorative but useful item imported from the Far East with,

---

[5] The differences between men and women were not significant (except for curtains which were recorded in 13 per cent of women's inventories and 8 per cent of men's) and are not considered further here.

as we shall see later, specific supply conditions. Curtains were decorative and enhanced comfort and privacy. Earthenware was associated with cookery and meals; it was modest in cost at less than a penny a piece. For each item cross-tabulations were produced (along with the chi-squared statistics) from which were calculated the probabilities that an item would be owned (expressed in the tables as a one-in-n chance of ownership), as well as the odds ratio between town and country.[6]

Wealth is hard to define from inventories for there are major problems in using the valuation of the whole inventory as a 'proxy'. For example, inventories can contain different capital items for different groups of people. The capital stock of farmers (crops and livestock) was included and at some times in the year could be substantial. On the other hand, the working capital of tradesmen was not valued in the same way and tools of the trades were often of more modest value than the farm equipment. This makes comparison unreliable, so I prefer to use the valuation of the total household element although this does not indicate wealth, merely the value of household items left after death.[7] The median was used as a measure of central tendency rather than the mean because the distribution was skewed, with a long tail of high values. For the purposes of this exploration the inventories were divided into two groups, 'high' and 'low', in order to investigate the hypothesis that wealth influenced ownership. The 'high' group contained the inventories that had valuations for household goods above the median for the whole sample. The 'low' group contained all those equal to or below the median.

---

[6]   The tables were constructed using cross-tabulations in SPSS and especially the chi-square statistic. I am grateful to Martin Charlton of the Geography Department in Newcastle University for introducing me to SPSS and chi-square. There are many books on these methods but I found Walsh, A., *Statistics for the Social Sciences* (New York: Harper Row, 1990) to be the most helpful. The chi-square test of independence is a test of significance that is used for data in the form of frequencies, percentages or proportions. It can be used to determine the dependence or otherwise of two categorical variables. The multi-variate analysis in the tables is based on bi-variate and second-order partial relationships, also using chi-square. The p-value is the probability of error and thus is a measure of significance. The higher the p-value, the more likely it is that we should accept the null hypothesis that the variables are independent. Accepting the null hypothesis means that we conclude that location (in town or country) was not a factor in ownership. If the p-value is less than 0.05 the null hypothesis is rejected and the conclusion made that the variables are dependent, that is that location and ownership were associated. Even if we show that location and ownership were associated, this does not mean that the relationship was one of cause and effect. The odds ratio is a calculation based on the probabilities of ownership in town and country. If it is around 1, then the probabilities in town and country are equal and so the conclusion that location has no influence on ownership is a reasonable one. Higher figures suggest relationships between ownership and location.

[7]   Shammas has used different approaches for her economic account of similar data; see Shammas, *The Pre-industrial Consumer in England and America,* pp. 100–112, especially Table 4.11, and pp. 169–88, Tables 6.5 to 6.9.

Table 2.3

Town versus country: the influence of wealth 1675–1725

Books

Wealth group	Influence of location		Probability of ownership		Odds ratio
	Chi-square	p-value	town	country	
Both	8.034	0.005	1 in 4.5	1 in 6	1.1
Upper	0.352	0.553	1 in 3.5	1 in 3.5	1.0
Lower	6.396	0.011	1 in 8	1 in 14	1.8

Clocks

Wealth group	Influence of location		Probability of ownership		Odds ratio
	Chi-square	p-value	town	country	
Both	0.759	0.384	1 in 5	1 in 6	1.1
Upper	1.752	0.182	1 in 4	1 in 3	1.0
Lower	2.357	0.125	1 in 14	1 in 21	1.5

Earthenware

Wealth group	Influence of location		Probability of ownership		Odds ratio
	Chi-square	p-value	town	country	
Both	7.722	0.055	1 in 2	1 in 3	1.4
Upper	2.097	0.148	1 in 2	1 in 2	1.0
Lower	2.166	0.141	1 in 3	1 in 4	1.4

China

Wealth group	Influence of location		Probability of ownership		Odds ratio
	Chi-square	p-value	town	country	
Both	58.091	0.000	1 in 14	1 in 73	5.7
Upper	34.978	0.000	1 in 10	1 in 46	5.0
Lower	15.361	0.000	1 in 26	1 in 153	6.0

Curtains

Wealth group	Influence of location		Probability of ownership		Odds ratio
	Chi-square	p-value	town	country	
Both	98.070	0.197	1 in 5	1 in 17	3.9
Upper	56.292	0.000	1 in 3.5	1 in 9	3.3
Lower	24.404	0.000	1 in 13	1 in 59	4.8

Notes: Upper wealth n = 1260; Lower wealth n= 1275.
Source: See text and note 6.

Table 2.3 takes account of both location in town or country and wealth group. This table shows the chi-squared measure of association between ownership and location in each of the wealth groups, for each of the five possessions under scrutiny. The odds ratio is a calculation based on the probabilities of ownership in town and country. If it is around 1.0, then the probabilities in town and country are equal and so the conclusion that location has no influence on ownership is a reasonable one. Higher figures suggest relationships between ownership and location. These show that some items were more influenced by location than others and that location had more influence over some wealth groups than others. This demonstrates two things. Firstly, the influence of towns is still apparent for some items within each wealth group and so it can be concluded that the differences and similarities were not due to a hidden effect of wealth. Secondly, taking account of wealth shows some interesting patterns and in particular that the higher wealth groups were (as we might expect) more likely to own everything, even things of modest value. The effect of the combination of wealth and location varied according to the item. Owners of books were four times more likely to be in the upper wealth group than in the lower; but owners of clocks were eight times more likely to be in the upper wealth group. On the other hand, wealth made little difference to the ownership of earthenware. Curtains and china both show a stronger tendency, in both wealth groups, to concentrate in towns. A comparison of the odds ratios for location and wealth are listed in Table 2.4. This indicates that location was not a determining factor for three of the items, clocks, books and earthenware; for curtains, wealth was more important than location; only for china was location more important than wealth.

Table 2.4
Odds ratios for wealth and location

	Wealth	Location
Books	4.1	1.4
Clocks	8.0	1.1
Earthenware	1.9	1.4
China	3.5	5.7
Curtains	6.1	3.9

Source: See text and note 6.

Social position appears easy to define from inventories because occupations or status designations are frequently given; in practice these are more complicated than seems the case at first sight. After much experimenting it was decided to group the occupations and status designations in much the same way that I have done in previous work but with a few simplifications.[8] In order to be able to work with as few groups as possible the intermediate- and high-status trades have been combined, but the low-status trades were left as they were because they do represent a different section of the population. Widows

[8] Weatherill, *Consumer Behaviour*, ch. 8; Weatherill, L., 'Consumer Behaviour and Social Status in England, 1660–1750', *Continuity and Change* 2 (1986), pp. 191–216; Mascuch, M., 'Social Mobility and the Middling Self-identity: the Ethos of British Autobiographers, 1600–1750', *Social History* 20 (1995), pp. 45–61.

Table 2.5
Town versus country: the influence of status, 1675–1725

Books

Status	Influence of location		Probability of ownership		Odds ratios
	Chi-square	p-value	Town	Country	
Gentry	0.492	0.483	1 in 2	1 in 2	1.2
Trade	0.604	0.437	1 in 3.5	1 in 4	1.2
Yeomen	2.131	0.144	1 in 11	1 in 6	2.1
Low trade	2.091	0.148	1 in 9	1 in 6	1.6
Husb. / lab.	0.627	0.428	1 in 14	1 in 31	2.3

Clocks

Status	Influence of location		Probability of ownership		Odds ratios
	Chi-square	p-value	Town	Country	
Gentry	4.917	0.027	1 in 3	1 in 2	2.2
Trade	1.066	0.302	1 in 4	1 in 4.4	1.3
Yeomen	0.002	0.965	1 in 5	1 in 5	1.0
Low trade	0.226	0.634	1 in 7	1 in 6	1.2
Husb. / lab.	0.788	0.375	1 in 14	1 in 34	2.5

Earthenware

Status	Influence of location		Probability of ownership		Odds ratios
	Chi-square	p-value	Town	Country	
Gentry	0.125	0.724	1 in 2.2	1 in 2.4	1.2
Trade	0.987	0.320	1 in 2	1 in 2.8	1.2
Yeomen	0.071	0.789	1 in 3	1 in 3	1.0
Low trade	0.174	0.676	2 in 3	2 in 3	1.0
Husb. / lab.	3.190	0.074	1 in 2	1 in 4	2.6

China

Status	Influence of location		Probability of ownership		Odds ratios
	Chi-square	p-value	Town	Country	
Gentry	2.130	0.144	1 in 10	1 in 25	2.7
Trade	4.757	0.029	1 in 9	1 in 20	2.6
Yeomen	14.824	0.000	1 in 9	1 in 127	16.3
Low trade	4.424	0.035	1 in 19	1 in 66	3.6
Husb. / lab.	*	*	*	*	*

Curtains

Status	Influence of location		Probability of ownership		Odds ratios
	Chi-square	p-value	Town	Country	
Gentry	2.649	0.104	1 in 3	1 in 5	2.0
Trade	5.355	0.021	1 in 4	1 in 7	1.9
Yeomen	0.973	0.324	1 in 4	1 in 25	1.8
Low trade	12.739	0.000	1 in 7	1 in 19	3.7
Husb. / lab.	13.869	0.000	1 in 7	1 in 85	14.0

Notes: Gentry n=147; Trade n=318; Yeomen n=933; Low trade n=374; Husbandmen / labourers n=354.

Source: See text and note 6.

are included if it was obvious what their occupation or status had been, otherwise they are 'unknown'; labourers and husbandmen are combined. I have argued elsewhere that the distinctions between trades and others were important but a simple dichotomy between 'trades' and 'others' was not meaningful, and a sense of hierarchy was retained by using more groups. The disadvantage is that the sample sizes became very small in some of the tables.

Table 2.5 shows the same statistics as Table 2.3 and was constructed in the same way. Very little distinction between town and country is apparent within most social groups for books, clocks and earthenware, except for the lowest groups who were not the most important consumers of these items. The influence of towns is clearer for china and curtains. Overall, it seems that the influence of social position was stronger than location, and even curtains were less clearly an urban phenomenon for the gentry and upper trades groups. The pattern for china is somewhat similar in that the more likely influence was social position for gentry and trades because within each group the influence of town or country is not significant. Ownership was rare amongst the yeomen and others, so here social position was hidden if we look only at the urban/rural dichotomy. Clocks were equally likely in town or country for yeomen but marginally more likely in the country for other groups; they were progressively less likely down the social hierarchy.

Regional differences themselves, measured here by the differences between the dioceses, were substantial (Table 2.6). There were wide variations in ownership across the dioceses examined, for example earthenware was common in Kent (occurring in one in three inventories) whereas in Winchester it was unusual (occurring in one in nine inventories). Curtains and china were strongly urban; for the others the patterns are varied with some dioceses (notably Durham) showing stronger distinctions between town and country than others.

Table 2.7 shows the influence of a combination of location, wealth and status. Each of the inventories in the status groups is further divided according to the wealth group into which they fell in town and country. In a very few instances the broad distinction between town and country remains, notably in the ownership of curtains in the trades group (upper wealth), and in the ownership of clocks and books amongst the trades and yeomen groups (lower wealth). Otherwise, the upper wealth groups were more likely to own things and there are few distinctions between town and country. This suggests that status and wealth acting together were (as the earlier tables imply) more influential in determining ownership than whether someone lived in town or country.

Table 2.6
Town versus country: taking account of diocese, 1675–1725

Books

Diocese	Influence of location		Probability of ownership		Odds ratios
	Chi-square	p-value	Town	Country	
Durham	6.315	0.012	1 in 7	1 in 9	3.0
Carlisle	0.633	0.426	1 in 5	1 in 6	1.4
Winchester	1.211	0.271	1 in 5	1 in 4	1.5
S. Lancs.	1.579	0.209	1 in 4	1 in 5	1.6
Kent	8.469	0.004	1 in 2.5	1 in 4	2.2
Ely	0.854	0.355	1 in 6	1 in 9	1.5
Staffs. / Salop	16.151	0.000	1 in 3	1 in 8	4.0

Clocks

Diocese	Influence of location		Probability of ownership		Odds ratios
	Chi-square	p-value	Town	Country	
Durham	11.841	0.001	1 in 5	1 in 15	3.6
Carlisle	1.435	0.231	1 in 9	1 in 15	1.9
Winchester	0.001	0.975	1 in 14	1 in 14	1.0
S. Lancs.	0.000	1.000	1 in 3	1 in 3	1.0
Kent	0.465	0.495	1 in 3	1 in 3	1.0
Ely	2.968	0.085	1 in 17	1 in 7	2.8
Staffs. / Salop	0.618	0.432	1 in 11	1 in 16	1.6

Earthenware

Diocese	Influence of location		Probability of ownership		Odds ratios
	Chi-square	p-value	Town	Country	
Durham	17.290	0.000	1 in 3	1 in 7	3.3
Carlisle	1.507	0.220	1 in 3	1 in 5	1.6
Winchester	7.968	0.005	1 in 4	1 in 10	2.9
S. Lancs.	1.972	0.160	5 in 6	2 in 3	2.0
Kent	1.848	0.174	2 in 3	1 in 2	1.6
Ely	0.729	0.398	1 in 3	1 in 3	1.3
Staffs. / Salop	3.074	0.080	1 in 4	1 in 6	1.9

China

Diocese	Influence of location		Probability of ownership		Odds ratios
	Chi-square	p-value	Town	Country	
Durham	11.633	0.001	1 in 7	1 in 33	5.4
Carlisle	9.436	0.002	1 in 14	1 in 116	8.6
Winchester	*	*	*	*	*
S. Lancs.	*	*	*	*	*
Kent	0.668	0.414	1 in 23	1 in 40	1.7
Ely	0.158	0.691	1 in 51	1 in 34	1.5
Staffs. / Salop	*	*	*	*	*

Table 2.6 contd.

Curtains

Diocese	Influence of location		Probability of ownership		Odds ratios
	Chi-square	p-value	Town	Country	
Durham	17.669	0.000	1 in 5	1 in 22	5.7
Carlisle	4.334	0.037	1 in 22	1 in 116	5.6
Winchester	11.441	0.001	1 in 6	1 in 26	5.0
S. Lancs.	2.648	0.104	1 in 7	1 in 13	2.1
Kent	8.172	0.004	1 in 3	1 in 6	2.3
Ely	24.520	0.000	1 in 4	1 in 16	5.8
Staffs. / Salop	16.437	0.000	1 in 8	1 in 69	9.3

Notes: Durham n=325; Carlisle n=390; Winchester n=260; S. Lancs. n=390; Kent n=390;
Ely n=390; Staffs. / Salop n=390.
* insufficient data.
Source: See text and note 6.

Table 2.7
Town versus country: the influence of wealth and status, 1675–1725

Books

Status	Wealth group	Influence of location		Probability of ownership	
		Chi-square	p-value	Town	Country
Gentry	Upper	0.005	0.942	1 in 2	1 in 2
	Lower	*	*	*	*
Trade	Upper	0.000	0.992	1 in 3	1 in 3
	Lower	4.321	0.038	1 in 10	1 in 24
Yeomen	Upper	1.742	0.187	1 in 8	1 in 4
	Lower	0.411	0.522	1 in 18	1 in 10
Low trade	Upper	1.759	0.185	1 in 5	1 in 4
	Lower	1.563	0.211	1 in 27	1 in 11
Husb. / lab.	Upper	*	*	*	*
	Lower	*	*	*	*

Clocks

Status	Wealth group	Influence of location		Probability of ownership	
		Chi-square	p-value	Town	Country
Gentry	Upper	2.059	0.151	1 in 2	2 in 3
	Lower	*	*	*	*
Trade	Upper	0.780	0.377	1 in 3.5	1 in 3
	Lower	0.358	0.550	1 in 11	1 in 8
Yeomen	Upper	0.745	0.388	1 in 5	1 in 3.5
	Lower	3.440	0.064	1 in 4	1 in 17
Low trade	Upper	0.197	0.657	1 in 4	1 in 3.5
	Lower	0.971	0.321	1 in 27	1 in 14
Husb. / lab.	Upper	*	*	*	*
	Lower	2.358	0.125	1 in 10	1 in 44

Table 2.7 contd.

Earthenware

Status	Wealth group	Influence of location		Probability of ownership	
		Chi-square	p-value	Town	Country
Gentry	Upper	0.021	0.884	1 in 2	1 in 2
	Lower	*	*	*	*
Trade	Upper	1.061	0.303	2 in 3	1 in 2
	Lower	0.057	0.811	1 in 5	1 in 4
Yeomen	Upper	0.281	0.596	1 in 2	1 in 2.5
	Lower	0.049	0.825	1 in 5	1 in 4
Low trade	Upper	0.345	0.557	1 in 2	1 in 10
	Lower	0.141	0.707	1 in 3	1 in 3
Husb / lab.	Upper	*	*	*	*
	Lower	0.739	0.390	2 in 3	1 in 4

China

Status	Wealth group	Influence of location		Probability of ownership	
		Chi-square	p-value	Town	Country
Gentry	Upper	3.103	0.073	1 in 8	1 in 23
	Lower	*	*	*	*
Trade	Upper	3.007	0.083	1 in 8	1 in 16
	Lower	*	*	*	*
Yeomen	Upper	9.478	0.002	1 in 13	1 in 105
	Lower	*	*	*	*
Low trade	Upper	0.797	0.372	1 in 20	1 in 40
	Lower	*	*	*	*
Husb./ lab.	Upper	*	*	*	*
	Lower	*	*	*	*

Curtains

Status	Wealth group	Influence of location		Probability of ownership	
		Chi-square	p-value	Town	Country
Gentry	Upper	3.455	0.063	1 in 3	1 in 5
	Lower	*	*	*	*
Trade	Upper	4.342	0.037	1 in 3	1 in 5
	Lower	1.252	0.263	1 in 8	1 in 16
Yeomen	Upper	1.545	0.214	1 in 8	1 in 17
	Lower	*	*	*	*
Low trade	Upper	9.494	0.002	1 in 4	1 in 12
	Lower	1.636	0.201	1 in 18	1 in 48
Husb./ lab.	Upper	*	*	*	*
	Lower	4.738	0.029	1 in 10	1 in 77

Notes: Upper wealth group: Gentry n=128; Trade n=224; Yeomen n=552; Low trade
n=175; Husbandmen / labourers n=36. Lower wealth group: Gentry n=19; Trade
n=94; Yeomen n=381; Low trade n=199; Husbandmen / labourers n=318.
         * insufficient data.
Source: See text and note 6.

The foregoing statistical analysis demonstrates well the spread of goods to various social groups and to different parts of the country. However, it tells us less about the ways in which people in the late seventeenth and early eighteenth centuries used and viewed these goods. Whilst it is tempting to try to 'explain' these results, it is more effective at this stage to view material culture and the ownership of property in other ways. It is to this that we now turn.

Households: material culture and property

What did people do that required them to have these material goods? What did they need to have in order to live a full life in ordinary middle-ranking households at the time? These questions force us to consider material culture in terms of the inner workings of the household, the practices of everyday life and the goods that accompanied them. This is a powerful, if somewhat imprecise, way of looking at the problem because it is clear that consumers in both town and country had an enormous choice of domestic items: they could have pewter, earthenware or wooden plates and bowls; they could cook on an open fire or on an enclosed stove; they could decorate their walls with pictures, looking-glasses and/or window curtains; they could eat using cutlery; and so on.[9] The data from inventories suggests that choices were made on the basis of whether things could be afforded, what lifestyle people expected and where they lived. Ownership had meanings to the people using and owning the goods, even if we are not able to say exactly what those meanings might have been. Looking at the relationships between mundane household activities and material goods allows us to speculate whether people had any uses for new items and what they did with well-established possessions. So this section focuses on domestic activity and relates this to some of the goods recorded in inventories, not so much to 'explain' as to display these items within the experiences of the people who used them. In particular, food, mealtimes, drinking and leisure are examined, with the emphasis on the homes of middle-ranking people, excluding the better-off gentry on the one hand and wage-earners on the other, because it was these groups that were particularly well represented in probate inventories.

Middle-ranking households consisted of small groups of adults and children (typically three to seven people) who were well known to one another and who

---

[9] The idea that material culture conveys 'meaning' is documented in much anthropological literature and is the main theme of Weatherill, *Consumer Behaviour*. The best book on this remains Douglas, M. and Isherwood, B., *The World of Goods: Towards an Anthropology of Consumption* (New York: W. W. Norton and Co., 1978).

cared about the welfare of the others.[10] Household life was, by its very nature, imbued with social, economic and psychological meanings and households had considerable links beyond their local community in both town and country as other papers in this collection show.[11] There were variations in the basic functions of domestic life, but, no matter who was present at different phases in the life-cycle and whether the household was located in the town or in the country, there were recognisable similarities. This in itself suggests that there might be similar mechanisms at work influencing ownership of property, and thus similarities between town and country. When it comes to the detail, we know strangely little about the day-to-day activities in households – indeed, it is relatively recently that the numbers of people living in them and their likely social relations have been unravelled. Furthermore, there are very few realistic illustrations of domestic scenes in British art, and the few that there are present only an idealised image of domesticity in which dirt and labour have no real place. The servants or cooks in many pictures (especially the Dutch and Flemish ones) are intended to convey the moral value of domestic life, suggestive of an appreciation for the well-run household, but not for the details of the tasks themselves or the material goods associated with them.[12]

---

[10] Mean household size in the English listings was 4.8: Laslett, P., 'Size and Structure of the Household in England over Three Centuries', *Population Studies* 23 (1969), pp. 199–223.

[11] Ownership of goods and material life should be seen within the whole context of social relations, as in Levine and Wrightson, *The Making of an Industrial Society*, pp. 231–41. Most evidence about the domestic economy of early modern households comes from large establishments because the records of large establishments have survived in greater numbers; for example, most of the manuscript accounts in local archives and in the British Museum are from the larger gentry and aristocratic households: evidence from these should not be taken as typifying behaviour in middling households. Domestic activities are, however, often referred to *en passant* in many contemporary sources such as diaries; much of this evidence does originate from households of middle rank, especially from clergy, doctors and tradesmen, who were the most able to express themselves in letters, diaries and autobiographies. There are examples of domestic organisation in Marshall, J. D. (ed.), 'The Autobiography of William Stout of Lancaster', *Chetham Society*, 3rd series, 14 (1967); Jackson, C. (ed.), 'A Family History begun by James Fretwell', *Surtees Society* 65 (1875), pp. 163–244. Others are listed in the bibliography to Weatherill, *Consumer Behaviour*, pp. 240–43. The most interesting and best-illustrated book on housework is Davidson, C., '*A Woman's Work is Never Done': A History of House-work in the British Isles, 1650–1950* (London: Chatto and Windus, 1982).

[12] Dutch and Flemish interiors are a useful way of seeing into households in these countries but they are not realistically applicable to Britain because the conventions about furniture, the shapes of the fireplaces and other details were different. See Wilenski, R. H., *Flemish Painters, 1430–1830* (London: Faber and Faber, 1960), which gives an account of the careers of Flemish painters that visited London; Bernt. W., *The Netherlandish Painters of the Seventeenth Century*, 3 vols (London: Phaidon, 1970); Sutton, P. C. (organiser), *Masters of Seventeenth Century Dutch Genre Painting: Exhibition Catalogue* (Royal Academy of Arts and Philadelphia Museum of Art, 1984). Some Flemish artists did work in Britain, but their work is not well documented. One such artist, Van Aken, produced a few very interesting interiors. He came to England before 1720 and painted draperies for portrait painters and a few

Food

What people ate was important, not just in maintaining physical health, but also in providing occasions for social bonding.[13] Provision of food and drink was skilled work: 'a perfect skill and knowledge in Cookery' was held to be foremost in a housewife's repertoire of knowledge, and thus cookery was an activity of high status within the household.[14] People in the middle ranks generally ate simply-prepared food, as Misson (a French visitor in the 1680s) said:

> English eat every thing that is produced naturally ... I say naturally in Opposition to the infinite Multitude of our made Dishes; for they dress their Meat much plainer than we do.[15]

Cooked meat was expected at meals, together with bread and vegetables. Misson, of the middling sort of people, said:

> The English eat a great deal at Dinner ... they chew meat by whole Mouthfuls ... they have ten or twelve Sorts of common Meats, which infallibly take their turns at their Tables, and two Dishes are their Dinners; a Pudding, for instance, and a Piece of roast Beef.[16]

Spit-roasting could be done in any room and it was also the 'traditional' way of cooking meat. In all households, meat was also boiled or stewed in a pot; such methods were extremely convenient, for the pot could be used over any kind of fire, even one unsuitable for roasting. If nothing went wrong (for pots could boil over) it was a clean and economical way of providing large amounts of hot food. Puddings and vegetables could be cooked alongside the meat; soup or

---

scenes of interiors. There is an outline of his career in Edwards, R., 'The Conversation Pictures of Joseph Van Aken', *Appollo* 132 (February 1936), pp. 79–85. There are illustrations, including Van Aken and Collett, in Weatherill, *Consumer Behaviour.*

[13] Cookery, as done in households of middle rank in the late seventeenth century, is not well documented because collections of 'traditional' recipes tend to have a nineteenth-century origin, although they can give useful insights. The most useful contemporary cookery book referring to the middling ranks is Mrs Hannah Glasse, *The ART of COOKERY made Plain and Easy* (1st edn, London, publisher unknown, 1747).

[14] Markham, G., *The English Housewife* (London, 1683), p. 49.

[15] Misson, H., *Memoirs and Observations in his Travels over England* (trans. Mr Ozell, London, 1719). He visited in 1685.

[16] Misson, *Travels*, under the topic of 'Table'. The extent to which people expected to eat meat is not easily demonstrated. Gregory King, in calculating the per capita consumption of meat, commented that about half the population never, or rarely, ate meat, including unweaned children. Of the rest, there were some families (440,000) who 'by reason of their poverty ... eat not flesh above 2 days in 7' and a further 440,000 'who receive alms and consequently eat not flesh above once a week' – King, G., 'An ESTIMATE of the Yearly Consumption of FLESH in the Nation', reproduced in Laslett, P. (ed.), *The Earliest Classics* (Farnborough: Gregg International, 1973).

pottage could also be made. In Scotland, the central hearths were particularly well suited to this kind of cookery, with the pot suspended over the fire, as the scenes of domestic life by David Allan in the later eighteenth century so well show. Bread was normally baked by the household and inventories show that many houses had appropriate equipment, but bread was also purchased – even Richard Latham's accounts record a few purchases of ordinary bread although 'corn' and 'flower' was often bought, apparently for bread.[17] Flat bread, characteristic of northern England and Scotland, was easier to make over an open fire, on girdle pans and baking stones. Smoking bacon and ham was common, but beef was salted and various fruit preserves were possible with the increasing availability of sugar. It is something of a problem in knowing how much food preparation was done in middling households, especially those of small farmers and tradesmen. Latham's accounts suggest that food was preserved, for salt and sugar were purchased but not in very large amounts, whilst the complexity of the domestic economy is shown by frequent purchases of some staple foods.

Many of the possessions listed in probate inventories were associated with food preparation and these are represented in Tables 2.1 and 2.2 by cooking pots and saucepans. As Table 2.1 shows, the differences between town and country were not significant for the ubiquitous and well-established cooking pots but ownership of saucepans was significantly different between town and country. Furthermore, saucepans were associated with methods of food preparation (not necessarily sauces) on smaller, enclosed stoves and fires. These were, as Table 2.2 illustrates, quite new in the late seventeenth century; at this time they were equally rare in town and country, but they became more common in towns by 1725. By contrast, there were no significant differences over time and between various groups in the ownership of pots, which had established uses and were ubiquitous. This points to differences between 'traditional' and other goods; that this is so is clearer when we look at property associated with meals.

Meals

Meals were, as they still are, important social events at which people sat down together, ate and talked. Dinner was the main meal, eaten at midday by virtually everyone in the seventeenth century, but there were some changes in the half century before 1750 that have a bearing on social meanings and

---

[17] 'The Account Book of Richard Latham, 1723–1767', Lancashire Record Office, DP385. Weatherill, L. (ed.), 'The Account Book of Richard Latham, 1724–1767', *British Academy Records of Social and Economic History*, NS 15 (1990). This can also be searched on the World Wide Web at http://seastorm.ncl.ac.uk/latham/.

material culture.[18] The 'traditional' way of serving any meal was that all dishes of food were placed on the table at once and each person had their own plate or trencher onto which they carved or helped themselves from the serving dishes. Food was eaten with a knife or fingers, except for pottage, which was eaten with a spoon. With some food, and in some households, it was taken directly from a large vessel and not served onto a person's own plate at all. Of mid-eighteenth-century Scotland, one observer recalled later that 'it was the custom with the gentry, as it still is with our substantial tenants, for the whole company to eat broth out of one large plate'. We must not assume that shared utensils and the lack of cutlery as we know it necessarily resulted in indelicate and unmannerly behaviour. Even eating from a common dish with a spoon and pieces of bread could be done neatly, although later changes in behaviour at table led many of the old mores to be associated with poor manners and the lowest ranks in society.[19] New ways of serving gradually became apparent in the late seventeenth century with the table carefully laid and food served in a series of courses

There were many goods associated with 'traditional' eating patterns or table layouts. They can be seen together in 'Grace before a meal'[20] and are re-presented in inventories by pewter, tables, table-linen and some earthenware. Some of these items show no difference between town and country; by contrast the goods associated with new patterns of behaviour do show significant urban–rural differences. This is emphasised in Table 2.2. There had been little change in ownership of pewter, tables and table-linen between the late seventeenth century and the early eighteenth century, but there were notable changes in the items associated with changing mores and behaviour. This supports the observation that 'traditional' goods were to be found equally in town and country households. When new goods appeared, their use was more apparent in town than country although, as we have already seen, ownership was also associated with wealth and occupation.

---

[18] For general commentary on the meaning of meals, see Douglas, M., *Implicit Meanings: Essays in Anthropology* (London: Routledge and Paul, 1975).

[19] There is scattered commentary on eating patterns. The division of a meal into courses was a novelty in the later seventeenth century, confined at that time to the households of some of the fashionable elite in London; for instance, Pepys reports such a dinner in 1669 with Lord Sandwich and others, 'dinner was brought up, one dish after another, but a dish at the time'. At home, Pepys's meals were served in the traditional way, with numerous dishes if he had company and a couple of simpler dishes if he did not: Latham, R. and Matthews, W. (eds), *The Diary of Samuel Pepys: A New and Complete Transcription*, 11 vols (London: G. Bell, 1970–83), vol. 9, 23–1–1669/70, p. 423; vol. 1, 26–1–1660/61; and vol. 4, 13–1–1663/64, pp. 13–14. The best evidence for the behaviour of the 'middling' is in diaries, and most diaries before 1740 record dinner in the middle of the day.

[20] Van Aken, 'Grace before a meal', Ashmolian Museum, Oxford; reproduced in Weatherill, *Material Culture*, p. 7.

Drinking and domestic property

Drinking was a social activity and drinking at home with friends and family was important – many of the visits reported in diaries refer to drinking of some kind, the more so when tea became available and a visit could be described as 'taking tea' or 'drinking tea' with someone.[21] From the late seventeenth century tea- and coffee-drinking gradually became more frequent and massive increases in imports of both tea and coffee meant that tea was familiar to many people of middle rank by the early eighteenth century, even if it did not enter daily routines until later in the century. The circumstances of tea drinking were different from alcohol and it appealed to people, especially women, who wanted light refreshment during the day or in the evening. In some households drinking tea became something of a ceremony, with appropriate – but not necessarily expensive – equipment associated with it. Utensils used for hot drinks are recorded in the sample of probate inventories and, together with china, indicate that these new customs were already having an impact on some households by 1725. Utensils for hot drinks were significantly more common in towns and ownership of these grew from the late seventeenth century. In-depth analysis of china suggested that early ownership was concentrated in urban areas with the better-off gentry and tradesmen in town as leaders, a pattern not repeated for the other, better-established goods, even curtains, as Table 2.7 has shown.

Leisure and decoration

Leisure was essential for peoples' well-being and middling households provided the time and occasion for some leisure, even if it were no more than talking to friends. That people had to have leisure was certainly understood at the time, although this was often combined with a fear that too much leisure would lead to sloth and sin:

> Now recreation (which is the phisic for this disease of an over toiled body minde and spirit) is of several natures (which are in them selves Innocent, and harmlesse; but abused by excesse, then cease to be good, and becomes vaine and sinful)[22]

Diarists were, by keeping a diary at all, expressing intellectual and emotional

---

[21] Misson, *Travels* (see 'Visits'); Hobhouse, E. (ed.), *Diary of a West Country Physican, AD 1684–1726. Extracts from Dr. Claver Morris' Diary* (London: Simpkin Marshall, 1934); Morris, *Journeys of Celia Fiennes* (see entries for Tunbridge, p. 153; Lichfield, p. 194; Bath, p. 41; Epsom, pp. 379 and 391); Clark, P., *The English Alehouse: A Social History, 1200–1830* (London: Longman, 1983), pp. 195–242.

[22] Holme, R., 'The Academy of Armory and Blazon' (London, published for the Roxburgh Club, 1905), p. 55.

needs beyond the daily round of physical life and some are explicit that they had such needs, or could see them in others. The most frequently documented way that people spent non-working time was in talking and visiting. Virtually every diary, series of letters or autobiography, no matter what the age and occupation of the writer, records innumerable visits to friends and relatives, apparently for relaxation and social purposes. Marchmont, to quote one instance amongst many, records that he visited, or was visited, eight times in the first ten days of October 1714; he usually ate meals or had drinks on these occasions.[23] Misson's observations are of interest, for he comments that 'the ordinary Sort of People did not visit each other in a formal way in the evening but they go to see one another with their Work in their Hands and Cheerfulness in their Countenance, without Rule or Constraint'.[24] There were a number of essentially quiet and private activities that could occupy some people for many hours within the household itself. Amongst them were reading, drawing, writing, studying, religious devotions and just sitting. They were undoubtedly more common amongst the professional people and the better-off tradesmen, but we should not assume that quiet contemplation was confined to those who were able to write about it. Latham purchased books throughout the period of the accounts and subscribed to newspapers from 1746. The increase in public leisure, such as that observed by Celia Fiennes in several aspiring spas in the late seventeenth century, was unusual in that it was not available to everyone; non-working time at home was more important for most people.[25]

People are social animals and the ambience of their surroundings had meanings for them at any time that we know anything about – from the Neolithic to the present. Possessions were used to signify something about the owner, as markers of status and much more, even if they served practical needs at the same time. There was an active material culture associated with this social side of peoples' lives, represented in inventories by a range of goods serving different practical functions – books, clocks, decorative items like mirrors and curtains. Some decorative items were more common in towns, as Table 2.1 shows. When allowance is made for wealth and status, however, towns do not emerge as the only influence on ownership, especially amongst the more important groups of consumers, the gentry and tradesmen. Books, well known and popular for a long time before the seventeenth century, were equally likely in town and country; the main influence over ownership was wealth. Clocks and watches changed but were little different in town or country, the main influence again being wealth.

[23] Turner, E. (ed.), 'The Marchant Diary, 1714–28', *Sussex Archaeological Collection* 25 (1873), 1–11 October 1714, p. 167. He was a substantial yeoman-farmer and became agent to the Duke of Somerset after 1727.

[24] Misson, *Travels*, under 'Visits'.

[25] Morris, *Journeys of Celia Fiennes*, p. 391.

Supply

The discussion so far has drawn evidence from individual households. This final section turns the problem around and looks at it from the perspective of the supply of domestic property. Some goods were more readily available in some areas than others due to supply conditions. It is fortunate that there is some good information on the internal trade in china because china was unusually concentrated in urban areas.[26] China was new and was unusually prevalent in urban areas; it was also imported and distributed in a way that tended to focus supply in towns.

Chinaware was entirely imported and not made in significant amounts in England before the middle of the eighteenth century. It was imported in very large quantities from the later seventeenth century as the valuations on the customs ledgers show.[27] Table 2.8 shows that there were large annual fluctuations but that enormous amounts were distributed around the country from the late seventeenth century. Enough had been imported by 1725 to provide every household in the country with several pieces, although they were not (as we have seen) evenly distributed. Most of the pieces imported were relatively modest; the supracargoes' diaries in Canton show that the main items in the earlier eighteenth century were saucers, cups, small plates and images; tableware did not become frequent until the 1740s.[28] They were not ornate pieces and were probably worth about sixpence each on average. What is important is that chinaware was distributed through a sophisticated network of dealers. This began in London, where it was auctioned in large lots from the East India Company warehouses. Provincial dealers and shopkeepers got supplies through one of the chinaware merchants, who were already in business as 'chinamen' by the early eighteenth century. This tended to concentrate the sales network on London but it did provide a mechanism by which china quickly became available throughout the country. There were shops specialising in selling glass and earthenware who included china as soon as it was available, and there were dealers in most large towns and many small ones by the middle of the eighteenth century, and probably earlier. By the mid-1720s china was widely available through urban outlets, so might be expected to be better known to town dwellers and therefore purchased and recorded in

---

[26] Weatherill, L., 'The Business of Middleman in the English Pottery Trade before 1780,' *Business History* 28 (1986), pp. 51–76.

[27] Weatherill, L., 'The Growth of the Pottery Industry in England, 1660 to 1815', unpublished PhD thesis, London School of Economics, University of London, 1982, pp. 125–9 and 197. See India Office Library, East India Co. Records, Home Miscellaneous series, 10–14 (1710–24) for auction sales.

[28] Weatherill, 'Growth of the Pottery Industry', p. 175. India Office Library, East India Co. Records, G/12/

Table 2.8
Imports and retained imports of chinaware, 1696–1730

	Imports recorded in customs ledgers	Imports with values adjusted	Re-exports	Retained imports	Pieces of china (value assumed at 6d)
1696	£1,316	£3,948	£1,397	£2,551	122,448
1697	£5,306	£15,918	£677	£15,241	731,568
1698	£555	£1,665	£58	£1,607	77,136
1699	£4,346	£13,038	£982	£12,056	578,688
1700	£10,772	£32,316	£910	£31,406	1,507,488
1701	£3,431	£10,293	£4,160	£6,133	294,384
1702			£4,386		
1703	£9,272	£27,816	£4,108	£23,708	1,137,984
1705	£34,942	£104,826	£1,463	£103,363	4,961,424
1706	£26,088	£78,264	£1,830	£76,434	3,668,832
1707	£2,415	£7,245	£763	£6,482	311,136
1708	£12,297	£36,891	£1,789	£35,102	1,684,896
1709			£1,443	-£1,443	-69,264
1710	£4,099	£12,297	£906	£11,391	546,768
1711	£5,219	£15,657	£490	£15,167	728,016
1712					
1713	£20,671	£62,013	£1,669	£60,344	2,896,512
1714	£8,704	£26,112	£2,660	£23,452	1,125,696
1715	£5,294	£15,882	£1,314	£14,568	699,264
1716	£337	£1,011	£1,034	-£23	-1,104
1717	£2,010	£6,030	£413	£5,617	269,616
1718	£48,600	£145,800	£1,277	£144,523	6,937,104
1719	£1,400	£4,200	£3,341	£859	41,232
1720	£1,191	£3,573	£964	£2,609	125,232
1721	£10,437	£31,311	£928	£30,383	1,458,384
1722	£32,800	£98,400	£2,901	£95,499	4,583,952
1723	£12,846	£38,538	£4,822	£33,716	1,618,368
1724	£13,547	£40,641	£3,598	£37,043	1,778,064
1725	£3,559	£10,677	£1,750	£8,927	428,496
1726	£3,800	£11,400	£1,870	£9,530	457,440
1727	£5,990	£17,970	£1,960	£16,010	768,480
1728	£14,604	£43,812	£2,104	£41,708	2,001,984
1729	£21,950	£65,850	£4,501	£61,349	2,944,752
1730	£20,860	£62,580	£5,224	£57,356	2,753,088

Source: Weatherill, 'Growth of the Pottery Industry', pp. 446–8.

in towns more often than in rural areas. This is not to deny that people from the countryside did visit towns – partly to buy provisions – and could thus be aware of new products. So the mechanisms behind the ownership of china were influenced both by a recognition that china would be good to have but also that it was more readily available in urban centres.

The influence of the supply of china can be seen in the patterns of ownership over the seven regions examined here, indicated in Table 2.6. It was most common in north-east England where china formed part of the return trade from London in domestic and other goods. It was least common in areas where trade with London was less marked, notable in the North West. The relationship between ownership and supply is less well documented for most domestic goods. Some goods were locally made and their supply well established. Some of the new items were often imported; for example, pictures and prints were mostly imported and show patterns similar to those for china. Clocks were made in Lancashire and were more common there. However, earthenware was not more common in Staffordshire where it was made in both the north and south of the county; it was made in Lancashire and was more common there. Supply and the inland trades should not be overlooked, for a rural–urban dichotomy could be based on the influence of trading networks rather than on 'something' about life in towns themselves. It is an area which clearly demands much fuller investigation.

Conclusion

In order to own something, wherever a household was situated, several steps were needed and each of these represents a different set of influences over the ownership of property. Firstly, a household had to know about and be able to get any item, old or new. The sales networks and the existence of shops and other outlets in towns meant that ownership was easier (all other things being equal) in towns, especially for new and imported goods. New items could be seen at markets and in shops, other people might have them and there were other ways of learning of their existence (including advertisements). So certain limited supply conditions would lead to concentration in urban areas where most sales outlets were concentrated. Where an item was widely produced, well known and widely distributed, the influence of location in town or country would be muted or non-existent. Secondly, a household had to have some purpose for any property. The purpose could be practical or emotional or social and there was certainly a combination of reasons for desiring any item of property. It is under this heading that the idea that material culture in some way satisfied social needs has been expressed, and many writers see these as important in ownership. The idea of goods giving 'pleasure' is also helpful here in preventing a purely utilitarian approach. Internal dynamics of the household and social position are favoured as explanatory variables by this approach. In cases where ownership of an item was related to behaviour, we would not expect a great deal of difference between town and country because household function was not greatly dissimilar in town and country. Thirdly, a household had to be able to buy property (or, unusually for the property dealt with here, inherit it) which means that wealth was important, even if it does not explain everything.

The various influences on ownership worked at different levels of the economy and society. On the one hand, there was continuity over time and between different places. The activities of domestic life and the meanings associated with them were not greatly different by 1730; households in town and country fulfilled similar functions. The things associated with continuity tended to be fairly evenly distributed throughout society and between town and country. On the other hand, some property was more easily available in towns through growing numbers of shops and traders. These contrasts suggest a variety of mechanisms, linked to what people actually did and wanted, and not a simple dichotomy between town and country.

Chapter 3

Meanings of property and the world of the petite bourgeoisie

Geoffrey Crossick

The cultural meanings attached to property in specific social settings are essential to an effective understanding of property ownership. The process of transferring and recording property after death may transform it into money equivalents, though even the act of will-making represented an effort to maintain the relational aspects of property *post mortem*,[1] but for the historian similarly to treat property primarily in terms of its total financial valuation is to neglect some of the most socially significant of its influences. The aggregate value of property is of major importance, but a simple ranking in wealth hierarchies can distract attention from the distinct meanings attached to property in different parts of the social system, and in different geographical locations. The problem should not be conceptualised in terms of two antithetical approaches, one focusing on consumption and artefacts, and rooted in cultural history, the other on the act of owning and bequeathing wealth, and based on quantitative analysis. Whilst the former makes little sense without an understanding of the material dimensions of what people owned, the latter needs to be understood through the meanings which people attached to those possessions and to the act of acquiring them. The ownership of property, the definition of what constitutes property, the cultural and political meanings attached to property of different kinds, are all issues which have until recently been neglected by social historians of modern Europe,[2] excessively attached as they have been to the study of those without property or to an often schematic

---

[1]   Morris, R. J., 'Reading the Will: Cash Economy, Capitalists and Urban Peasants in the 1830s', in Kidd, A. and Nicholls, D. (eds), *The Making of the British Middle Class? Studies of Regional and Cultural Diversity since the Eighteenth Century* (Stroud: Sutton, 1998), pp. 120–22.

[2]   This is perhaps nowhere more evident in Britain than in the long debate on bourgeois landownership in the nineteenth century. We have an increasingly sophisticated, albeit still contested, understanding of who owned land, but a far weaker grasp of why they acquired it and what significance they attached to its ownership. See Daunton, M. J., '"Gentlemanly capitalism" and British industry, 1820–1914', *Past and Present* 122 (1989), p. 130–31; Crossick, G., 'La bourgeoisie britannique au 19ᵉ siècle. Recherches, approches, problématiques', *Annales. Histoire, Sciences Sociales* (1998), pp. 1121–2 and the references there.

approach to those with it. This is evident in the attempts to use wealth hierarchies to partition social space; indeed, to identify social groups.[3]

The petite bourgeoisie of small shopkeepers, small manufacturers and master artisans in nineteenth-century Europe are the focus of this essay, with special emphasis being laid on evidence from Britain and France.[4] The petite bourgeoisie provides a good case study of the meanings of property, for it was the social group most clearly defined by its attachment to property in a very specific sense. As has been observed of contemporary Britain, 'at the centre of the social world of the petit-bourgeois lies petty property'.[5] Unlike the working class it generally owned real property, whether for business use or investment, whilst unlike more substantial bourgeois this property tended to be relatively concrete and immobile, tied to specific forms and places long after flexibility had come to characterise the holdings of the wealthy. The ability of petit-bourgeois property to generate resources was also closely linked to the labour of owners and their families, again in contrast to larger bourgeois. In the words of a Belgian social catholic observer in 1914, 'the *classe moyenne* both labours and owns at one and the same time'.[6]

Ownership and investment

What did these petits bourgeois own? Studies of property and investment suggest a distinctive pattern which drew upon the cultural and social imperatives of the world of small enterprise. As Chaline observes in his study of the bourgeois of nineteenth-century Rouen, in the property that people accumulate 'there is a choice of investments and sources of income that is heavy with social implications and which is often extremely revealing about deeply-rooted mentalities'.[7] The theme is particularly revealing of the world of small enterprise. The characteristic binding together of family and enterprise might be expressed through the specific property of the shop or workshop,

---

[3]   This approach is best articulated in the work of Adeline Daumard and the thesis-based French studies associated with her. See Daumard, A., *La bourgeoisie parisienne de 1815 à 1848* (Paris: École Pratique des Hautes Études, 1963) and Daumard, A. (ed.), *Les fortunes françaises au XIXe siècle* (Paris: Mouton, 1973).

[4]   For a broad analysis of the petite bourgeoisie in nineteenth-century Europe, see Crossick, G. and Haupt, H.-G., *The Petite Bourgeoisie in Europe 1780–1914. Enterprise, Family and Independence* (London: Routledge, 1995).

[5]   Bechhofer, F. and Elliott, B., 'Petty Property: the Survival of a Moral Economy', in F. Bechhofer and B. Elliott (eds), *The Petite Bourgeoisie. Comparative Studies of the Uneasy Stratum* (London: Macmillan, 1981), p. 194.

[6]   Duplat, G., *La classe moyenne. Son rôle social. Son action politique. Sa situation économique. Les réformes urgentes* (Brussels, 1914), p. 22.

[7]   Chaline, J.-P., *Les bourgeois de Rouen. Une élite urbaine au XIXe siècle* (Paris: Presses de la Fondation nationale des sciences politiques, 1982), p. 137.

though the ownership of the site of the business was not the normal expectation. Oldham shopkeepers in the 1830s and 1840s did not generally own their business premises,[8] whilst artisans and shopkeepers in mid-century Amsterdam were much less likely to have capital tied up in their own business premises than were merchants and industrialists, in spite of a greater attraction to real property in general.[9] Nonetheless, surpluses for investment tended to be disproportionately placed in real property – land and especially housing – rather than personal property – stocks, shares, loans and so on. Although there was some trend amongst petits bourgeois towards investment in the latter, it was not universal and was far less marked than amongst other wealth-holding groups. In maintaining through the nineteenth century its broad preference for investment in real property, the petite bourgeoisie resisted what Pierre Léon called 'the triumph of mobile capital'[10] – a striking cultural as much as economic feature of this group.

Surpluses were often invested in real property rather than in the business itself, a feature which is partly explained by the characteristics of small enterprise, where the risks of business expansion were considerable and the benefits of growing beyond what limited and localised markets could bear uncertain. The search for secure investments was also a response to the insecurity endemic in small business, sustained by credit networks whose fragility was a source of continuing anxiety. The business characteristics of small enterprise in increasingly complex capitalist economies was thus one factor shaping the investment mentality of petits bourgeois. Their dominant place amongst the owners of tenement property in later nineteenth-century Edinburgh has been interpreted as a form of insurance as much as an investment.[11] Petits bourgeois appear to have had a smaller percentage of their wealth tied up in the enterprise than wealthier groups. Berg has shown that the priority for the owners of small-scale industry in eighteenth-century Birmingham and Sheffield was not to increase the size of the production unit, but to acquire workshop and especially residential property to let out for rent, suggesting clear threshold sizes for manufacturing units.[12] A similar pattern can be seen amongst Lyon's bakers in the middle decades of the nineteenth century,

[8]   Winstanley, M., 'Owners and Occupiers: Property, Politics and Middle-Class Formation in Early Industrial Lancashire', in Kidd and Nicholls, *The Making of the British Middle Class*, pp. 106–7.

[9]   De Vries, B., 'Amsterdamse Vermogens en Vermogensbezitters, 1855–1875', in *AAG Bijdragen*, 28, *Dertig Jaar Afdeling Agrarische Geschiedenis*, Wageningen 1986, p. 204.

[10]   Léon, P., *Géographie de la fortune et structures sociales à Lyon au XIXe Siècle (1815–1914)* (Lyon: Presses Universitaires de Lyon, 1974), p. 265.

[11]   Elliott, B. and McCrone, D., 'Landlords in Edinburgh: Some Preliminary Findings', *Sociological Review* 23 (1975), p. 559.

[12]   Berg, M., 'Small Producer Capitalism in Eighteenth-century England', *Business History* 35 (1993), pp. 17–39.

with profits used not for a second oven or an enlarged shop, nor even to improve the domestic space, but lent or invested for interest. This was even true of prosperous bakers such as Jean-Benoît Brouailler, whose substantial investments in stocks and shares and personal loans seemed to barely match the humble shop with its modest equipment as described by the *notaire* who drew up the inventory on his death.[13] In July Monarchy Paris, 39 per cent of petit-bourgeois wealth at death was tied up in the business, compared with 69 per cent in the case of merchants and industralists.[14] The character of small enterprise shaped the culture of its owners to ensure that surpluses were turned into investments that were seen as more secure.

This concern for security was translated into a fixation on real rather than personal property, with the role of petits bourgeois in the ownership of rental housing its best-known manifestation.[15] The purchase of houses and apartments for rental to workers was common amongst the small investors of European towns – small *rentiers*, widows, and the owners of small businesses. The three groups often overlapped, certainly through the life-cycle. Housing proprietors in the 1st arrondissement of Brussels in 1866 were dominated by two groups: 44 per cent were retailers and artisans, 31 per cent *rentiers*.[16] In Berlin at the end of the century the landlord class contained small businessmen, shopkeepers, senior clerks, lesser professionals, and of course widows.[17] Their borrowing from mortgage banks reminds us that property ownership of this kind was not simply about finding a location for surplus income, but also about finding a framework of secure and diverse investments. Petit-bourgeois ownership of working-class housing is a recurrent theme of contemporary analysis, for example in the replies of parish officials to the inquiries made on behalf of the 1834 Royal Commission on the Poor Laws in Britain, with tradesmen, small businessmen, and *rentiers* singled out regularly for special mention. Winstanley's analysis of the overseers' replies for Lancashire indicates a more variegated pattern, one in which small landlords prevailed in longer-established towns and the suburbs of large towns, whereas manufacturers and larger landed and commercial capital dominated in newer industrial towns and city centres.[18] This may have been no more than a temporary stage, for in Lancashire as in much of Europe larger manufacturing

---

[13] Angleraud, B., 'Les boulangers lyonnais aux XIXe–XXe siècles (1836 à 1914). Une étude sur la petite bourgeoisie boutiquière', Doctoral thesis, University of Lyon 2, 1993, vol. 2, pp. 431–2, 446–7.

[14] Daumard, *La bourgeoisie parisienne*, pp. 484–5. A similar pattern can be shown for a wide range of French towns as the above books by Daumard (ed.), Chaline and Léon reveal.

[15] See Crossick and Haupt, *The Petite Bourgeoisie*, pp. 123–6.

[16] Van den Eeckhout, P., "Brussels", in M. Daunton (ed.), *Housing the Workers, 1850–1914. A Comparative Perspective* (Leicester: Leicester University Press, 1990), pp. 78–9.

[17] Bullock, N., 'Berlin', in Daunton, *Housing the Workers*, p. 203.

[18] Winstanley, 'Owners and Occupiers', p. 96.

capital was by mid-century withdrawing from the ownership of working-class housing: whether, as in Preston, because others were now willing to provide it or, as in the northern French textile town of Roubaix, because the shift from outwork to concentrated production meant that manufacturers no longer felt in need of this form of labour control. Their role was assumed by shopkeepers and artisans.[19] Generalisations about petit-bourgeois ownership of working-class housing need to be qualified by type of town, by chronology, but also by trade. A survey in Leipzig in 1893 established that 41 per cent of butchers and 40 per cent of bakers owned housing property, 20 per cent of joiners, and just 3 per cent of shoemakers.[20]

The ownership of rental housing was one dimension of an attachment to real property, which was evident when the owner was active in business and not simply as preparation for retirement. Our picture of the composition of petit-bourgeois property is most thorough for France, whose notarial archives provide detailed information on property-holding at death, though less systematic evidence for Britain, Germany and other countries points in a similar direction. In July Monarchy Paris petits bourgeois became proprietors long in advance of retirement – indeed, they did so even if it meant indebtedness. For larger bourgeois such investments, other than in their own business premises, awaited the approach of retirement. Reinforcing a persistent localism of petit-bourgeois property ownership, Parisian small-businessmen bought property in their own *quartier*, close to where the wealth had been made. This persisted through the traumatic upheavals of Haussmannisation.[21]

There could be business as well as cultural reasons for this attachment to real property, for such investments could be used to guarantee the credit and loans often needed in vulnerable enterprises.[22] There were wider cultural imperatives at work, however, which shaped the prominent place of real property in petit-bourgeois investment. A study of Amsterdam probate

---

[19] Bedale, C., 'Property Relations and Housing Policy: Oldham in the Late-nineteenth and Early-twentieth Centuries', in J. Melling (ed.), *Housing, Social Policy and the State* (London: Croom Helm, 1980), pp. 50–51; Deyon, P., 'Roubaix dans la première moitié du XIXe siècle', in M. Garden and Y. Lequin (eds), *Construire la Ville XVIIIe–XXe siècles* (Lyon: Presses Universitaires de Lyon, 1983), pp. 117–29. See also Winstanley, 'Owners and Occupiers', pp. 92–112.

[20] Bücher, K., 'Eigentumsverhältnisse der Leipziger Handwerker', in Schriften des Vereins für Socialpolitik, 67, *Unterschungen über die Lage des Handwerks* vol. 6 (1897), pp. 699–705.

[21] Daumard, *La bourgeoisie parisienne*, p. 488; Bourillon, F., 'Etude de la sociabilité dans un milieu pré- et post-Haussmannien. Le quartier des Arts et Métiers à Paris entre 1850 et 1880', Thesis (3ème cycle), University of Paris X, Nanterre, 1985, pp. 576–605.

[22] For examples see Berg, 'Women's Property', p. 35; Young, C., 'Financing the Micro-scale Enterprise: Rural Craft Producers in Scotland, 1840–1914', *Business History Review* 69 (1995), pp. 412–13; Jacquemet, G., *Belleville au XIXe siècle. Du faubourg à la ville* (Paris: Éditions de l'ÉHSS, 1984), p. 291.

inventories between 1855 and 1875 reveals that 40 per cent of shopkeeper and artisan wealth was in real property, compared with a figure below 20 per cent for all other middle-class groups. This was not the business premises but other acquisitions by a petite bourgeoisie much less attracted to the shares and bonds rapidly growing in popularity elsewhere in the middle class.[23] The best evidence comes from studies which draw on inheritance and inventory records for a range of French cities. Notwithstanding some unevenness rooted in local circumstances, the dominant place of *immobilier* (real property) over *mobilier* (personal property) in petit-bourgeois wealth at death is clear, as is its persistence long after other sections of the bourgeoisie had moved emphatically towards different forms of investment. By the early twentieth century, when *mobilier* prevailed in larger bourgeois fortunes, studies of Paris, Lille, Bordeaux and Lyon all show the continuing strength of real property amongst the petite bourgeoisie.[24] In Lille, for example, 65 per cent of petit-bourgeois wealth at death in 1821 was tied up in *immobilier*, compared with 56 per cent of all fortunes. In 1908 the average place of *immobilier* in all fortunes had declined to 30 per cent (17 per cent for industrialists, 26 per cent for merchants, and 23 per cent for professions), but it stood virtually unchanged at 66 per cent for shopkeepers and artisans.[25] In the fairly traditional town of Rouen, a larger bourgeoisie concerned for security and stability – one which was socially and economically fairly conservative – nonetheless shifted from real property to personal investment whilst petits bourgeois moved, if anything, in the opposite direction. Equally interesting in Rouen is the shifting composition of the personal property. Larger bourgeois saw *créances* (personal loans) decline, to be replaced by government stocks, debentures and to a lesser extent shares, whereas that shift was much less marked amongst the town's retailers and artisans.[26] Petits bourgeois did not ignore stock-market investment completely, but they embraced it much less enthusiastically than did other groups.

As the Rouennais attachment to *créances* suggests, personal investment was personal not just in the formal legal sense, but also because it was tied up in genuinely personal loans. Petit-bourgeois investment typically involved mortgages to family or to individuals in the local or other known communities. The investment inventory of Marius Barrat, a plasterer and grocer in the 3ème arrondissement of Lyon who died in 1875, was primarily composed of very personal loans: *billets à ordre* at 5 per cent to a succession of local individuals,

---

[23]   De Vries, 'Amsterdamse Vermogens', p. 204.

[24]   See Daumard, *Les fortunes françaises*; Léon, *Géographie sociales à Lyon, passim.*

[25]   Codaccioni, F.-P., 'Les fortunes à Lille (1821–1908)', in Daumard (ed.), *Les Fortunes Françaises*, pp. 275–428. See also Dupeux. G. and Herpin, J., 'Les fortunes bordelaises', in Daumard (ed.), *Les fortunes françaises*, pp. 431–551; Boyer, M., 'Les métiers de la viande à Lyon de 1860 à 1914', Thesis (3ème cycle), University of Lyon 2, 1985, p. 219.

[26]   Chaline, *Bourgeois de Rouen*, pp. 127–60, and Figure 23 (non-paginated).

a loan to a small farmer at Saint Georges where Barratt had once owned land.[27] Local shopkeepers were often also the neighbourhood's money-lenders, as the record of their wealth at death revealed. There was also the more informal credit to customers that was a necessary part of maintaining a clientele, of whatever social level, and which always constituted a significant part of shopkeepers' wealth at death.[28] Book debts were one of the largest elements of wealth left, for example, by Glasgow's small businessmen in 1861, for whom loans in general were much more important than amongst larger bourgeois.[29]

As the relative importance of personal loans declined amongst petits bourgeois, we find a trend towards secure rather than speculative investments, including the growing importance of life assurance in both Britain and France.[30] Security was often identified with the local and the known. Hence the predilection of small businessmen for investing in local railway, water and gas companies, and banks.[31] 'If they ventured into the world of stock market investment,' wrote Angleraud of Lyon's bakers in the closing decades of the century, 'they did so without moving out of the regional space, which was for them a source of reassurance'.[32] Local savings banks could similarly seem more stable than their national counterparts, especially where the distrust of the larger state was reinforced by political localism. Cologne's petits bourgeois strengthened their commitment to the local savings bank during the crisis year of 1847, seeking security in their local municipality.[33]

The core characteristics of petit-bourgeois property ownership thus emerge. A preference for the secure and the local; a preference for real property over personal; and, amongst the latter, a preference for the known over the impersonal. David Morgan, a small but increasingly prosperous draper in the South Wales town of Pontlottyn, provides an illustration. He came from a small-scale farming background, opened two small shops in nearby towns, and displayed in his early business years a typical petit-bourgeois difficulty in separating business from household expenditure in his shop accounts. By the time that he had decided to move to a more ambitious shop in Cardiff, his investment preferences were clear. He set them out in a mortgage application in

---

[27] Archives Départmentales du Rhône: 3E 10857.

[28] On the importance of credit to customers, see Crossick and Haupt, *The Petite Bourgeoisie*, pp. 180–86.

[29] Nenadic, S., 'The Structure, Values and Influence of the Scottish Urban Middle Class: Glasgow 1800 to 1870', PhD thesis, University of Glasgow, 1986, pp. 134, 142.

[30] Morris, R. J. and Nenadic, S., 'The Family and the Small Firm: Edinburgh 1861–1891', ESRC End of Award Report, 1992, pp. 16–17; Boyer, Les métiers de la viande, p. 233.

[31] Nenadic, 'Scottish Urban Middle Class', p. 142.

[32] Angleraud, 'Les boulangers lyonnais', p. 444.

[33] Ayçoberry, P., 'Histoire sociale de la ville de Cologne (1815–1875)', Doctoral thesis, University of Paris 1, 1977, pp. 320–21.

1879. He had the leases on four shops along with twenty-four cottages in Pontlottyn, the freehold of a small farm near Brecon, the inevitable book debts, and shares in a range of local utilities, including the Ystrad Gas and Water Company, and the Rhymney Gas Company. The only industrial investment was a debenture bond in the local Rhymney Iron Company.[34]

In a century that saw an increasing anonymity of investment, a declining ability to watch over one's savings, and an increasing investor passivity, petits bourgeois may not have entirely resisted these trends, but they sought to hold on to a more personal vision of wealth. The local dimension of property was for them a powerful imperative, shaping, for example, the resistance in 1830s Britain to the establishment in London of a general register of deeds. Security for property, opponents argued, required local proprietors, local solicitors and local procedures, so that local knowledge would prevail. The very security that lay behind the acquisition of small property in the first place seemed to be undermined by rendering it national. The importance of local storage of deeds was reinforced by the fact that when held locally they could be rapidly deployed to sustain credit networks.[35]

The distinctive petit-bourgeois pattern of property-holding thus constitutes a personal, local and very concrete relationship with property. Faced with the threat that Cardiff's shipping elite could move to docks elsewhere, the city's councillors protested: 'To the Cardiff Chamber of Commerce the Cardiff Docks are a convenient and economical means of carrying on their business. To the ratepayers of the town they are an absolute necessity of existence'.[36] The wealthy elite of the city might have been able to move their capital and their business elsewhere, but the interests of Cardiff's small enterprise were tied to property that was both specific and local. Morris has identified what he calls the 'urban peasant', those in the Leeds of the early 1830s whose wills did not require that their estate be turned into cash before being divided amongst the beneficiaries according to instructions, but who left specified items of property, named and identified. The division might still be meant to be equal, but the distribution was of things (specific real property, investments, goods, the business, and so on) rather than cash. He suggests that these were will-makers of lower economic status, 'peasants' because their income derived from their own capital, labour, skill, credit and real estate.[37] In their resistance to the

[34] Morgan, A. N., *David Morgan. 1833–1919. The Life and Times of a Master Draper in South Wales* (Risca: Starling Press, 1977), pp. 81–2.

[35] For the case of Stockport, see the forthcoming University of London thesis of Owens, A., 'Small Fortunes: Property, Inheritance and the Middling Sort in Stockport, 1800–57'. I am grateful to Alastair Owens for this point.

[36] Quoted in Daunton, M. J., *Coal Metropolis. Cardiff 1870–1914* (Leicester: Leicester University Press, 1977), p. 156.

[37] Morris, 'Reading the will', pp. 128–9.

notion that property was really only its cash value, they articulated a conception of property shared by the petite bourgeoisie with whom they overlapped.

Property, politics and culture

Relationship to property and the meanings attached to property were one element in the process by which the owners of small enterprise came to separate themselves from the world of the people, to separate themselves from corporate ideals, to construct a distinctive group attached to the larger bourgeoisie. The world of small enterprise was at the heart of the shift that took place, between the late eighteenth century and the middle decades of the nineteenth century, from perceptions of property bound up with corporate and community rights and therefore also obligations, to a more individualistic and exclusive sense of the term.[38] This need was less a different conceptualisation of property, which remained a bundle of rights, more a narrower definition of the ways in which these rights were conceived. Even if the distinction between multiple use rights subject to wider moral forces and a new set of absolute property rights is in practice too simplistic a dichotomy, the rhetoric of absolute rights became politically powerful.[39]

Within the world of the small urban trades before the nineteenth century, the concept of 'property' included many types whose ownership was constrained by some wider community or, more precisely, whose ownership lay in membership of a community or group on which the rights depended.[40] To be a fully independent person meant the exercise of property regulated by a community. The regulation provided by the community of which you were a member was a 'privilege', that is to say a right which itself constituted a form of property. If property was the basis of independence, this was meant not in some narrowly material sense but also in terms of the privilege and status (for example as a guildsman or burgher) that was itself property. The archetypal example of such regulatory communities was the corporate trades, where the guild or corporation regulated the master's use of property whilst at the same time giving him[41] rights which were themselves conceptualised as property.

---

[38] For a survey of this ideological transition for France see Sewell, W. H., *Work and Revolution in France. The language of labour from the old regime to 1848* (Cambridge: Cambridge University Press, 1980), pp. 114–42.

[39] Brewer, J. and Staves, S. 'Introduction', in J. Brewer and S. Staves (eds), *Early Modern Conceptions of Property* (Routledge: London, 1995), pp. 17–18.

[40] For a variant of this approach applied to Chartist discourse, see Somers, M. R., 'The "misteries" of Property. Rationality, Rural-industrialization, and Community in Chartist Narratives of Political Rights', in Brewer and Staves, ibid., pp. 62–92.

[41] Female corporations existed but were rare, and widows admitted to male corporations were denied full rights. See Crossick, G., 'Past Masters: in Search of the Artisan in

When the tradesmen and artisans, whose support in the Dutch town of Deventer had underpinned the town's municipal revolution in the 1780s, began to distance themselves from the reforms being put in place by the town's elites, they petitioned against the way in which the new constitution undermined 'the most holy and inalienable privileges' of the guilds and burghers.[42] Similarly, when the *loi d'Allarde* abolished corporations in France in March 1791, the master wigmakers of Bordeaux, like many other corporations, protested that they had a right of property in the mastership which they had obtained at a good price.[43] Sewell has argued for *ancien régime* France that the property of a mastership was actually more important than the capital involved in the business, notwithstanding the fact that the latter was financially greater.[44] However, excessive emphasis on the way in which property and privilege were woven together in *ancien régime* France, and other societies with strong corporate structures, can deflect us from the more general situation which included Britain: the place in small entrepreneurial ideology of an artisanal conception of property that saw it as defined and constituted by the regulation of a community, a corporate ideal that could exist without the institutional structure of corporations.[45] This was an alternative definition of the rights to property to that conceived of within political economy, an alternative which embraced the right to work at one's trade and to defend its customs and privileges against intruders and the state alike.[46]

A more individualistic conception of property came to serve as one point of attachment to a larger bourgeois world for the owners of small enterprise, as the moral community of the trade fractured in the first half of the nineteenth century under the pressure of changing productive relations.[47] In Britain as in France, a significant proportion of masters detached themselves from the restrictions of the older conception of property, restrictions which their predecessors had once seen as their rights and their defence. As the idea of property became leaner and more individualistic, petit-bourgeois political

---

European History', in G. Crossick (ed.), *The Artisan and the European Town, 1500–1900* (Scolar Press: Aldershot, 1997), pp. 13–15 and the references there.

[42]   Te Brake, W., *Regents and Rebels. The Revolutionary World of an Eighteenth-Century Dutch City* (Oxford: Basil Blackwell, 1989), pp. 103–4.

[43]   Pontet, J., 'Craftsmen and Revolution in Bordeaux', in Crossick, *The Artisan and the European Town*, p. 124.

[44]   Sewell, *Work and Revolution in France*, pp. 118–19.

[45]   Note the English usage of the 'community of the trade', and the fact that the French *corporation* was in fact much more commonly referred to as a *communauté*.

[46]   This was part of a wider artisanal conception within which skill was seen as property. See Rule, J., 'The Property of Skill in the Period of Manufacture', in P. Joyce (ed.), *The Historical Meanings of Work* (Cambridge: Cambridge University Press, 1987), pp. 99–118.

[47]   See Crossick and Haupt, *The Petite Bourgeoisie*, pp. 16–63; Behagg, C., *Politics and Production in the Early Nineteenth Century* (London: Routledge, 1990).

relationships became bound up with the contested meanings of property. Many petits bourgeois, and by no means always the smallest, refused to accept the narrowing of the obligations bound up with property, and resisted within the framework of a wider popular radicalism. For others, an acceptance of these newer conceptions of property was one dimension of their separation from the world of wage-labour. Yet the older conception of property did not entirely disappear from the world of small enterprise, remaining as a potential – albeit residual – resource. This was particularly noticeable in those parts of Europe where independent enterprise, corporate status and political rights interlocked, such as the German free cities and what Mack Walker dubbed 'Home Towns'.[48] In many countries (most notably Germany, Sweden and Austria-Hungary) the political and juridical identity of urban citizenship – as burghers, burgesses, freemen and so on – was closely intertwined with becoming a craft master, in other words with acquiring the dual property of business and mastership.

Even as guild rights were curtailed and abolished, they were replaced by rights of residence and representation which maintained implicit attachments to independent enterprise. Political representation, and the traces and memories of older patterns of representation, thus maintained the links between corporate status, small property and civic rights, and allowed it to function both as a force limiting democracy and as one reinforcing a particular municipal, small-propertied version of it. In the middle decades of the nineteenth century it provided the basis of much oppositional politics, resisting local oligarchic elites on the one hand and working-class associations on the other. Indeed, corporate notions of trade as property, drawing on an older discourse supposedly displaced by individualistic (and in France republican) ideas, reappear in petit-bourgeois movements of the late nineteenth century. In this discourse, small property and small enterprise were vested with Jacobin or Jeffersonian republican virtues, or with moral superiority in the defence of a healthy social order. Property's symbolic meanings presented it as an expression of stability rather than as a tool for accumulation and growth. For much of the petite bourgeoisie, property came to represent independence, autonomy and security.[49]

The late abolition of corporations and the continuing existence of *Innungen* gave artisans a particularly influential role in petit-bourgeois mobilisation in late nineteenth-century Germany, and the corporatist conception of their trade strongly shaped the demands of German petit-bourgeois organisations. A distinctively corporatist sense prevailed of the property that was guild

---

[48]   Walker, M., *German Home Towns. Community, State, and General Estate 1648–1871* (Ithaca: Cornell University Press, 1971).

[49]   For these values in the twentieth century, see Bechhofer, F. and Elliott, B., 'A Progress Report on Small Shopkeepers and The Class Structure', SSRC Research Report, 1975.

membership.[50] Although corporate projects had little appeal in France, where republican ideals precluded intermediary bodies between the citizen and the state, the corporatist assumptions of the shopkeeper *Ligue syndicale de travail, de l'industrie et du commerce*, founded in Paris in 1888, are undeniable. The *Ligue syndicale* presented a vision of a republic of small property owners, fragmentation of property (*morcellisme*) against monopoly, and nostalgia for a past in which small enterprise provided the basis for a popular republican democracy. As petit-bourgeois politics began to move to the right, it carried with it many of its older values. The key to the *Ligue syndicale*'s defence of the small shop against the department store and the organised economy was specialisation – that each person should have one trade and only one trade, and that the right to practice and live by that trade was in effect each individual's property.[51] Thus, in a radical petit-bourgeois vision, the trade as one's property was reasserted, a corporatist ideal without the corporatist framework. The shifting conception of property within small enterprise was thus one of emphasis more than of abrupt transition, and older conceptions of property could survive as a residual resource of surprising longevity.

Even within an individualistic sense of property, however, political discourse had long linked small property to a radical conception of independence. In this radical vision, an ordinary, useful and productive people was distinguished from the rich and the parasites who monopolised wealth and power. This ideology of modest means, hard work and independence took shape in the writings of Tom Paine and Thelwall, as well as in the ideals of the Parisian *sans-culottes* during the French Revolution, and it was developed in popular political movements in Britain and France in the first half of the nineteenth century. In this vision of the world, the ownership of property was not a significant point of social or political division, and small property often provided the independence to reject the client economy and its associated dependence and hierarchy.[52] This was clearly present in late eighteenth-century reform ideas in Britain, providing one element of the ideology of popular radicalism over the following decades. Wilkite reform ideology redefined Country ideas by removing the requirement that independence be rooted in substantial landed property, and by attaching the concepts of independence and property to a smaller middling group who were at the heart of the Wilkite cause. Property remained fundamental to independence, but in this radical formulation the property was more limited in scale, not necessarily landed, and

---

[50] Volkov, S., *The Rise of Popular Antimodernism in Germany: The Urban Master Artisans 1873–1896* (Princeton: Princeton University Press, 1978).

[51] Nord, P., *Paris Shopkeepers and the Politics of Resentment* (Princeton: Princeton University Press, 1986), pp. 261–301.

[52] See Crossick and Haupt, *The Petite Bourgeoisie*, pp. 147–53.

the basis for resisting the client relationship.[53] Metropolitan radicals of the
1760s and 1770s still held to a propertied franchise, but it would rest on the
small property of shopkeepers, craftsmen and others 'whose property is
sufficient to render them independent and secure them, if they please, from
undue influence'.[54] The doctrine was subsequently extended to all ratepayers
and taxpayers, en route to universal manhood suffrage, but in its eighteenth-
century flowering it saw widely diffused small property as the basis of a
healthy political system that would safeguard liberty. This radical vision drew
on a continuing eighteenth-century conception of small property as the basis of
a healthy and balanced society in which independence provided the roots of
democracy and liberty of ideas. At its heart lay a republican vision that can be
traced back to Machiavelli's Discourses, a vision in which the virtuous citizen
could only be found amongst those whose small property allowed them the
independence necessary for sound political judgement, the ability to resist
corruption, and above all made them a force for political virtue. The radical and
virtuous potential of small property found many expressions (in the English
Commonwealth tradition, Jeffersonian and artisanal ideals in early America,[55]
or the sans-culottes in the French Revolution), and it continued to influence the
ideas of popular movements in Britain and France before fading in the middle
decades of the nineteenth century.

The division between those with property and those without it was thus not
yet the fault-line within European society, and in this continuing vision small
property would constitute not a threat to a democratic egalitarian order but its
very foundation. Small property held a variety of meanings, which included the
ownership of land or buildings or enterprise without being limited to that, and
the ideological detachment of the petite bourgeoisie from that popular milieu
had not yet played its part in making the defence of small property an issue for
the political right. In this context the Birmingham Political Union of the 1830s
and 1840s was an attempt to draw a section of the town's petits bourgeois into
a reform alliance with larger business interests, combining the language of
popular radicalism with insistence on a propertied franchise.[56] The slow

---

[53] Brewer, J., 'English Radicalism in the Age of George III', in J. G. A. Pocock (ed.),
Three British Revolutions. 1641, 1688, 1776 (Princeton: Princeton University Press, 1980), pp.
344–8.

[54] Reflexions on Representation in Parliament (1776), quoted in Dickinson, H. T.,
Liberty and Property. Political Ideology in Eighteenth-Century Britain (London: Methuen,
1977), p. 226.

[55] New York's democratic small masters and journeymen in the late eighteenth and
early nineteenth centuries 'exemplified a belief that independent men of relatively small means
were both entitled to full citizenship and best equipped to exercise it'. Wilentz, S., Chants
Democratic. New York City and the Rise of the American Working Class, 1788–1850 (New
York and Oxford: Oxford University Press, 1984), p. 102.

[56] Behagg, Politics and Production, esp. pp. 158–83.

detachment of petits bourgeois from wider popular movements was a continuing thread of European social history during the nineteenth century. It is hard to pinpoint the period when small property came to be conceived not as the foundation of the virtuous republic nor as a force for radical independence, but as the basis for social and political conservatism; when it became a notion of the political right. In the first half of the nineteenth century a narrower conception of property developed as a determinant of civic and political rights in Britain, France, Belgium and elsewhere in industrialising Europe, but it would be rash to see this as the moment when the distinct sense of property came to underpin a perception of the social order in which propertied and propertyless occupied different sides of a political divide. It should be seen as no more than a beginning, not least because what we call a propertied franchise was in reality much more than that, as a variety of signs of stability emerged in Western Europe as the basis for admissibility to the political nation. Winstanley has rightly pointed to property as 'the yardstick by which democratic reforms were debated and judged', defining eligibility to vote and serve on a plethora of municipal bodies in early to mid-nineteenth-century Britain. But with equal significance he stresses the concern for the occupation as well as the ownership of property. The French *censitaire* suffrage effectively made tax payment a surrogate for the ownership of property, and the July Monarchy added the payment of the *patente*, essentially a small-business licence tax, to earlier and narrower definitions. As late as Belgium's 1893 franchise reform the search for safeguards to accompany universal male suffrage led to extra votes for those with real property of 2000 francs value or more, but also occupation of housing at a designated level of tax, as well as for those with university degrees.[57] In the course of the nineteenth century, property and security did indeed become ideologically aligned in an increasingly precise fashion in Western Europe, but it was rarely property alone which counted. In any case, it is doubtful whether independence rooted in small-scale property ever completely lost its radical edge. The petits bourgeois who were drifting to the right throughout Europe in the later nineteenth century were not so much conservatives adjusting to a new set of circumstances, but in many ways populists protesting against the faults of existing parliamentary systems and condemning the activities of large-scale financial and commercial capital.[58]

---

[57] Winstanley, 'Owners and Occupiers', p. 93; Wolloch, I., *The New Regime. Transformations of the French Civic Order, 1789–1820s* (New York: W. W. Norton, 1994), p. 111; Witte, E. and Craeybecks, J., *La Belgique politique de 1830 à nos jours* (Brussels: Editions Labor, 1987), pp. 118–19.

[58] Nord, P., 'Les mouvements de petits propriétaires et la politique (des années 1880 à la première guerre mondiale)', *Revue historique* 558 (1986), pp. 407–33. For the recurrence of older radical themes in a more right-wing political setting, see Crossick and Haupt, *The Petite Bourgeoisie*, p. 163–5.

Property was in this sense always an ambiguous force within the world of small enterprise, capable of expressing radical as well as defensive visions. Yet it was also expressive of a distinctive petit-bourgeois culture as that took shape. The culture became more protective and introspective as the societies within which small enterprise operated changed between the middle of the nineteenth century and the First World War. And so, too, did the meanings of property. As has already been observed localism, personal relations and security became more distinctively important, not only in daily life but in property and investment as well. Small-scale property came to be articulated more as a source of achievement and pride than as a force for change. The ownership of property now came to distinguish the petite bourgeoisie from the working class in general and from their own employees in particular. For Pierre-Louis Marcelin, a small tinsmith and lampmaker with a handful of journeymen in late nineteenth-century Nîmes, the thing which set him apart from his workforce was not his labour, for he worked alongside them, nor his craft, for they shared that too, but the independence which went with property. The business was, of course, part of that property, but in his recollections of his upbringing, his son Paul stressed the importance of other smaller, but very concrete, forms of property in setting the family apart. The great point of difference was the security that property provided. 'My father, because he had become a *patron* fairly young and because he had worked so hard, had been able to save what was needed to build, bit by bit, two houses in the suburbs, worth about 30,000 Francs in 1924'.[59] This was to be his security, a source of stability and an independent old age. But there were also the *mazets nîmois*, rustic simple cottages with a field, up to 3 or 4 kilometres from the town, where olives, vines, almonds and figs could be cultivated. The *mazets* were owned by petits bourgeois and by artisanal workers, and though some cultivated their land themselves, the Marcelins could hire someone to do the work, confirming their *mazet* as a place for leisure. These *mazets* were not abstract property, but something embedded deep in the artisanal world.[60]

As concrete and specific property came to distinguish the owners of small enterprise from workers, so we encounter the normative and expressive dimensions of property ownership, which came to constitute almost an end in itself. It was graphically portrayed in the postcard-photographs which retailers had taken of themselves in front of their shops in turn-of-the-century Europe. These photos were about family as much as business, with the small shopkeeper, wife and children often framed by the shop doorway, the employees set at a distance along the shopfront. The postcards were distributed

---

[59]   Marcelin, P., 'Souvenirs d'un passé artisanal', *Les cahiers rationalistes* 253 (1968), p. 45.

[60]   Ibid., pp. 56–8.

to family, to friends and to customers. They expressed the pride of their owners – pride in the ownership of the business, maybe pride in the building though this was less important except as a signal of the scale of the enterprise. The photographs represented something that was very personally bound up with the owner of the enterprise, and the messages often indicate the ways in which they were presentations of the business, an affirmation of success, a search for approval. The size of the enterprise needed to be pointed out. 'This is a view of our shop', wrote the daughter of an English watchmaker and jeweller, 'the entrance to the front door is on the left, but it is not shown here'.[61] Or from a Parisian pattern maker: 'I am sending you the postcard of the business – two windows are missing'.[62] The messages can also remind us of the very personal associations of property in this petit-bourgeois world. 'The house father built in 1887', one finds on a message from a bakers and confectioners in Crediton, Devon; 'There Mabel was born, from which I married in 1898. There Dorothy was born. There dear Frank died in 1906 – taken on the last morning when Alice was leaving'.[63]

If one turns the postcards and reads the photographs rather than the messages, one sees the presentation of pride in the very concrete reality of the shop which represented the success of the family or the individual. The sober pride of the Townshends, framed in the doorway of their double-fronted hairdresser's and umbrella repairer's (Plate 3.1); the staff amidst the meticulous display of merchandise outside Smith's butchers and supply stores (Plate 3.2); the Yeoman family grocer's and greengrocer's, with the owner and son framed again in the doorway and the assistants and lads carefully marking out the space (Plate 3.3); the simple pride of the owners of the corner household stores, the photograph taken to embrace the shop, now expanded into what were once two houses, the merchandise, and the articulation of family in front of the doorway, with the couple, their son, and the pet in the wife's arms (Plate 3.4). The understated pride in ownership of a successful small business expressed in photographs such as these was sometimes more assertive and explicit. L. Gonord, third from the left in the photograph, one foot proprietorially in the doorway and the other forcefully forward on the pavement, had taken over the ironmonger's business in Montargis from which he sent this card to 'Messieurs les employés' (the staff), Herouart ironmonger's, in rue Notre Dame de Nazareth, Paris. He had written no more than a few words on the back: 'A friendly handshake from your former colleague' (Plate 3.5). The pride in success shown by L. Gonord in the photograph and confirmed by his message

---

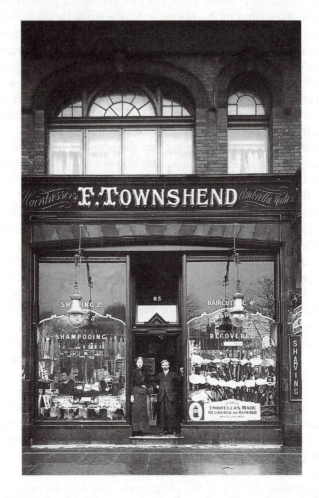

Plate 3.1: F. Townshend, hairdresser and umbrella repairer. Place unknown, c. 1900–1914

was left to the image alone in the postcard of Jones, decorator and hardware merchant, as the proprietor gestures proudly to his shop, with the women carefully set in the domestic space to one side (Plate 3.6). This is not the place to explore the potential of such photographs as self-presentation by the owners of small enterprise, but pride in the business and in the property associated with it are a recurrent (though not exclusive) theme of such images in both Britain and France in the early part of the twentieth century. In her autobiographical

Plate 3.2: Barnes and Smith, butcher and general supply store. Place unknown, c. 1900–1914

Plate 3.3: F. C. Yeoman, tea dealer and bacon factor. Place unknown, c. 1900–1914

Plate 3.4: Claremont Household Stores. Place unknown, c. 1900–1914

Plate 3.5: L. Gonord, ironmonger. Montargis, Loiret, c. 1910

Plate 3.6: Syl Jones, practical decorator and hardware merchant. Place unknown, dated 1921

recollections of her childhood in her family's small *café-épicerie* (café and grocers) in a Normandy town in the 1920s, Annie Ernaux's description of one family photograph captures the way in which these images articulated the pride of ownership, one that found cultural expression in very personal and precise ways. She starts with her father:

> About fifty, still in the prime of life, head held very straight, an air of concern as if worried that the photo might be spoiled, he is wearing an outfit, dark trousers and light jacket over a shirt and tie. Photo taken on a Sunday, in the week he was in overalls. In any case, one always had one's photo taken on a Sunday, because there was more time and one was better dressed. I am standing by his side in a flounced dress, one foot on the ground, both hands gripping the handlebars of my first bicycle. He has one arm dangling by his side, the other hand on his waste. In the background there is the open door of the café, flowers on the windowsill, and above the door the bar licence plaque. One had oneself photographed with the things one was proud to own – the business, the bike, later the 4CV, on the roof of which he rested one hand in a gesture that pulled up his jacket. He never smiles on any photo.[64]

---

[64]   Ernaux, A., *La place* (Gallimard: Paris, 1983), pp. 55–6.

Inheritance, patrimony and the discourse of property

The role of property within the world of the petite bourgeoisie shifted during the course of the nineteenth century, and as it became more associated with stability and continuity, so the ideas of inheritance and succession assumed increasing ideological significance. How important was the building of a patrimony for nineteenth-century owners of small enterprise? Property should not be conflated with that which is inherited, not least because some of the historian's richest sources for the analysis of property ownership are those generated by death and inheritance. This is especially true of England, where although records of wealth at death were limited in comparison with other countries, detailed statements of wealth at other moments in the life cycle, above all the marriage contract, were even less common outside the elite.

Although property of a precise kind was so significant for the petite bourgeoisie, the inheritance of property and wealth may not itself have been a central force. Acquisition at precise stages of the life cycle certainly mattered, but it was at marriage rather than at death that the most significant property transfers for small enterprise probably took place. Marriage was, throughout Europe, a moment to start new enterprises, partly because many such businesses rested on the work of a married couple, but also because the dowry was an indispensable supplement to other sources of capital. Dowries in the Lyon bakery trade, for example, often matched the purchase price of the new business.[65] For the mass of owners of small enterprise, passing the business as a patrimony to a child or to their children was not a real expectation, not even in the idealised craft structures of eighteenth and nineteenth-century Austria. Ehmer has shown how the sons of artisans served their apprenticeship and worked as journeymen in other households, and that if they themselves became masters it was by acquiring influences and resources from the parent rather than craft and enterprise.[66] The limited level of business succession was accentuated in France by the abolition of corporations in 1791 and by the new inheritance laws which produced a clear shift in inheritance practice. The patrimonial property of the *ancien régime*, where a small business had been in theory, at least, bound up with the rights of mastership and public status, gave way to family inheritance that narrowed to more formal possessions and detached from the small enterprise. The latter was a way to generate resources for children as a whole rather than a resource to be preserved and transmitted to a single heir.

---

[65] Angleraud, 'Les boulangers lyonnais', pp. 136–45. For the same pattern in Malmö: Edgren, L., *Lärling Gesäll Mästare. Hantverk och hantverkare i Malmö 1750–1847*, (Lund: Universitetsförlaget Dialogos, 1987), p. 400.

[66] Ehmer, J., 'The artisan family in nineteenth-century Austria: embourgeoisement of the petite bourgeoisie?', in G. Crossick and H.-G. Haupt (eds), *Shopkeepers and Master Artisans in Nineteenth-Century Europe* (London: Methuen, 1984), pp. 195–218.

The core relationship of the business was now a married couple rather than a father and son.[67] The limited attachment to succession between generations was surely one reason why widows in small-enterprise families tended to inherit outright.[68] The interference and authority of the husband need not, of course, disappear with his death. At least not in his own intentions. Thomas Carr, a fairly successful draper whose house and business stood on south London's Old Kent Road, made his will in 1858 (eighteen years before his death). He left the business and the buildings, and indeed all his property, to his wife Ellen, who was his sole executrix. The will would have been a good deal shorter had he stopped at that point, but he proceeded to use most of the will to give her detailed instructions as to what she might do with the property: to maintain and insure the houses; to accept a good offer for the business should it be forthcoming; to invest the proceeds in government stock; how much she should spend on another house to live in should the issue arise; whilst all the time insisting that she would, of course, be free to make her own decisions.[69]

The main concern in petit-bourgeois families was not the passage of the business to the next generation but a broader family continuity and the passing on of social position. Owens has concluded from his study of Stockport succession strategies in the first half of the nineteenth century that the real issue reflected in the wills was not continuity of the business but provision for wife and children in the short and long term. In the majority of cases this meant disposing of the firm, either on death or within a specified period of time. Where the business was passed on, it was to the wife not the children, thus conforming to the general European pattern.[70] Artisanship or a capacity to organise a small enterprise was passed on rather than the actual business, and by the later nineteenth century, as the options for independent small enterprise seemed less promising, resources were increasingly deployed to ensure that children were provided with cultural capital with which to sustain their social position. Continuing petit-bourgeois status for children was not only more difficult to achieve, it was becoming less attractive. The new opportunities that were appearing in office and clerical occupations, including expanding state bureaucracies, and in new minor professions such as elementary schoolteaching, offered the prospects of moving sideways within a world increasingly defined as lower middle class or *classe moyenne*. This trend may

---

[67] Darrow, M. H., *Revolution in the House: Family, Class and Inheritance in Southern France, 1775–1825* (Princeton: Princeton University Press, 1989).

[68] For Britain see Davidoff, L. and Hall, C., *Family Fortunes: Men and Women of the English Middle Class 1780–1850* (London: Hutchinson, 1987), pp. 198–228.

[69] Will of Thomas Carr, Old Kent Road. Proved 1876. General Register Office, Somerset House, London.

[70] Owens, A., 'Inheritance and the Life-cycle of Family Firms in Early Nineteenth Century England', unpublished paper.

have disturbed many friends of small enterprise, for it weakened the petite bourgeoisie whilst enlarging a group far less able to play the role of social intermediary, but it proceeded apace. A dual strategy of limiting family size and investing in secondary education enabled the resources of French petits bourgeois in the first half of the twentieth century to be focused on educating their children for white-collar occupations, in what has been called a strategy of reconversion.[71] It was one that had its roots in the later nineteenth century. The Director of the Ecole Turgot in Paris reported in 1875 that his school recruited largely from workshop masters and the like. 'The principal goal of the great majority of both children and parents,' he observed, 'is office employment'.[72] The relationship between property acquisition, transmission, and social reproduction was thus a complex one.

The inheritance of a patrimony was paradoxically considered by others to be important in a milieu in which its occurrence was somewhat limited. A conservative social discourse at the turn of the century amongst a section of followers of Frédéric Le Play, and an overlapping strand of social catholics, found in an idealised world of small enterprise and its owners the source of stability and moderation in polarising societies.[73] Victor Brants, a Belgian social catholic economist and one of the key figures on the academic wing of this movement, observed that 'these small manufacturers build a patrimony and transmit it with their home and with their industry'.[74] In this discourse it was not property that defined the idealised *classes moyennes*, but rather property mixed with their other key features, particularly family, labour and independence. Georges Duplat argued that 'the support of possessions is not enough for the carrying out of their economic function; they must add labour; furthermore, this union of labour and property, which is characterised by the mixture of oneself and one's own, produces an average [*moyenne*] between possessions and labour which is the basis of social equilibrium'. Duplat concluded that 'the *classe moyenne* is the group which works at the same time that it owns'.[75] The harmony which that balance of labour and property could provide was the source of the stability which a thriving world of small

---

[71] Gresle, F., *L'univers de la boutique. Les petits patrons du Nord (1920–1975)* (Lille: Presses Universitaires de Lille, 1981), pp. 84–90. Bourdieu, P., Boltanski, L. and de Saint-Martin, M., 'Les stratégies de reconversion. Les classes sociales et le système d'enseignement', *Information sur les Sciences Sociales* 12 (1973), pp. 61–113. For this process of reconversion in Britain and Germany as well as France, see Crossick and Haupt, *The Petite Bourgeoisie*, pp. 83–6.

[72] Gaillard, J., *Paris, la Ville (1852–1870)*, (Lille, 1976), p. 404.

[73] See Crossick, G., 'Metaphors of the Middle: The Discovery of the Petite Bourgeoisie 1880–1914', *Transactions of the Royal Historical Society* 6th series, 4 (1994), pp. 251–79.

[74] Brants, V., *La lutte pour le pain quotidien. Précis des leçons d'économie politique* (Paris: H. Champion, 1885), p. 188.

[75] Duplat, *La classe moyenne*, pp. 12 and 22.

enterprise would bring to society. Hector Lambrechts, the workhorse and spokesman for this movement, saw those who lived off property ownership alone – *rentiers* – as a threat to social stability, for the moral virtue of property held true only when associated with labour.[76] In Duplat's terms, goods are owned by the petite bourgeoisie 'as economic utility rather than as egotistical pleasure', and the virtues such as foresight, saving and orderliness that were necessary for the accumulation of property within the world of small enterprise were precisely those needed for the well-being of society.[77]

In certain circles there was thus an ideological need to establish patrimony and a particular vision of property at the core of a middling intermediary group. The distinctive nature of the property had some grounding in the world of small enterprise itself, though a large number of more marginal petits bourgeois would have found it hard to recognise the description. The idea of patrimony was less well rooted, at least as far as the business was concerned, but the passing of small resources between generations was, indeed, one of the distinguishing features of the petite bourgeoisie. As the twentieth century advanced, the ability of patrimonial enterprise to constitute the basis of a *classe moyenne* became even more tenuous, and the idea of patrimony shifted uneasily in response. The concept of patrimony was reshaped in inter-war France in an attempt to define the *classe moyenne*, finding in the personal character of its property a point of contrast with the anonymity of the capital of large business and large-scale wealth, and a means to link the *rentier* to the owners of small enterprise whose labour and savings had once legitimised this wealth. Personal and family savings, not for security but to constitute a patrimony for its own sake, has been seen as the defining feature of the twentieth-century *classe moyenne*.[78] It is in this formulation that the idea of the patrimony as a defining characteristic – perhaps as the defining characteristic of the *classe moyenne* – took shape. Property was, in this conception, rooted in family, place and the personal. As such, patrimony came to define a morally necessary *classe moyenne*, but it also led relentlessly away from finding the heart of that social group amongst the owners of small enterprise.[79]

For Frédéric Le Play himself, the intellectual father of many of these ideas, it was not so much small enterprise that was the source of social order and stability, but its attachment to a specific piece of agrarian property or peasant holding. It was a distinction to which his successors were generally much less attentive. Nonetheless, we need to know a good deal more about the

---

[76] 'Hego' (Hector Lambrechts), *La Métropole*, 29 April 1897.

[77] Duplat, *La Classe Moyenne*, pp. 26 and 125–8.

[78] Capdevielle, J., *Le fétichisme du patrimoine. Essai sur un fondement de la classe moyenne* (Paris: Presses de la Fondation nationale des Sciences politiques, 1986).

[79] See Boltanski, L., *Les Cadres. La formation d'un groupe social* (Paris: Les Éditions de Minuit, 1982), pp. 91–102.

comparative importance of peasant proprietorship for conceptions of property within the petit-bourgeois world and in the wider discourse about it. There are distinct issues here: the rural origins of urban small enterprise; the ownership of rural property by urban petits bourgeois, and the presence of ideologies of peasant proprietorship in different national cultures. All would need to be explored in any full analysis and only some broad points can be offered in the limited space available here. Each marks out an area of distinction between England and France which is relevant not only to the specific analysis of petit-bourgeois property, but to the wider culture and politics of the petite bourgeoisie as a whole. The rural origins of the owners of urban small enterprise in France, above all those of retailers, signals the way in which rural family capital was frequently transferred into urban property and enterprise. Nearly two-thirds of Parisian petits bourgeois in the early nineteenth century were of rural origin, and subsequent expansion of the city's grocery trade rested on migrants from the Paris basin bringing family savings into the capital. This was equally true of smaller towns like Caen, or of a provincial capital such as Lyon where 86 per cent of the city's bakers in the period 1836 to 1852 were of rural origin, and still 78 per cent in the period 1878 to 1914.[80] Urban traders in France were consistently more rural in origin than a town's population as a whole, whereas it is significant that the reverse seems to have been the case in England.[81]

Such urban ambitions in France required no sharp break with the rural past – indeed, rural resources, whether peasant or from other small family enterprises, had a continuing role to play. The owners of small artisanal and retail enterprises in Paris tended to marry wives from the same region, whilst Parisian grocers frequently obtained loans from their home district.[82] One consequence of this distinctive relationship to the countryside on the part of French urban petits bourgeois was their continuing ownership of rural property. This was especially the case with respect to retailers: whereas the master artisans of

---

[80] Daumard, *La bourgeoisie parisienne*, p. 126; Faure, A., 'The Grocery Trade in Ninetenth-century Paris: a Fragmented Corporation', in Crossick and Haupt, *Shopkeepers and Master Artisans*, p. 170; Le Yaouanq, J., 'Aspects de l'immigration departementale à Paris au xixe siècle: les commerçants et artisans ligeriens', *Cahiers de l'Institut d'Histoire de la Presse et de l'Opinion* 3 (1974–75) pp. 7–39; Désert, G., 'Immigration et ségrégation à Caen', in M. Garden and Y. Lequin (eds), *Habiter la Ville. XVe-XXe Siècle* (Lyon: Presses Universitaires de Lyon, 1984), p. 180; Angleraud, 'Les boulangers lyonnais', p. 111.

[81] See the data in Crossick and Haupt, *The Petite Bourgeoisie*, pp. 70–72. In London in 1851 the proportion of shopkeepers born outside the capital (not only in rural areas) was almost identical to that of the adult population as a whole, 45 per cent and 46 per cent respectively. Sample of London enumeration districts in 1851 Census. For further details of this see Crossick and Haupt, *The Petite Bourgeoisie*, p. 253, n. 3.

[82] Le Yaouanq, J., 'Trajéctoires sociales à Paris au XIXᵉ Siècle: le monde de la boutique', *Bulletin du Centre Pierre Léon d'Histoire Économique et Sociale* 4 (1993), pp. 25–40; Faure, 'Grocery trade in Paris', p. 170.

Bourg-en-Bresse, for example, tended to have their property in the town itself, the town's retailers were more likely to own land for rental outside the town. Rural investment actually grew amongst Lyon's retailers in the second half of the nineteenth century, for whom a small vineyard or field, or a house in the countryside, remained an attraction.[83]

The relative importance of rural origins and rural property amongst urban petits bourgeois in France was reinforced by broader cultural connections. There was the potential for peasant ideas of enterprise and property to be articulated in the world of urban small enterprise: small-scale property conceived as the basis of a household economy directed not so much at profit or at business expansion, but at continuity and survival. The Auvergnats who set up so numerously in small business in Paris have been presented as reconstructing their peasant ideals within an urban setting. According to Raison-Jourde, money was conceived as the value of effort rather than as some separate reality open to any fruitful use. They articulated a culture of frugality, economy, hard work and a reluctance to display what wealth they had made, values that connected their urban businesses as café-owners or coal and metal dealers to their peasant origins in central France.[84]

British parallels were rare. Thomas Lipton, who went on to found one of Britain's largest retail grocery chains, recalled how his parents had fled from their smallholding in Ireland after the Famine, and opened in Glasgow a small shop that drew much of its ham, butter and eggs from an Irish farmer. A stay in the United States of America taught Lipton business methods which he found quite different from those of his parents, whose shop seemed to provide for them the security that the family smallholding had once done.[85] This link between peasant mentality and urban enterprise was unusual in Britain. The flow of children from small, intensive, family pastoral farms in the northern Dales into Liverpool, where with a little family capital they would set up in business as cowkeepers, was a rare parallel to the much more common pattern in French urban retailing. These Liverpool cowkeepers came from tenant farming backgrounds, where changes of farm were fairly frequent, rather than classic peasant holdings. A period of years in the Liverpool dairy trade formed part of an intergenerational family life-cycle pattern, with close links retained between migrants in these better-class Liverpool dairying enterprises and the

---

[83] Defaudon, B., 'Bourg-en-Bresse: aperçu d'une société urbaine au debut du XIXe siècle 1815–1848', Mémoire de maitrise, University of Lyon 2, 1976, pp. 212–13, 224; Léon, *Géographie sociales à Lyon*, pp. 208–9, 245. On the way in which links to rural areas of origin continued, see Crossick and Haupt, *The Petite Bourgeoisie*, p. 71.

[84] Raison-Jourde, F., *La colonie auvergnate de Paris au XIXe Siècle* (Paris: Ville de Paris, Commission des Travaux Historiques, 1976), pp. 121–160, 380.

[85] Mathias, P., *Retailing Revolution. A History of Multiple Retailing in the Food Trades based upon the Allied Suppliers Group of Companies* (London: Longman, 1967), pp. 40–44.

Dales communities from which they had come, and to which they would return, or to which they would at least dream of returning. The cowkeeping income eased pressure on the rural small-farming family, if only by removing dependants, and it allowed some accumulation of savings for a return to farming.[86]

The much closer relationship in France between the countryside and urban small enterprise raises the question of the importance of a peasantry within national society for wider conceptions of small property. Small enterprise was largely ignored by politicians and commentators in England in the later nineteenth and early twentieth centuries, whether as a social problem or as a social solution, in comparison with many other European countries.[87] It is notable that it was their experience of organising small peasant farmers that provided the basis for Belgian catholic activity in organising urban small enterprise.[88] How far can the weakness of the voice of small enterprise in Britain at this time, and the reluctance to articulate a distinctive social and cultural vision of small property, be traced in part at least to the absence of a significant and numerous peasantry, and the absence of links between such a peasantry and urban small business? Small urban enterprise with rural origins occurred most in regions of England and Wales with a marked degree of viable small agrarian proprietorship. In addition to the flow of Dalesmen and women into the Liverpool milk trades, one can point to the small-scale hill-farming districts of Cumberland where yeoman capital enabled migrants to set up as shopkeepers or trading artisans in coastal industrial towns in the middle of the nineteenth century, or the emigrants from peasant farming districts of south-west Wales who opened shops in the mining communities of South Wales towards the end of the century, drawing supplies from friends and relatives back home.[89] Such links were, however, rare in nineteenth-century Britain (though they have been little explored for Scotland) which, even if large-scale farming was not as dominant as the traditional picture would have it, was far less characterised by peasant agriculture and peasant aspirations than were many other parts of Europe. The viable small farms which Winstanley

---

[86] Grundy, J. E., 'The Origins of the Liverpool Cowkeepers', M. Litt. thesis, University of Lancaster, 1982, pp. 244–54, 280ff; on continuing links to their home areas see pp. 315–26. I am grateful to Michael Winstanley for drawing my attention to this thesis.

[87] See Crossick, G., 'Formation ou invention des classes moyennes? Une analyse comparée: Belgique-France–Grande-Bretagne 1880–1914', *Revue belge d'histoire Contemporaine* 26 (1996), pp. 105–38.

[88] Van Molle, L., *Chacun pour tous. Le Boerenbond belge 1890–1990*, (Leuven: Universitaire pers Leuven, 1990).

[89] Marshall, J. D. and Walton, J. K., *The Lake Counties from 1830 to the Mid-Twentieth Century* (Manchester: Manchester University Press, 1981), pp. 90–91; Jenkins, D., *The Agricultural Community in South-West Wales at the turn of the Twentieth Century* (Cardiff: University of Wales Press, 1971) p. 251.

identifies in his important study of industrial Lancashire saw a rapid turnover of tenanted properties and an intensive level of market responsiveness which does not mesh (even in revisionist approaches) with more traditional peasant attachment to specific pieces of property. The most significant element was perhaps the mobility of these farmers who, similar to the Dales families described above, were not attached to a particular piece of land, whether by owner-occupation or long tenancies, but were highly mobile in response to changing family structure and changing market opportunities.[90] The classic peasant relationship to property was missing.

In comparison with other European industrial countries at the end of the nineteenth century, small enterprise in Britain does not become an issue for self-assertion or for wider political debate. When small property emerges as a political issue, it takes a form that has little to say about small enterprise or the petite bourgeoisie, being connected instead with proposals for smallholdings to stabilise the working population, and it made little headway as an ideal. The same was true of conservative concerns to achieve 'the individualisation of property', with a view to protecting large-scale property (especially large landed estates) against the perceived threats of democracy and socialism. The partisans of such ideas focused on small-scale property – the owner-occupation of housing, allotments and so on – rather than small enterprise. In Britain by the 1890s the conservative emphasis on small property as a social principle was concerned with the diffusion of small proprietorship, not an engagement with small enterprise of a kind found at this time amongst conservative circles in France, Germany and Belgium. It found expression in Bateman's attack on primogeniture, Lord Randolph Churchill's support for leasehold enfranchisement, or a stress on owner-occupation of housing.[91] Here was one reason why the political mobilisation of petits bourgeois in Britain in these years had such limited impact – small property's appeal to social conservatism did not associate it primarily with the owners of small enterprise. Rather than associations or political movements articulating a distinctive social and political vision of the kind that can be seen in other European countries, British petits bourgeois mobilised as ratepayers and as the owners of rented housing.

---

[90] Winstanley, M., 'Industrialization and the Small Farm: Family and Household Economy in Nineteenth-Century Lancashire', *Past and Present*, 152 (1996), pp. 157–95. An interesting debate about the existence of an English peasantry was sparked by Reed, M., 'The Peasantry of Nineteenth-Century England: A Neglected Case?', *History Workshop Journal* 18 (1984), pp. 53–71. See also Reed, M., 'Nineteenth-century Rural England: a case for "Peasant studies"?', *Journal of Peasant Studies* 14 (1986–87), pp. 78–99. This has been important in reasserting the significance of rural pluriactivity against an oversimplifying picture of rural proletarianisation, but has not succeeded in establishing a peasantry of a kind familiar to historians of other parts of Europe.

[91] Harris, J., *Private Lives, Public Spirit: a Social History of Britain, 1870–1914* (Oxford: Oxford University Press, 1993), pp. 119–20.

House owners' associations grew from the 1880s to construct lists of bad tenants, help landlords recover arrears, and restrain municipal spending. House owners' associations organised only a small proportion of the proprietors of rented property, but their place in representing petit-bourgeois interests reflects the generally weak political formation of the owners of small enterprises. What was a limited political presence in comparative European terms has been used to explain the ease with which petty landlords were marginalized in Britain, as state housing policy steadily abandoned the interests of the small landlord. Rent controls during the First World War and then the policy of council housing left small landlords as a declining force with no significant political groups seeking to defend them.[92]

Conclusions

It has been recently argued that 'at the micro level, property relations form the myriad ways in which people build up their social identities through holding and using a variety of "things" in their environment'.[93] Although a call to attend to the meanings of property, and to the variations in those meanings, may need pressing less urgently than it might have done a decade or so ago, it remains true that this approach to property has had far more impact on research for the early modern period than for the nineteenth and twentieth centuries. This essay has not sought to offer a systematic exploration of the nature of petit-bourgeois property, not least because of the absence of the detailed research which would form the basis for such conclusions. Instead, and drawing on a range of evidence from Britain and France as well as other countries, it has sought to show how such an attentiveness to the meanings of property can help understand a group whose small proprietorial character made it such a critical element in the nineteenth-century social and political order. For a social milieu ambiguous and fragile in its structural position,[94] the petite bourgeoisie's conception of property was peculiarly important for its changing identity.

---

[92] Englander, D., *Landlord and Tenant in Urban Britain 1838–1918* (Oxford: Clarendon Press, 1983), pp. 51–81; McCrone, D. and Elliott, B., 'The Decline of Landlordism: Property Rights and Relationships in Edinburgh', in R. Rodger (ed.), *Scottish Housing in the Twentieth Century* (Leicester: Leicester University Press, 1989), pp. 223–8.

[93] Hann, C. M., 'Introduction: The Embeddedness of Property', in C. M. Hann (ed.), *Property Relations. Renewing the Anthropological Tradition* (Cambridge: Cambridge University Press, 1998), p. 3.

[94] Crossick and Haupt, *The Petite Bourgeoisie,* pp. 3–10.

Chapter 4

Property, will making and estate disposal in an industrial town, 1800–1857

Alastair Owens

Historians' interest in wills has largely been confined to reconstructing patterns of property ownership and analysing inheritance practices. In general, there has been an emphasis on studying the outcomes of property transmission rather than the processes by which such activities were effected. Remarkably little attention has been paid to will-making practices or the various activities associated with the disposal of estates.[1] The aim of this chapter is to examine these matters. In part, this is done in order to provide a background to other contributions to the volume which explore in detail patterns of wealth holding, inheritance strategies and the social uses of property. However, a second and more important objective is to explore the social significance of will making and estate disposal within urban communities. By focusing on the wider social context of property transmission in towns, the chapter investigates a side of inheritance usually ignored by historians concerned with the domestic context of estate disposal. It investigates the everyday social relations of property transmission, exploring the networks of people, sources of expertise and forms of knowledge that enabled the making of wills and disposal of estates. Ultimately, therefore, the chapter aims to look at the way in which will making and estate disposal were embedded within the social fabric of the urban public sphere. This is done in recognition of Jeffrey Longhofer's claim that 'in order to make sense of inheritance practices ... it is necessary to understand the structure of the formations (household, community and social) within which

---

[1] This is especially the case for nineteenth-century urban contexts. A broad introduction to will making is provided by Camp, A. J., *Wills and Their Whereabouts* (London: published by the author, 1974) pp. ix–xl. Philip Riden's edited collection of essays *Probate Records and the Local Community* (Gloucester: Alan Sutton, 1985) addresses will making in an early modern context, as does Ralph Houlbrooke in *Death, Religion and the Family in England, 1480–1750* (Oxford: Clarendon Press, 1998), pp. 81–109. Finch, J., Mason, J., Masson, J., Wallis, J. and Hayes, L., *Wills, Inheritance and Families* (Oxford: Clarendon Press, 1996), pp. 39–65, provide an interesting contemporary comparison.

these practices are formed, codified and contested'.[2] Whilst it is impossible, in the space available here, to explore all of the structures and formations through which inheritance took place, an investigation of the key activities relating to will making and estate disposal makes it possible to access some of the motives for, and meanings of, property transmission in urban contexts.

In considering will making and estate disposal the chapter inevitably pays considerable attention to legal matters. As Janet Finch and her colleagues have recently observed, 'the law creates the very concept of a will as a mechanism for the transmission of property'.[3] The law was an important social referent and without some understanding of the legal background to will making, both in terms of the rules it established for the transmission of property and the way in which legal knowledge was used in the construction of wills, it is not possible to fully appreciate strategies of inheritance. As Janet Finch and Judith Wallis have argued elsewhere, legacies and bequests recorded in wills often reflect professional norms, rather than personal desires about how property should be passed to family and kin.[4] This chapter describes the legal context for the transmission of property by will in early nineteenth-century England and Wales. It also examines some of the ways in which this legal knowledge was accessed and 'consumed' within towns. It identifies the main sources of legal expertise used in the making of wills and disposal of property. Finally, it also highlights some of the ways in which the consumption of legal knowledge was embedded within the social structures of urban communities.

The setting for this study is the northern industrial town of Stockport during the first half of the nineteenth century. Stockport was, in many ways, a classic example of a 'new' industrial town. Like many of the other urban centres of northern England in the nineteenth century, its growth and fame was built upon the textile industry. The town's population increased from just under 15,000 people in 1801 to a little below 57,000 people in 1861. This expansion was largely driven by its importance as a centre of cotton manufacture. In 1851 over a third of the adult population were engaged in the industry and the town was, after Manchester, the second-largest centre of cotton production in the world.[5] Whilst contemporaries were often appalled at the social inequalities generated by industrialisation in Stockport – Engels memorably described the town as 'excessively repellent' – it was still regarded, like the rest of the manufacturing districts, as a land of opportunity where dazzling fortunes could

    2   Longhofer, J., 'Toward a Political Economy of Inheritance: Community and Household among the Mennonites' *Theory and Society* 22 (1993), p. 340.
    3   Finch, et al., *Wills, Inheritance and Families*, p. 20.
    4   See Finch, J. and Wallis, L., 'Death, Inheritance and the Life Course', in D. Clark (ed.) *The Sociology of Death* (Oxford: Blackwell, 1993), pp. 50–68.
    5   Kirk, N., *The Growth of Working Class Reformism in Mid-Victorian England* (Beckenham: Croom Helm, 1984), pp. 47–53.

be made.[6] Typical of other industrial towns associated with the accumulation of wealth and property by an emerging middling sort over the first half of the nineteenth century, Stockport therefore provides an informative context in which to consider how this wealth was transmitted to others.

The chapter draws upon a variety of sources. Central to the discussion is the analysis of a random sample of some 500 Stockport wills proved at the Consistory Court of Chester, 1800–1857.[7] This figure accounts for 52 per cent of all Stockport wills proved at that court over the period. Whilst testamentary documents have mostly been used to study inheritance practices, they also furnish considerable insights into the processes of will making and disposing of estate. The actual text of the will provides, amongst other things, information on authorship, the use of professional expertise, the style of construction, the timing of will making, and the names of people appointed to oversee the disposal of estate. Further information can be gleaned from the written act of probate endorsed on the back of the will. In most cases this gives details of the date of a testator's death, the date of probate, the name of the official who granted probate, a sworn estimation of the gross value of personal estate, the names of the persons who took executorship and the nature of the oath that they swore. This and other information was abstracted from each of the 500 wills to form the basis of the analysis in this chapter. Where appropriate, other sources, such as newspapers and legal manuals, were used to supplement the material and animate the will-making process.

Wills, property transmission and the law

First and foremost a will was a mechanism for transmitting property. However, wills also served as a vehicle by which a testator could direct how their body should be disposed of and make arrangements for the guardianship of children.[8]

---

[6]   Engels, F., *The Condition of the Working Class in England*, (London: Granada Publishing, 1969, originally published in English in 1892), pp. 76–7.

[7]   The sample was derived systematically from an alphabetical list of all wills and administrations of Stockport persons proved at the Consistory Court of Chester 1800–1857. Analysis ends in 1857 due to major changes to the law in January 1858. The sample does not include Stockport wills proved at the Prerogative Courts of Canterbury and York. Analysis of indexes suggests that few Stockport wills were proved these courts. Roughly 90 per cent of Stockport wills were proved at Chester.

[8]   In general, see Camp, *Wills and Their Whereabouts*. See also, Green, D. R. and Owens, A. 'Metropolitan Estates of the Middle Class: Probates and Death Duties Revisited' *Historical Research* 70 (1997), pp. 294–311. The clearest and most thorough contemporary account prior to the 1837 Wills Act can be found in PP. 1833 XXII, *Law of Real Property, Fourth Report: Wills;* after that date lucid summary of the new laws can be found in Hudson, J. C., *Plain Directions for Making Wills in Conformity with the Law* (London: Longman and Co., 1838).

Making a will thus enabled an individual to 'regulate the rights of others over his or her property or family after his or her death'.[9] However, disposal of property by will was just one of at least three ways by which estate might be transmitted to others after a property owner died. The transfer of property by will is known as testamentary succession. However, property could also pass by legal succession or administration. To comprehend the significance of testamentary succession, and to try and understand why people decided to make a will, it is necessary to consider these latter modes of transmission in more detail.

Legal succession occurred where the 'destiny' of property was settled according to common law or other legal rulings. The succession of property might already have been established by the will of an ancestor who attempted to ensure that a portion of his (and, less frequently, her) estate was kept intact over several generations. The most common form of legal succession was where land, freehold buildings or other real estate passed according to the rules of entail. Here, upon death, property would automatically pass by the tradition of primogeniture to the eldest male heir. He would retain a lifetime interest in the estate but without power to sell or 'alienate' the property. Upon his death the interest in the property would pass to his son. In reality, the laws of legal succession were rather more complex, but increasingly during the eighteenth and nineteenth centuries traditions of entail were being broken and periods of perpetuity – the length of time an estate could remain intact – were being limited.[10] Legal succession of settled property has been subject to thorough investigation by legal and social historians as a feature of eighteenth- and nineteenth-century landed social life.[11] The significance of this kind of property transmission within urban industrial contexts such as Stockport appears to be limited. Certainly, few wills amongst the sample under analysis made any reference to settled property.[12]

The transmission of estate according to the laws of administration occurred when a property owner died without making a valid will. It is often assumed that intestate succession took place where an individual forgot or, through some misfortune, was unable to make a will. However, this is to preclude the possibility that intestate succession was a deliberate strategy on the part of some property owners. It avoided the expense and trouble of executing a will, whilst the rules of intestate succession offered a kind of normative frame for

---

[9]   Camp, *Wills and Their Whereabouts*, p. ix.

[10] See Offer, A., *Property and Politics* (Cambridge: Cambridge University Press, 1981), ch. 1; and Holcombe, L., *Wives and Property: The Reform of Married Women's Property Law* (Oxford: Martin Robinson, 1974).

[11] See for example Spring, E., *Law, Land and Family: Aristocratic Inheritance in England, 1300–1800* (Chapel Hill: University of North Carolina Press, 1990).

[12] Of course there would be no need to mention property already settled in a will and alternative sources would need to be investigated to probe this issue in more depth.

the transmission of estate. Indeed, the rationale behind intestate succession was to make sure that after the death of a property owner heirs were provided for in some kind of 'equitable' way. The division of an intestate's property privileged family and kin. Yet, contemporary legal pamphleteer Richard Dickson felt that leaving the distribution of property to the laws of intestacy was undesirable, for 'it is very seldom that the distribution of property in this way is consistent with the relative merits of the parties amongst whom it is distributed, far less the intentions of the deceased'.[13] Another lawyer – Joseph Hudson – went further, warning against the 'evils of intestacy'.[14] Although he recognised that intestate succession existed as a mechanism for protecting the heirs of property owners who did not make a will, he saw a knowledge of the law relating to the division of intestates' estates as a 'powerful inducement' to make a will.[15] To him, the laws of administration were too blunt a tool for providing for needy dependants who might fall beyond the critical proximity of intestate provision. Despite obvious financial self-interest, the comments of Hudson and Dickson do highlight the importance attached to the ability to control and personally direct the future uses of property within contemporary legal discourses of inheritance.

The transmission of wealth by intestate succession occurred when a property owner died without making a valid will. For both real and personal estate the division of an intestate's property privileged immediate family and kin. In the case of the former type of property, freehold estate passed under common law by the tradition of primogeniture to the eldest male child of the deceased. Where an intestate had no male children the property was divided equally between the daughters. In the absence of any children, real property was conveyed to the eldest collateral male heir. The distribution of an intestate's personal property was a regulated by ecclesiastical rather than common law. The power of distributing the estate was vested in an administrator. Appointed by an ecclesiastical court, this person was usually the deceased's next of kin.[16] He or she was required to dispose of property according to the statute of distributions or customary ecclesiastical laws. The Consistory Court of Chester granted letters of administration on some 484 Stockport estates between 1800 and 1857, compared with 967 grants of probate on wills.[17] Deliberate or not, intestate succession was thus an important mechanism for the transmission of deceased persons' estates.

---

[13] Dickson, R., *A Practical Exposition of the Law of Wills* (London: Sherwood, Gilbert and Piper, 1830), p. 4.

[14] Hudson, *Plain Directions for Making Wills*, p. 78.

[15] Ibid., p. 6–11.

[16] See the chapter by Jon Stobart in this volume.

[17] Data are taken from the Cheshire County Record Office's Consistory Court of Chester Wills and Administrations database. This figure excludes 'administrations with the will annexed' where, usually in default of executors being appointed, administration of the estate was granted on condition that the property was disposed of by the terms of the will.

Testamentary succession was realised by the execution of a will. The term 'will' is nearly always used incorrectly to describe an individual's last will and testament.[18] The former disposed of real estate, such as freehold land and buildings, whilst the latter dealt with personal property, which included personal possessions, cash, stocks, shares and the value of leasehold property and annuities.[19] Most kinds of estate could be disposed of by will including that in possession or reversion, contingent property, and rights of entry.[20] For the period under consideration here, the distinction between different forms property is more important prior to 1838 when different rules existed as to the execution of wills of real and personal property.[21] Most wills were constructed as a series of instructions relating to the disposal of various items of property. As indicated earlier, they might also detail funeral arrangements and make provisions for the guardianship of children. They varied enormously in length, ranging from one or two lines to twenty or more pages. According to the law, the will became a legally binding document once it had been signed by the testator and witnessed in the required manner. However, a grant of probate, which prior to 1858 had to be sought from an ecclesiastical court, was required before any estate could be disposed of in order to register the will, ascertain its validity, and pay probate and other duties.[22]

Not everyone could make, or needed to make, a will. Furthermore, not everyone needed to seek probate. Only those with *bona notabilia* – personal 'goods worth mentioning' – valued at £5 or more (or, by custom, £10 in the diocese of London) were required to have their wills proved by a church court.[23] Following the 1837 Wills Act, children under the age of twenty-one were prevented from making a will.[24] Prior to this, they could publish a testament to dispose of personal property, but could not transmit real estate by will. Lunatics, prisoners and those who had been excommunicated were similarly not able to make valid wills. A more significant rule preventing

---

[18]   But to avoid confusion and follow convention the term 'will' will be used from now on to describe both the will and testament which in practice were usually contained within the same document.

[19]   Though the distinction between real and personal property was not always clear, see P.P. 1833 XXII *Law of Real Property; Fourth Report: Wills*, pp. 14–15.

[20]   The 1837 Wills Act attempted to unify the law with respect to the disposal of different descriptions of property. The rules prior to 1837 are detailed in PP 1833 XXII *Law of Real Property; Fourth Report: Wills*, pp. 23–5 and after 1837 by Hudson, *Plain Directions for Making Wills*, pp. 22–41.

[21]   See PP 1833 XXII *Law of Real Property; Fourth Report: Wills*, pp. 4–20.

[22]   In 1858 the ecclesiastical courts were abolished and replaced by the state-run Central Probate Registry. See Manchester, A. H., 'The Reform of the Ecclesiastical Courts' *American Journal of Legal History* 10 (1966), pp. 51–75.

[23]   As probate helped confirm the validity of the will, it is likely that estates valued at less than £5 still sought probate.

[24]   1 Victoria c. 26.

freedom of testamentary disposition applied to married women. By common law, married women faced severe restrictions in the control and disposal of their own property.[25] Although rules varied according to the nature and type of property, the ownership of most property became vested in a woman's husband upon marriage. The freedom to dispose of property by will was also surrendered to a woman's spouse. Occasionally, however, married women were able to make a will disposing of a limited amount of property if they obtained the consent of their husband and drew up a marriage settlement. In spite of these significant exceptions, England and Wales were considered to have a permissive testamentary regime and there were few other restrictions on free disposal of property.[26]

Various estimates have been made of the number of persons disposing of property by will in the early-nineteenth century. Anthony Camp suggests that at the end of the eighteenth century approximately 6 per cent of those who died in England and Wales made wills.[27] In 1841 roughly 10 per cent of the total number of dying adults in England and Wales made a will.[28] Camp suggests that by 1873 8 per cent of dying persons made wills.[29] Given the incompatibility of probate jurisdictions and civil registration districts it is only possible to estimate the number of people leaving wills in early nineteenth-century Stockport. Taking evidence for 1841, it appears that a relatively low proportion, just 5 per cent, of the town's dying adults left a probated will. The low number perhaps reflects the dominance of the town's poorer population. It was remarked by one Londoner who visited to Stockport in the early 1860s that 'there are but few wealthy residents in the place'.[30]

Who made wills?

Evidence from the sample of Stockport wills suggests that will making was predominantly a male activity. Given the restrictions women faced in making wills, it is not surprising that only 21 per cent of the sample of Stockport wills were made by females. This proportion is very similar to that found by Maxine Berg in her study of eighteenth-century Birmingham and Sheffield wills, where women left 22.8 per cent and 18.1 per cent of the total number of wills

---

[25] See Holcombe, *Wives and Property*.

[26] Compare with the more restrictive regime in Scotland outlined in the chapter by Ann McCrum in this volume.

[27] Camp, *Wills and Their Whereabouts*, p. xxxviii.

[28] Green and Owens, 'Metropolitan Estates of the Middle Class', p. 296.

[29] Camp, *Wills and Their Whereabouts*, p. xxxviii.

[30] Barlee, E., *A Visit to Lancashire in December 1862* (London: Sheeley, Jackson and Halliday, 1863), p. 8.

respectively.[31] Berg argues that these proportions are much higher than that which is indicated in studies of other parts of the country for the late eighteenth century, where typically women left 10 per cent of wills. However, the proportion of female testators in Sheffield and Birmingham in the eighteenth century and Stockport in the early nineteenth century, is considerably lower than the proportion of women leaving wills in nineteenth-century London. Figures provided by Green and Owens suggest that in 1800, 32 per cent of testators were women, and that in 1850 women made 34 per cent of all metropolitan wills.[32] One further observation on the Stockport sample is that widows account for by far the largest proportion of female testators (over 60 per cent) and there are only three examples of married women's wills.

The preamble to most wills contains what is properly referred to in law as an 'addition', which allows further investigation of the identity of will makers.[33] The addition contained the testator's surname, Christian name, place of abode and occupation. In the case of women a description of their condition – spinster, widow or wife – was usually considered sufficient instead of a trade and occupation. Occupations of Stockport testators were classified using the Armstrong index (see Figure 4.1). Those persons engaged in manufacturing industries formed the largest occupational category of will makers accounting for roughly a quarter of all testators. In a town dominated by the textile industry, this is not surprising. The second-largest group of will makers were those involved in dealing or retail trades – shopkeepers, publicans and the like.

By comparing the occupational data derived from the wills with that available from the 1851 census it is possible to gain a clearer picture of the relative propensity of different occupational groups to make probated wills (see Figure 4.2). Whilst the results must be treated with caution, not least because of the temporal incompatibilities of the two data sets, the material suggests that certain occupational groups were more inclined to make wills than others. Retailers and other dealers, professionals and property-owning males were proportionally more numerous amongst will makers than the population as a whole. Whilst the latter two of these groups – because of their wealth and status – might have been expected to make more wills, the high proportion of retailers who disposed of their property by will requires further explanation. At a simple level, retailing activities clearly generated personal property, such as leasehold premises and stock-in-trade, that could be passed on by will. At a more pragmatic level, wills could have been used by retailers as a mechanism for settling business transactions and ensuring that property associated with the

---

[31] Berg, M., 'Women's Property and the Industrial Revolution' *Journal of Interdisciplinary History* XXIV (1993), p. 237.

[32] Green and Owens, 'Metropolitan Estates of the Middle Class', p. 310. See also the chapter by David R. Green in this volume where he addresses these differences.

[33] Dickson, *A Practical Exposition of the Law of Wills*, pp. 8–9.

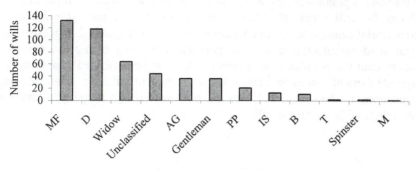

Armstrong occupational category

Figure 4.1: Occupational identity of will makers, Stockport, 1800–1857

Key to Armstrong occupational categories:

AG	Agriculture and breeding	B	Building
D	Dealing	DS	Domestic service
IS	Industrial service	M	Mining
MF	Manufacturing	PO	Property owning / independent
PP	Public service and professional	T	Transport
N/A	No occupation		

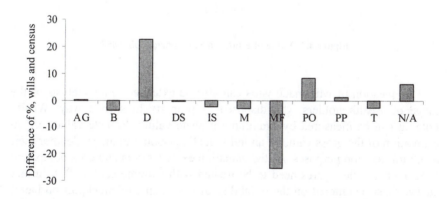

Figure 4.2: Comparison of occupational structure of male will makers 1800–1857 with occupational structure of male population according to 1851 census, Stockport

(For key to Armstrong occupational categories see Figure 4.1)

firm was transmitted to the right people. Amongst this petit-bourgeois segment of the town's population, the ability to transmit the accumulated fruits of one's labours by will might also have been regarded as a modest measure of proprietorial achievement.[34] In contrast to Figure 4.1, Figure 4.2 suggests those engaged in manufacturing were proportionally less significant amongst will makers than the population as a whole. This can be explained simply by the large numbers of cotton operatives who were categorised under manufacturing occupations in the census but who did not own enough property to make it worth their while making a will.

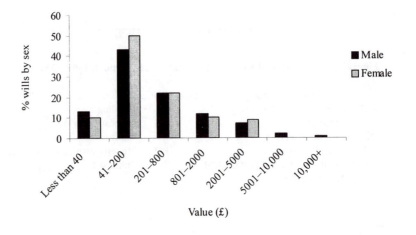

Figure 4.3: Value of estates in Stockport, 1800–1857

The question of who made wills can also be extended to an analysis of the range of wealth holders who disposed of property in such a way. Wealth holding can be measured by examining probate values. Probate values are an estimation of the gross value of an individual's personal estate made after their death for taxation purposes. As the valuation excludes debt and does not extend to real estate, the figures need to be treated with extreme caution.[35] A further caveat must be entered on the reliability of the sample of Stockport probates, which only includes wills proved at the Consistory Court of Chester. Wills

---

[34] On attitudes to property ownership amongst the petite bourgeoisie (comprised mostly of shopkeepers and small retailers) see the chapter by Geoffrey Crossick in this volume.

[35] A thorough discussion of the problems of using probate documents can be found in Green and Owens, 'Metropolitan Estates of the Middle Class', pp. 294–304 and Rubinstein, W. D. and Duman, D., 'Probate Valuations: a Tool for the Historian' *Local Historian* XI (1974), pp. 68–71.

proved at other courts with testamentary jurisdiction over Stockport – notably the Prerogative Courts of York and Canterbury – may well, because of the rules that determined jurisdiction, have been of greater value. However, given the small number of Stockport wills that were proved in these courts, the exclusion of such valuations is unlikely to affect the figures drastically. With these qualifications in mind, Figure 4.3 reveals the average size of estate to have been relatively small. The modal property valuation category was £100, whilst the mean value of the entire sample (excluding one very large estate) was £791. Significantly, 40 per cent of estates were valued at under £100 and there were only three estates valued at over £10,000.[36] However, whilst the average size of personal estates in Stockport appears to have been relatively low, the ownership of real estate amongst will makers was widespread. Some 70 per cent of testators possessed freehold property. In most cases the wills suggest this to have been cottage property.

In summary, will making in early nineteenth-century towns like Stockport was an activity dominated by males, but was not solely restricted to the wealthy. Those with more modest fortunes also made wills in large numbers, and retail traders and owners of real estate appear to have been particularly keen to dispose of their property in such a way. However, thinking about the identity of will makers in such functional terms ignores the material and symbolic importance of making a will. In examining the different stages of the will-making and estate-disposal process, the remainder of this chapter builds up a clearer picture of the social context within which testamentary disposition took place. In doing so it also begins to uncover some of the meanings and significance of inheritance within urban industrialising society.

When were wills made?

Richard Dickson provided the following advice on when wills should be made:

> let no man ... postpone this sacred duty until he is not able to perform it; for, as death is appointed to all men, and 'of the day and hour knoweth no man', we should not, through neglect, want of fortitude, or cowardice, betray so shameful neglect of our temporal concerns, till we are sick and the hand of death is upon us ... [and] if we delay the duty until we are sick, we may be under the necessity of calling in the assistance of those who may deceive us ... [If we delay the duty] until we are old, we may not be able to recollect our various obligations.[37]

---

[36] Compare with Green and Owens, 'Metropolitan Estates of the Middle Class', pp. 297, 310, for the London situation.

[37] Dickson, *A Practical Exposition of the Law of Wills*, p. 3–4.

Tinged with an element of professional self-interest, Dickson's remarks establish a sense of urgency in making a will by playing upon fears of what might happen if the such a 'duty' is left until too late in life. Joseph Hudson, in a notably gendered description of will making, also advised that a will should be made early on in an individual's life, depicting it as one of the key responsibilities of married family life. He recommended that

> a man ought to make his will as soon as he has married. Perhaps so grave a subject may be allowed to be put off until the honeymoon has entirely waned; for ... a will is required to be made when a testator is in a sound and disposing mind, memory and understanding; but it ought, certainly, to be among the most prominent subjects of a married man's thoughts, upon returning to sober and serious reflection.[38]

The exigencies of will making in relation to changing life-course circumstances are a feature of the comments of both Dickson and Hudson and offer a springboard for further discussion of the issue of the timing of will making.

Hudson's identification of marriage with will making is significant. Marriage was an important stage in the life course of both men and women when property rights were defined and settled. For most women it was a time when the right to will property was ended; any will that had been published previously was automatically revoked.[39] For a minority of women – just four out of the sample of 105 female testators in early nineteenth-century Stockport – entry into wedlock was the time when limited rights to alienate property and dispose of it by will were confirmed by a marriage settlement. Up until the 1837 Wills Act a man's will was also automatically revoked upon marriage and a new one had to be published.[40] More generally, marriage was a time when expectations about the future uses and deployment of property changed and ideas of family provision began to emerge. Unfortunately, the impact of marriage on will-making activities is difficult to assess. Although, as Hudson suggests, getting married was a powerful incentive for publishing a will, few wills dating from this stage in an individual's life end up as the testamentary document proved by an ecclesiastical court. For some people, to make a will at marriage was to tempt fate, and so it was left until much later in life.

As the wording of most wills indicate, the document which settled property upon death was an individual's 'last will and testament'. The 1837 Wills Act reaffirmed the rule that had existed under previous legislation that the publication of a new will, executed according to the proper legal formalities, was sufficient to revoke a former will. Dickson recommended that a married

---

[38] Hudson, *Plain Directions for Making Wills*, p. 70.
[39] Traditional dower or 'thirds' rights of married women to their husband's estate were abolished by the 1833 Dower Act. See Holcombe, *Wives and Property*.
[40] A will was also revoked by the birth of a first child.

man should review his testamentary affairs on a regular basis, altering his will according to changed circumstances.[41] Certain key life-course events, such as the birth of children or the death of family members, would probably require a new will to be drawn up. Of course, most married women who made wills did so after their husband's death. A will made before marriage could not be revived and an entirely new document had to be published. It is therefore not surprising that widows made up the majority – some 63 per cent – of the sample of Stockport's female testators who had their wills proved at the Consistory Court of Chester between 1800 and 1857. A new will might also be required because of the acquisition, sale or disposal of property. With respect to the latter, a particular incentive for testamentary revision was where a gift of property to a family member, originally intended to be effected by will, was made *inter vivos*.

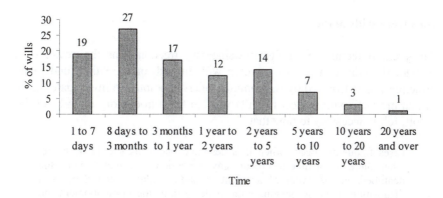

Figure 4.4: Length of time between date will made and date of death, Stockport testators 1800–1857

The sample of Stockport wills does provide insights into two issues that relate to the timing of will making. First, they contain accurate information on when last wills and testaments were made. Figure 4.4 shows the length of time between when a will was made and when a testator died. The most striking feature of the data is that most wills were made close to death, with nearly half of testators performing this act within three months of dying and nearly a fifth within one week. The results therefore reveal that however many wills were made over the life course, final decisions about the transmission of property

---

[41] Dickson, *A Practical Exposition of the Law of Wills*, p. 12

were often made in the face of death.[42] In this respect the findings are also suggestive of the conditions under which wills were made. The propinquity of will making to death suggests that most testators published their wills mindful of their impending fate, and therefore probably in a state of ill health.[43]

Secondly, the sample of Stockport wills offers some measure of the extent of the use of the codicil. Provided it was executed in the same manner as a will, a codicil was a device that allowed the contents of a will to be altered without complete republication. Most codicils simply altered one or two instructions contained within the main text of a will, such as a revocation of a legacy or the appointment of a new executor. Just 6 per cent of wills in the sample contained a codicil. Given that so many people made wills close to death it is not surprising that the figure is so low. Either people left will making so late that they did not have time to make alterations, or they made changes so substantial that complete republication was preferred.

How were wills made?

An essential feature of English testamentary freedom was the power of an individual to draw up his or her own will. Indeed, in 1833 this fundamental principle was reaffirmed by the commissioners appointed to investigate the law of real property with respect to wills who, in the introductory remarks to their report, felt it necessary to note that:

> cases frequently occur when it is desirable that wills should be made, when there is not time to procure any professional assistance, as on the deathbed, in the event of accident or sudden illness; and there is a disposition in many persons both to delay until the latest moment the making of a will, and to do it in secrecy, to which the law must, we think have regard.[44]

---

[42] Some commentators have argued that the dating of a will may not be a true indication of when the document was drawn up. Caroline Litzenberger, for example, claims that many wills were dated when they were read in front of witnesses – often some time after they were initially drafted. Some testators might have prudently postponed this until such time as death seemed close. Evidence here suggests this not to be the case. Most wills seem to have been witnessed by solicitors or their clerks, suggesting that the date of publication coincides with the date of drafting. Even if the attestation of a drafted will was postponed, this does not undermine the argument that final decisions about the disposal of property were left until late in a testator's life. See Litzenberger, C., 'Computer-Based Analysis of Early-Modern English Wills', *History and Computing* 7 (1995), p. 150, n. 5.

[43] Traditional religious preambles to wills often include a phrase providing some indication of the testator's health, such as them describing themselves as being 'sick and weak in body but of sound and perfect mind' or 'in good health and of sound mind memory and understanding'. Unfortunately, few Stockport wills contained such clauses.

[44] PP. 1833 XXII *Law of Real Property; Fourth Report: Wills*, p. 3.

So although the legislation which followed the report abolished nuncupative wills, it resisted calls for greater legal professionalism in the will-making process.[45] The commissioners dismissed calls for the application to wills of 'the strict rules by which the language of deeds is interpreted' because they believed 'it would impose too great a restraint upon the power of testamentary disposition'.[46] In theory, then, the liberty to transmit the benefit of property by will was vested in the individual through freedom of authorship. Such was the aim of reformers who wanted to make the process of transmitting property as simple as possible and accessible to all. In practice, however, evidence from Stockport suggests that will making was largely a professional legal activity.

The use of solicitors

Of the 500 Stockport wills under analysis some 427 (85 per cent) could be identified as having been drawn up by a solicitor. This evidence suggests that Stockport testators overwhelmingly viewed will making as something requiring professional expertise, a finding at odds with the view of Joseph Hudson who claimed that 'a very large proportion, perhaps as many as one third of the wills proved throughout England and Wales, are made, either by testators themselves, or by persons not belonging to the legal profession'.[47]

   Why did so many people go to the trouble and expense of getting a solicitor to make their will? It is obvious from further analysis of the wills that the kind of strategies of property transmission commonly being used by Stockport testators were complex and required legal expertise. Typical forms of post-mortem family provision involved the management of property in trust. Significantly, 62 per cent of the wills involved a trust being set up and trustees being appointed. The law of trusts was based in equity, a branch of the law largely beyond lay expertise. Indeed, if done properly, the setting up of a trust by a will was a complex business requiring the use of specialist legal terminology to give power and protection to trustees and thereby maximise the vitality of trust estate.[48] Quite simply, in order for testators to enable forms of property transmission consistent with pervasive ideologies of family provision, it was necessary to resort to legal expertise. Joseph Hudson's characterisation

---

[45]   1837 Wills Act (1 Victoria c. 26); a nuncupative will is one which is not written down.

[46]   PP. 1833 XXII *Law of Real Property; Fourth Report: Wills*, p. 3.

[47]   Hudson, *Plain Directions for Making* Wills, p. 12.

[48]   The protection of those appointed to dispose of the estate, such as executors and trustees, could have been a powerful inducement for seeking professional legal advice. Some of the perils of executorship are outlined in A'Beckett, T. T., *Law Reforming Difficulties Exemplified in a Letter to Lord Brougham and Vaux Accompanied by an Analysis of a Bill for the Improvement of the Law Relating to the Administration of Deceased Persons' Estates*, (London: Henry Butterworth, 1842).

of will making as 'the duty and paramount obligation of every considerate and rational man' captures the sense of urgency associated with testamentary disposition.[49] Not done properly – without recourse to the legal knowledge being made available in his pamphlet, or which could be bought from a local attorney – the whole process could fail with disastrous consequences, from expensive litigation to a ruined and pauperised family. With a similar whiff of financial self-interest, Richard Dickson also warned that 'everyman who is his own lawyer has a fool for his client'.[50] He believed that an accurate knowledge of the law was beyond lay capabilities. He continued, arguing that:

> the law is a difficult and a profound science and requires the period of a whole life to be expended in its service ... before its votaries can pretend a competent knowledge of its mysteries. It must therefore be evident to every professional man, that he is incurring a great risk, and putting in peril his whole property for the salvation of a few pounds, by ... performing for himself the office of a scribe.[51]

Elsewhere in Hudson's text the adoption of legalistic forms of wording in the construction of a will is presented as underpinning the successful transmission of property. For example, he advises that when making a legacy in a will, 'accuracy of description will frequently prevent litigation'.[52] Later he warns that if the will is not written clearly and accurately according to what the law demands 'the legacy fails and the legatee takes nothing'.[53] Using a solicitor therefore offered greater security and supposedly made it more likely that property would be passed in accordance with the testator's wishes and without further trouble and expense.

The use of a lawyer to draw up a will also helped to dramatise an activity strongly associated with the middling sort. Making wills, disposing of estates and receiving an inheritance were very visible, ever-present features of middle-class life. Indeed, the consumption of legal knowledge and expertise in the nineteenth century was driven by the needs of an increasingly propertied, middling sort like that resident in Stockport. Paying for solicitors to make wills was characteristic of the professionalism that marked the masculine, middle-class public sphere. Amongst family and kin, the use of professional expertise provided testators with an additional degree of authority over the property transmission process. A solicitor offered confidentiality, a space separate from

---

[49] Hudson, *Plain Directions for Making Wills*, p.78. Even Hudson remarked that 'persons of great wealth' should engage a lawyer to make their will rather than rely on his own text (p. 47).

[50] Dickson, *A Practical Exposition of the Law of Wills*, p. 7.

[51] Ibid.

[52] Hudson, *Plain Directions for Making Wills*, p. 48.

[53] Ibid. p. 54.

the emotionally complex terrain of home and hearth where decisions could be made more impartially. In the confines of a solicitor's office testators could usefully distance themselves from the personal implications of the provisions made in the will. By not writing the document in their own hand the text of the will became depersonalised – superseded by a series of formal legal instructions. This disembodiment from the process allowed the will to take on an authority of its own, instantly recognisable by its construction and use of a legalistic language. The use of a professional legal knowledge could therefore be interpreted as a strategy for claiming power and overcoming difficult and sensitive decisions about the transmission of estate.

Part of the explanation for such a large proportion of the wills being drawn up by solicitors probably relates to the supply of legal expertise in a rapidly expanding town like Stockport. Towns offered easy access to a range of professional services, not always available in rural areas. According to trade directory evidence, the number of solicitors' firms in Stockport rose from thirteen in 1814 to twenty-seven in 1865, perhaps reflecting the growing demand for legal expertise that accompanied industrialisation. Furthermore, Stockport was also close enough to Manchester to draw upon the legal services available there. A more detailed analysis of the solicitors used by Stockport testators points to specialisation by some attorneys in wills and probate business (Table 4.1). Jonathan L. Chetham, for example, a prominent town lawyer who practised from premises in Great Underbank, was responsible for the execution of some seventy-two wills – remarkably, 14 per cent of all wills in the sample.

Probing the question of why certain lawyers were used in preference to others is difficult. Of crucial importance must have been the cost of having a will made. Charges were generally dependent upon the length of the document, but it is unlikely that cost alone determined the choice of a lawyer. Personal allegiance could also be an incentive for choosing one solicitor over another, particularly where a professional had provided legal expertise in the past and therefore might already have been familiar with family or business property arrangements. In other instances the choice might be made on the basis of the reputation of solicitors. Lawyers were often very visible members of the social and political communities of nineteenth-century towns. When political allegiances became more marked in the post-reform era, some Stockport traders, notably publicans, complained of exclusive partisan dealing.[54]

---

[54] Various examples of complaints of exclusive dealing can be found in the *Stockport Advertiser* during the 1830s and 1840s (see, for example, 15 September 1837).

Table 4.1
Use of solicitors

Solicitor	Number of wills	% of all wills
Chetham	72	14
Lingard/Vaughan	36	7
Baddeley	27	5
Harrop	16	3
Coppock/Woollam/Oldham	15	3
Boothroyd	11	2
Herbert	10	2
Oakes	10	2
Lloyd/Paulden	9	2
Hall	7	1
Turner	7	1
Mann	7	1
Reddish	6	1
Hudson	6	1
Ferns	5	1
Walters	5	1
Winterbottom	5	1
Walker	5	1
Unknown	32	6

Source: Sample of 500 Stockport wills proved at the Consistory Court of Chester, 1800–1857.

It is plausible that similar kinds of issues affected the use of lawyers. Will drafter extraordinaire Jonathan L. Chetham was a prominent Whig councillor and one-time alderman who may have attracted hostility from his political opponents. Similarly, Stockport's remarkably energetic, yet always controversial, Liberal-Unitarian town clerk – Henry Coppock – practised as a lawyer with his partner William Woollam (and latterly with Samuel Oldham) and drew up a number of wills amongst the sample. Coppock was described by the editor of the *Stockport Advertiser* as a 'violent party man' and the newspaper reveals him to have made many enemies during the course of his political life. Indeed, one of Coppock's key opponents was fellow lawyer, will drafter and would-be town clerk John Kenyon Winterbottom, who was a prominent Anglican Conservative. In choosing a solicitor to make a will, it is therefore likely that existing economic, social and political allegiances influenced a testator's decision. Here, as at other times, will-making activities were embedded within the social relations of the locality.

Other sources of expertise

Whilst most testators sought the services of a solicitor when drawing up a will, other forms of advice were also available. A number of legal manuals, such as that by James Bird, aimed to 'recapitulate in familiar detail, such practical formalities and requisites as are material to be remembered and attended to by those whose particular inclinations, or peculiar situation ... may induce or oblige them to frame their own wills or other testamentary instrument.'[55] Whilst it is impossible to tell whether the home-made wills in the sample were drawn up using some kind of professional guide, there is one example of a will that used a simple pre-printed form that was customised by the testator.[56]

At a more general level the church provided an incentive for will making. Testamentary disposition was ecclesiastical in origin and, up until 1858, was partly regulated by ecclesiastical law. The church encouraged will making and some prayer books contained forms of wording appropriate for religious preambles to wills. Although not ensuring legal robustness, by making a will 'In the Name of God' an individual was invoking the highest 'natural' authority possible to sanction the disposal of property. Nevertheless, there is clear evidence from the sample of Stockport wills that the use of religious preambles was in decline over the period. Some 40 per cent of wills proved between 1800 and 1809 began with a religious preamble, falling to 11 per cent of wills proved between 1850 and 1857. In part, this shift reflects the decreasing use of religious preambles by solicitors. Attorney John Baddeley, who was responsible for twenty-seven wills amongst the sample, began nearly all with a religious preamble. However, Baddeley died in 1834 and other popular solicitors such as Jonathan L. Chetham began wills with a simple, secular form of wording. More generally, such a trend may reflect the growing secularisation of nineteenth-century society, a Nonconformist rejection of 'Anglicanised' wording and the increasingly 'legalistic' nature of testamentary disposition.[57]

In spite of the growing secularisation of will making the disposal of estates remained closely associated with the established church. As a result, another possible source of advice and expertise in testamentary matters was local clergymen. As is discussed further below, many Anglican clergy acted as surrogates for the ecclesiastical courts where wills were proved and were thus required to have some knowledge of the laws which governed their execution.

---

[55] Bird, J. B., *The Laws Respecting Wills, Testaments and Codicils*, 6th edn (London: W. Clarke and Sons, 1817), p. 48.

[56] Cheshire Record Office (CRO)/WS 1850 John Deaville of Stockport.

[57] Houlbrooke, R., 'Death, Church and the Family in England Between the Late Fifteenth and Early Eighteenth Centuries' in Houlbrooke, R. (ed.), *Death, Ritual and Bereavement*, (London: Routledge, 1989).

Fragmentary evidence suggests that clergymen were sometimes consulted for advice in matters relating to testamentary disposition. For example, a forgery trial reported in the *Stockport Advertiser* in the mid-1840s mentions that an executor who wanted to prove her deceased husband's will, consulted the town's rector – Reverend Charles K. Prescot – on what course of action she should take.[58]

Disposing of estates

Executors and trustees

The disposal of testamentary estate was a matter for executors and trustees. These were the people that a testator appointed to oversee the distribution of their estate and act as their living representatives. The distinction between the two roles of executor and trustee is a legal one; whereas trustees assumed the legal ownership of estate as part of the disposition strategy, executors did not. Executors were simply appointed to ensure that the disposition of property was carried out in accordance with the instructions laid down in the will. They were also responsible for getting the will proved by obtaining a grant of probate from a church court, calling in the deceased person's debts and paying his or her creditors. Trusteeship was arguably a more responsible activity because it involved taking on legal ownership of some or all of the deceased person's property. It also frequently entailed maintaining, selling and investing that property in order to meet the requirements of legacies paid to beneficiaries in the form of a regular provision income. Both roles could be time-consuming, expensive and fraught with difficulty.[59] Nevertheless, Shani D'Cruze has suggested that acting as a trustee or executor for a deceased relation, friend or colleague was an important part of male, middle-class life in towns.[60] Taking on this responsibility suggested status and, above all, that the individual

---

[58] *Stockport Advertiser*, 20 September 1844. The trial concerned was that of Mr. J. K. Winterbottom for forgery. Winterbottom stood accused of forging signatures to obtain the sum of £5000 insured upon the life of Thomas Isherwood of Marple who died in 1839. Winterbottom was Isherwood's attorney and the claim was made using his probated will. Isherwood's widow and executor Elizabeth was cross-examined to determine her role in the matter. During her cross-examination she mentioned seeking advice on how to prove the will from the rector of Stockport.

[59] Many wills contained clauses allowing executors to take expenses in order to pay for the disposition of estate and sometimes specific legacies were made to executors 'for their trouble'. Clauses also offered legal protection to executors and trustees who made sales of estate and who entered into contracts with other parties.

[60] D'Cruze, S., 'The Middling Sort in Eighteenth-Century Colchester: Independence, Social Relations and the Community Broker' in J. Barry and M. Brooks (eds), *A Middling Sort of People* (Basingstoke: Macmillan, 1994), pp. 181–2.

concerned could be trusted. Joseph Hudson advised that 'having resolved on making his will [a testator] should look round, amongst his kindred or friends, for a man of intelligence, activity and honour, to become his executor'.[61] An executor or trustee would gain an intimate knowledge of a testator's financial affairs, and would often be allowed considerable power and control over the use and investment of family property. They would also often be exposed to the private volatility of family relationships and might be expected to adjudicate in disputed testamentary claims. In an unstable economic environment trust was an important part of business life. Appointing someone as an executor or trustee was thus a real test of trust and sent out a public signal of confidence in an individual's capabilities to perform the necessary duties.[62] For those appointed to such a role, the duties of trusteeship and executorship offered a way of demonstrating competence and some degree of proprietorial acumen. Both were useful bourgeois masculine virtues in a business-oriented community. The activities of estate disposal in industrialising towns were thus enmeshed in broader social and economic contexts, drawing upon and reproducing existing social relations.

Evidence suggests that there were a number of individuals – men of 'intelligence, activity and honour', or people who D'Cruze might term 'community brokers' – who possessed the necessary skills and virtues to be a 'good' executor.[63] One example was the Stockport chemist Samuel Sims. Sims was a well-known townsman who came from an established family of Quaker chemists who settled in the town in the 1760s. Upon his death in November 1839 an obituary in the *Stockport Advertiser* noted that 'such was the general opinion of his sagacity and unsullied integrity, that no man was called upon more frequently to arbitrate the difference of parties, or to perform the difficult and delicate duties of executor and trustee in the affairs of others'.[64] The Sims family was renowned for good 'business habits and uprightness' which had gained them a favourable reputation amongst the townspeople.[65] According to the obituary, Sims had 'filled nearly every public office in the town, with the decided approbation of his fellow townsmen'.[66] He had proved his financial capabilities in acting as treasurer to the 'borough fund' and the savings bank.[67]

---

[61] Hudson, *Plain Directions for Making Wills*, p. 70.

[62] On the importance of trust and reputation in early modern urban communities see Muldrew, C., *The Economy of Obligation: The Culture of Credit and Social Relations in Early Modern England* (Basingstoke: Macmillan, 1998), esp. ch. 6.

[63] D'Cruze, 'The Middling Sort', p. 181.

[64] *Stockport Advertiser* 15 November 1839.

[65] Heginbotham, H., *Stockport: Ancient and Modern*, vol. II (London: publisher unknown, 1892), pp. 364–5.

[66] *Stockport Advertiser* 15 November 1839.

[67] *Stockport Bank for Savings: Minute Books*, D1620: DD/Tsb/1/1, Stockport Heritage Library. In the role of treasurer to the savings bank, Samuel Sims was preceded by his father Ollive Sims and succeeded by his nephew, also called Ollive Sims.

Sims was one of a number of prominent shopkeepers, businessmen and public office holders who were regularly appointed as executors. As well as being professionally competent, such people were clearly worthy folk with whom it was good for a testator , dead or alive, to be associated.

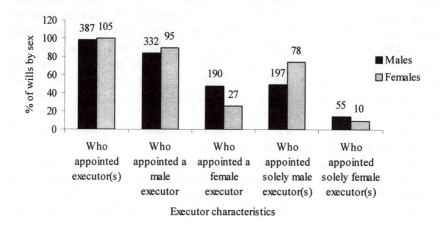

Figure 4.5: Executor characteristics, Stockport, 1800–1857

Given the need for executors and trustees to be trustworthy individuals who would gain an intimate knowledge of a testator's financial and familial affairs, it is perhaps not surprising that the majority of such persons appointed by Stockport will makers were close family relations. Some 371 (75 per cent) of the 492 testators who named an executor appointed at least one blood-relation to this role. Analysis of gender differences in the appointment of executors (see Figure 4.5) reveals that men were more often appointed executors than women. Interestingly, however, female testators tended to appoint more male executors than did male testators.[68] For example, whereas 74 per cent of the sample of women's wills appointed solely male executors, just 50 per cent of men's wills appointed solely male executors. Whilst this might partly be explained by the tendency of married men to appoint their wives as executors (some 84 per cent did so), it may also reflect pervasive gendered notions of dependency for widows and spinsters.

---

[68] Compare with Berg 'Women's Property and the Industrial Revolution', p. 239 and the chapter by David R. Green in this volume.

As well as family, other groups of people acted – sometimes in conjunction with kin – as executors or trustees. Supplementing family executors with non-family executors served a number of purposes. As suggested above, it signalled something of a testator's social standing. It also ensured some form of external adjudication to the property transmission process. In addition, a non-family executor could provide a source of expertise for the more complex or specialist aspects of estate disposal. For example, 16 per cent of testators appointed an executor of the same or a similar trade to their own. Where business estate was to be disposed of, or where the family firm was to be continued to support dependants, this expertise was undoubtedly useful. Finally, it is worth observing that most executors were also local people. Some 80 per cent of male testators and 62 per cent of female testators appointed executors from Stockport parish. The appointment of local folk was clearly done for practical reasons. However, this trend once again reflects the way in which the processes of property transmission were firmly embedded in the wider social relations of the community.

Seeking probate

Upon the death of a property owner the first task of an executor or family member was to ascertain whether the deceased had made a will. If a valid will had been made, then under normal circumstances its contents would be made known to the deceased's family, kin and friends. Wills were technically public documents 'published' for general inspection. Sometimes the disclosing of the contents of the will would become part of the post-mortem mourning rituals, alongside the funeral events and other public displays of mourning. Under these circumstances the will might be read before family and friends, usually by one of the named executors. This dramatised the activity, especially where the contents of the will had been kept under wraps and potential legatees learned for the first time of their gift or provision.[69] This was clearly a time when a will might also be contested, a process that could become a protracted, divisive and complex legal affair.[70] It is not possible to tell whether such sequences of events were followed by Stockport testators, although the nature of property transmission disclosed by their wills indicates that few testators adopted strategies of preferential gifting, suggesting that most will-reading events would not be dramatic revelations of an uneven distribution of property amongst family members.

---

[69] For a discussion see Jalland, P., *Death in the Victorian Family* (Oxford: Oxford University Press, 1996).

[70] This issue is not dealt with here. See Addy, J., *Death, Money and the Vultures: Inheritance and Avarice, 1660–1750* (London: Routledge, 1992).

Strictly, an executor took the authority to dispose of a deceased person's property from the will itself.[71] However, proof of the validity of a will could only be obtained in a court of law. A number of different courts had the power to prove the validity of a will with respect to different sorts of property, but it was the ecclesiastical courts that tried the validity of wills with respect to personal estate. Probate was required on all wills containing personal property and it was the duty of the executor named in a will to obtain a grant of probate. Furthermore, a grant of probate acted as proof of payment of probate duty (a legal requirement for all estates containing personal property) and as a prerequisite for the payment of estate and death duties, for which most estates were liable.

Stockport parish came under the jurisdiction of three main ecclesiastical courts: the Consistory Court of Chester, the Prerogative Court of York and the Prerogative Court of Canterbury.[72] Probate was sought from one or more of these courts depending on where the deceased person owned property, but in reality most Stockport wills were proved at the Consistory Court of Chester.[73] It was also rare for executors to travel directly to the court in order to apply for a grant of probate. In Stockport, most wills were sworn before a local Anglican clergyman acting as a surrogate for the court. One or more of the executors named in the will took a religious or solemn oath before the clergyman, swearing that they would faithfully carry out the instructions laid down in the will. The executor, for the purpose of calculating probate and other duties, swore an estimation of the gross value of the personal estate of the deceased.[74] This was made upon the basis of an inventory of the testator's effects provided by the executor. The figure recorded in the will and in other probate documents indicated the tax banding which the estate came under. It was therefore only an approximation of the total value of the deceased's personal property. A copy of this sworn oath was transmitted by the local clergyman to the relevant ecclesiastical court. Probate was then formally granted and the will deposited in an ecclesiastical registry. This process usually occurred soon after the testator's death. Indeed, 89 per cent of Stockport wills were proved within one year of the date of death.

---

[71] See PP. 1833 XXII *Law of Real Property: Fourth Report: Wills*, pp. 35–40.

[72] Wills from Stockport parish might also be proved in one of the courts of appeal of these three tribunals. However, such cases were extremely rare.

[73] For a general discussion of probate jurisdictions see Camp, *Wills and Their Whereabouts*, pp. xxv–xxxi.

[74] For a more detailed discussion of the process of estimating the value of an estate see Green and Owens, 'Metropolitan Estates of the Middle Class', pp. 300–301.

Table 4.2
Proving of will by Stockport surrogates

Name	Office	Active as surrogate	Wills proved	% of total sample
Charles Kenrick Prescot	Rector	1824–1857	189	38
William Bowness	Curate	1800–1807	59	12
Thomas Middleton	Master of grammar school	1832–1849	54	11
Joseph Taylor	Curate	1846–1857	49	10
Charles Prescot	Rector	1808–1820	44	9
Kelsall Prescot	Perpetual curate, Marple	1815–1823	36	7
		Total	431	87

Source: Sample of 500 Stockport wills proved at the Consistory Court of Chester, 1800–1857.

Recognised local clergymen were responsible for granting probate on 87 per cent of wills in the sample (Table 4.2). The effect of this practice was to divorce testamentary disposition from the legal institutions that regulated it. It was also a practice that sustained the close links between testamentary disposition and the established Church of England. Only where a will was disputed would it be necessary for the parties concerned to travel to Chester, York or London to appear in an ecclesiastical or other court. Even then, they would often be represented by a solicitor. Legal expertise was thus produced and consumed locally whilst the authority upon which it rested remained distant. As Table 4.2 reveals, one local ecclesiastical family – the Prescots – dominated the proving of wills in Stockport. Charles Prescot was succeeded by his son Charles Kendrick Prescot into the freehold incumbency of the parish of St Mary Stockport, and both were active will-provers. Charles Prescot's second son, Kelsall Prescot, who held a perpetual curacy at Marple until his death in 1823, was also engaged in probate duties, as was Prescot's third son, William, who succeeded Kelsall to the Marple curacy until 1826 and who later officiated at nearby Handforth Chapel.[75] It is hard to imagine that this domination did not create unease amongst some of Stockport's inhabitants. Evidence from the local newspaper suggests elements of anticlericalism amongst the town's population. Furthermore, the Prescots were a controversial family. Charles Kendrick Prescot became embroiled in local politics on a number of occasions

---

[75] On the Prescot family, see Heginbotham, *Stockport Ancient and Modern*, vol. I, p. 322 and vol. II, pp. 194, 235.

in the 1830s and 1840s and was clearly unpopular amongst the radical-Whig town government (many of whom were nonconformist Quakers or Unitarians) for his staunch conservative and constitutional views. In this respect, the local proof of wills embedded universal legal cultures in local political ones.

Disposing of property

Without a detailed exploration of executors' accounts and papers (few of which survive) it is difficult to discover exactly how estates were disposed of. However, it is possible to reconstruct at least part of the process by examining notices and advertisements relating to the disposal of estates published in local newspapers. Notices issued by executors and solicitors reveal something of the timings and stages of property transmission, whilst advertisements of sales of a deceased person's estates published by auctioneers provide a rich source of information on the property that was disposed of. Indeed, the process of inheritance helped to support a small economy of professionals who specialised in the conveyance of property from the distressed, destitute and dead, to the enterprising, energetic and entrepreneurial. The publication of newspaper notices and advertisements by these people rested on a number of factors. Evidence suggests that substantial estates, where disposition arrangements involved the sale of large amounts of property, were most likely to be disposed of through newspapers. A good example is the estate of Thomas Steel who died in February 1837 and whose will was proved at the Consistory Court of Chester in June 1837.[76] Steel was a wealthy cotton manufacturer, former mayor and Justice of the Peace for Stockport. Between 17 February 1837 and 26 January 1838, John Turner, who had been given the task of disposing of Steel's estate by public auction, published eleven different advertisements of sales of Steel's property, ranging from the auction of his private book collection to the disposal of his house and other real estate in nearby Edgeley, and the sale of his cotton-spinning factories and machinery in and around the town.[77]

The professional activities of solicitors also sometimes led to the publication of legal notices relating to the disposal estates. Thus, the solicitors dealing with the disposal of Steel's estate – Winterbottom and Wright, and Lingard, Vaughan and Lingard – published a notice in the *Stockport Advertiser* on 17 February 1837 calling for debtors to pay what they owed to the estate and inviting creditors to submit their demands.[78]

---

[76] CRO/WS 1838 Thomas Steel of Stockport.

[77] *Stockport Advertiser*, 17 February 1837, 24 February 1837, 17 March 1837, 7 April 1837, 28 April 1837, 26 May 1837, 28 July 1837, 13 October 1837, 17 November 1837, 29 December 1837 and 26 January 1838. This excludes re-advertisements of sales at intermittent dates.

[78] *Stockport Advertiser*, 17 February 1837. Although wealthy, evidence suggests that

Finally, executors and solicitors sometimes used newspaper advertisements when the identity or address of potential estate beneficiaries was not known. Following the death of Stockport widow Nancy Pollitt in 1836, for example, a newspaper notice was published calling forward all legatees listed in her late husband's will. George Pollitt (Nancy's husband) had died in 1807 but his legatees did not become entitled to their share of his estate until the death of his wife. Nearly thirty years later it was clearly difficult to identify these people. The advertisement made a plea for all claimant legatees to come forward within the following six months, after which time George Pollitt's trustees would make a division of the property.[79]

Newspaper notices and advertisements therefore provide a glimpse of the ways in which estates were disposed of and property was transmitted to legatees. They form another part of the public side to property transmission. To contemporaries, such notices were the ultimate revelation of a testator's wealth. They also reminded individuals of their own mortality and highlighted the need for setting proprietorial affairs in order. As a tangible outcome of the mechanics of inheritance, they provided propertied individuals with an indication of how they might fashion and manage their own property transmission strategies. In short, newspaper advertisements and the activities of solicitors, auctioneers and executors were another part of the community structures of towns through which inheritance was defined and codified.

One striking feature of the evidence is the length of time that it often took to settle and dispose of property. In some cases the process took several years. William Shuttleworth, a celebrated Stockport artist, died on Saturday 28 March 1829 aged forty-four.[80] His will was proved by the rector of Stockport, Charles Kendrick Prescot, on 21 November 1829 and probate was granted by the Consistory Court of Chester in January 1830. Shortly after his death, local auctioneer John Turner announced a public auction of Shuttleworth's 'household furniture, plate, glass, china, linen, brewing utensils, books, prints, paintings and items of vertu', including artwork by 'eminent masters', to take place at Shuttleworth's residence in Churchgate between 13 and 16 April.[81] Further sales were organised at the end of April and in the middle of May.[82] Clearly, William Shuttleworth had died leaving unpaid debts, for in August and September 1831 newspaper notices were published inviting creditors to meet his executor, local bookseller Thomas Claye, and his solicitors, Vaughan and

---

Steel died heavily indebted. A notice published in the *Stockport Advertiser* on 27 April 1838 announced that the family cotton-spinning firm had gone bankrupt.

[79] *Stockport Advertiser*, 28 October 1836. George Pollitt's will was proved at the Consistory Court of Chester on 4 July 1807.

[80] *Stockport Advertiser*, 3 April 1829 – death notice and brief obituary.

[81] *Stockport Advertiser*, 10 April 1829. As well as the front-page advertisement placed by Turner, the paper carried a small report drawing attention to the sale.

[82] *Stockport Advertiser*, 24 April 1829 and 15 May 1829.

Walker, at the Warren Bulkeley Arms in Stockport 'for final arrangement of estate and dividends'.[83] However, it was not until October 1835 that an advertisement appeared in the paper announcing that his creditors could receive final dividends from the estate by applying to Thomas Claye.[84] The example of Shuttleworth serves to illustrate just how visible the disposal of estates could be in early nineteenth-century towns. In the months or years following a testator's death, newspapers, auctioneers, solicitors and executors made an individual's private property into a public matter.

Conclusion

The purpose of this chapter has been twofold. Its first aim has been to describe processes of will making and property disposal in an attempt to provide a background for other chapters within the book. This has involved an investigation of some relatively basic issues of how many and what sorts of people made wills. It has also entailed a consideration of the ways in which the activities of will making and property disposal were managed by individuals and a discussion of the forms of knowledge and expertise that were required to effect a successful transmission of property. The second purpose of the chapter has been to demonstrate the multiplicity of ways in which property transmission was a social activity. The activities surrounding the making of wills and disposal of estates reveal that property ownership both routinely generated and reproduced social relations within industrial towns.[85]

In identifying these social relations the chapter has also demonstrated that inheritance, the study of which is so often centred around the family, had a public side as well as a private one. Studies of inheritance need to be aware of this wider context of property transmission both in terms of the material social practices that underpinned estate disposal and the meanings of property transmission that were created through these practices. It is clear from the evidence presented above, for example, that notions of professionalism and status which were central to the so-called masculine public sphere in towns also impinged upon the activities surrounding will making and estate disposal. Ultimately, therefore, a discussion of how people disposed of their property at death leads to a consideration of why people made wills. Whilst this is clearly a question that requires further research, some of the broader social meanings of will making are captured in the writings of lawyers. In concluding his manual on how to make wills, Richard Dickson proclaimed that

---

[83]   *Stockport Advertiser*, 26 August 1831 and 2 September 1831.

[84]   *Stockport Advertiser*, 2 October 1835.

[85]   Further consideration of these social networks of property transmission can be found in the chapter by Jon Stobart in this volume.

it is the duty and paramount obligation of every considerate and rational man ... as early as possible to make his will, in order to preserve the further peace and harmony of his family and prevent those irremediable disputes among them which are the consequences of intestacy ... No person ... who is desirous of leaving behind him the character of a just, kind, and wise member of society should delay or defer to perform the simplest and most easy act of human obligation ... This is an obligation binding on all men who are possessed of property, but more especially those who have families, and those who are engaged in the connections of business. Could any man of sense who died without a will, return to this world to see his family almost beggared, his children scattered on the wide world, his business embarrassed so as to be worth nothing; how would he grieve to think that all this confusion arose from his culpable neglect of performing so simple a duty as that of making his will.[86]

In a similar vein Joseph Hudson remarked that

few minds are so dull as to be utterly insensible of the pleasure which is afforded by the prospect of posthumous regard; and to be accounted hereafter as an affectionate husband and father, a considerate relation, and a sincere friend, is within the power of every man, by making a proper disposal of his estate and effects in his last will and testament.'[87]

The dramatic comments of Dickson and Hudson suggest that making a will in early Victorian England was viewed as more than a simple, functional exercise in transmitting property. They associate will making with a particular form of bourgeois masculinity characterised by rational thinking, good citizenship, familial cohesion and harmony, and personal esteem. In exploring will making and estate disposal practices in early nineteenth-century Stockport, this chapter has revealed many of these traits to be at the heart of the wider social relations of property transmission. The use of lawyers, the exploitation of social connections, the involvement of family members and significance of proprietorial status which have been outlined as central to the process of property transmission, all fit with this vision of will making. It is therefore with these powerful social meanings of property transmission in mind that strategies of inheritance discussed in other parts of this book, and elsewhere, need to be viewed.

---

[86] Dickson, *A Practical Exposition of the Law of Wills*, pp. 2–3.
[87] Hudson, *Plain Directions for Making Wills*, p. 78.

Chapter 5

Social and geographical contexts of property transmission in the eighteenth century

Jon Stobart

The processes of will-making and property transmission examined in the previous chapter took place within social and geographical networks which both reflected and defined the life-worlds of testators, their executors and legatees. These networks provided financial, legal and moral support for their members and helped to shape flows of goods, people and ideas as well as moulding local and regional markets, cultures and identities. Most importantly in the context of this volume, they formed the context in which property was owned and its meanings created or reinforced, and in which property management and transmission took place. And yet we know relatively little about these networks, beyond the commonplace that they were comprised of family and friends. What role did these two sets of people play and how did they connect with each other in spatial and social terms?

Work by McFarlane, Stone and others in the 1970s and early 1980s emphasised the primacy of the nuclear family in early modern society.[1] More recent studies, though, have placed greater emphasis on the extended family who, as Levine and Wrightson argue, 'constituted a resource: a network of trusted individuals bound by special obligation, a pool of assistance and support which could be drawn upon when occasion demanded'.[2] Networks of kin were important in commercial and industrial activities, in shaping migration to towns and as an emotional and economic support system.[3] They

---

[1] Cressy, D., 'Kinship and Kin Interaction in Early Modern England', *Past and Present* 113 (1986), pp. 38–44. For detailed arguments on the rise of the nuclear family, see Macfarlane, A., *The Family Life of Ralph Josselin* (Cambridge: Cambridge University Press, 1970); Stone, L., *The Family, Sex and Marriage in England, 1500–1800* (New York: Harper and Row, 1977); Laslett, P., *The World We Have Lost, Further Explored* (London: Methuen, 1983).

[2] Levine, D. and Wrightson, K., *The Making of an Industrial Society: Whickham 1560–1765* (Oxford: Oxford University Press, 1991), p. 338.

[3] Wrightson, K. and Levine, D., *Poverty and Piety in an English Village: Terling 1525–1700* (2nd edn, Oxford: Oxford University Press, 1995), pp. 29–36; D'Cruze, S., 'The

could remain strong over wide geographical areas and were resilient in the face of marked change in social and economic conditions.[4] Equally, as Tadmor has shown, wider kin often penetrated the geographical space of the nuclear family: the eighteenth-century household was constantly changing its size, constituents and dynamics as distant relations, friends and domestic servants came and went.[5]

Overlapping these family networks were others based on politics, occupation, religion or neighbourhood, often brought together through key individuals or community brokers.[6] The product was a series of social systems, each occupying distinct if overlapping spatial territories. This concept of local country is central to the work of Wrightson and Levine on both Terling and Wickham and, in essence, links the closely defined nuclear family to dense clusters of locally-resident friends and more dispersed networks of kin.[7] Although King has argued that such ideas are hard to sustain in areas of high population turnover, where behaviour and interaction were socially constrained and social networks became geographically limited,[8] this remains the most widely accepted conceptualisation of eighteenth-century social worlds. Unfortunately, these constructions (and their critiques) are based on research which focuses largely on rural areas and often on single settlements or parishes. Relatively little work has been carried out for the eighteenth century on urban-based social networks; the wider networks of contacts which linked towns, town and country, and even counties and regions; and the geographical constitution of such networks.[9] We might reasonably expect urban social networks to be substantially different from those of the countryside. Vann suggests that, due to heightened social dislocation, kin are likely to be more important in towns, whilst Dennis, Daniels and Pooley amongst others have

---

Middling Sort in Eighteenth-Century Colchester: Independence, Social Relations and the Community Broker', in J. Barry and C. Brooks (eds), *The Middling Sort of People: Culture, Society and Politics in England, 1550–1800* (London: Macmillan, 1994), p. 187; Pooley, C. and D'Cruze, S., 'Migration and Urbanization in North-west England circa 1760–1830', *Social History* 19 (1994), pp. 339–58; Anderson, M., *Family Structure in Nineteenth Century Lancashire* (Cambridge: Cambridge University Press, 1971), pp. 152–66; Cressy, 'Kinship and Kin Interaction', p. 42.

[4]   Cressy, 'Kinship and Kin Interaction', pp. 44–53; Levine and Wrightson, *Making of an Industrial Society*, pp. 295–307.

[5]   Tadmor, N., 'The Concept of the Household-family in Eighteenth-century England', *Past and Present* 151 (1996), pp. 111–40.

[6]   D'Cruze, 'Middling Sort in Eighteenth-Century Colchester', pp. 182, 190–99.

[7]   Levine and Wrightson, *Making of an Industrial Society*, p. 338; Wrightson and Levine, *Poverty and Piety*, p. 74.

[8]   King, S., 'Migrants on the Margin? Mobility, Integration and Occupations in the West Riding, 1650–1820', *Journal of Historical Geography* 23 (1997), p. 286.

[9]   A rare exception is Lane, P. 'An Industrialising Town: Social and Business Networks in Hinckley, Leicestershire c.1750-1835', in J. Stobart and P. Lane (eds), *Trade, Towns and Regions* (forthcoming).

emphasised the changing role of community and neighbourhood in shaping, as well as spatially defining, nineteenth-century social interaction.[10] At a broader level, the greater geographical mobility and external linkages of towns would argue for geographically wider networks:[11] if the local country did indeed define life-worlds in the eighteenth century, then these would presumably be far less local for towns than for villages.

The first aim of this chapter, then, is to throw some extra light on the social and geographical networks of townspeople. Evidence for this is drawn from probate records for Cheshire and southern Lancashire for the period 1701–60. The region was experiencing the early stages of industrialisation during this period, a process which involved increased movement of people within and beyond the North West, and brought individuals into contact with more people in a growing range of social and economic contexts. That said, such processes had not reached the intensity seen in the nineteenth century with the spread of factory production, large-scale urbanisation and the attendant social and geographical dislocation. The study therefore provides an insight into the life-worlds of individuals at arguably the last stage when the individual was still central to the social and economic worlds of production and consumption. Accordingly, the social and geographical structure of these urban-based networks are explored through analysis of the identity, familial status, occupation and location of the executors and administrators named in a sample of 2,606 wills and administration bonds.[12] Probate records are economic, social and cultural as well as legal documents and so reflect many aspects of an individual's life-world.[13] Wills, in Cressy's words, 'are sensitive indicators of family awareness' and, notwithstanding the fact that they clearly make mention of only a subset of the testator's family and friends, they have frequently been used to trace social networks.[14] Administration bonds have not

---

[10]   Vann, R., 'Wills and the Family in an English Town: Banbury, 1550–1800, *Journal of Family History* 4 (1979), pp. 363–6; Dennis, R. and Daniels, S., '"Community" in the Social Geography of Victorian Cities', *Urban History Yearbook* (1981), pp. 7–23; Dennis, R., *English Industrial Cities of the Nineteenth Century: A Social Geography* (Cambridge: Cambridge University Press, 1984), pp. 280–85; Pooley, C., 'Residential Differentiation in Victorian Cities: A Reassessment', *Transactions, Institute of British Geographers* 9 (1984), pp. 131–44. See also Earle, P., *The Making of the English Middle Class* (London: Methuen, 1989), *passim*.

[11]   Pooley and D'Cruze, 'Migration and Urbanization', pp. 339–58.

[12]   The sample included records from the Consistory Court at Chester and its counterpart at Richmond (for Preston probates) as well as the Prerogative Courts at York and Canterbury. This means that all types of estate and all levels of wealth (above an obvious minimum) are included in the study.

[13]   See the chapters by David Green and Alastair Owens in this volume.

[14]   Cressy, 'Kinship and Kin Interaction', p. 53. For the use of the wills see, *inter alia*, Wrightson and Levine, *Poverty and Piety*, pp. 75–9; Cressy, 'Kinship and Kin Interaction', pp. 53–9; D'Cruze, 'Middling Sort in Eighteenth-Century Colchester', p. 190; Johnston, J., 'Family, Kin and Community in Eight Lincolnshire Parishes, 1567–1800', *Rural History* 6

been so well utilised, but they, too, can indicate interpersonal links of friendship, kin or neighbourliness. Although signatories to these documents were clearly not nominated by the deceased, they must have known and been sufficiently close to him to be willing to enter into the legal processes involved in acquiring letters of administration. Indeed, it seems likely that these people were drawn from the most immediate family and friends, probably those whom the widow could most readily identify and trust amongst her dead husband's and her own close circle. Mapping the relative social and spatial position of executors and administrators thus gives a clear picture of the networks of social interaction which bound together individuals and places; but this is by no means the same thing as understanding the nature of (geographical) communities. More detailed work would be needed to discover the reasons for friendship and social interaction; the ways in which individuals interacted with and viewed their neighbours, family and friends; the precise relationship between place, communion and community, and the role of property in all these processes. Nonetheless, the present analysis allows us an insight into some of the social and spatial dimensions of townspeople's life-worlds, and on a scale not hitherto attempted.

Probate records are much more than simply a convenient and reliable register of significant life relations, however. Their distinctiveness comes from the fact that they identify the subset of these relationships which were significant at death and important for the transfer of property. The relationships signalled in wills and administration bonds are, at one and the same time, amongst the most public and the most private an individual might have. Being an executor or administrator publicly identified a person as trustworthy and gave them status; it also brought them into intimate contact with the finances and social workings of the deceased's household and family.[15] Given the significance of inheritance in securing social status and family coherence, and in cementing the wider social and cultural meanings of property,[16] the relationships defined within the probate records formed not merely the context, but also a significant part of the process of property transmission. Executors and administrators were, in effect, important conduits of social, cultural and economic reproduction. The second aim of the chapter is to highlight this significance, in part by analysing who acted in these positions of responsibility and in part by linking the broader social networks to the specifics of property transmission. The latter involves, in the first instance, a general review of the strategies adopted by testators with surviving wives and children. More detailed information is then presented for a much smaller number (just twenty-

---

(1995), pp. 179–92; Lane, 'Social and Business Networks'.

[15] D'Cruze, 'Middling Sort in Eighteenth-Century Colchester', pp. 181–2. See also the chapter by Alastair Owens in this volume.

[16] See the chapters by Ann McCrum and Geoffrey Crossick in this volume.

five wills) of individuals without this nuclear family. Clearly, this sample is not statistically significant and any findings must be treated with some caution, but it serves to illustrate the range of influences, linkages and strategies which shaped property transmission in early industrial England, not least the 'property relationships' of testator, executor and administrator.

Social and geographical networks

A total of 5091 executors and administrators were identified in the 2606 probate records, representing links to a vast range of family and friends (Table 5.1). However, discovering the precise nature of the relationships reflected by these links is problematical. For instance, 'friend' could include individuals related by blood or marriage, whilst 'cousin' encompassed a range of distant relations and associates. In the end, we are forced to accept that, if no family association is discernible from the documents, then none existed.[17] Notwithstanding the undercounting of kin that this probably entails, the data reveal some striking patterns. Only around one-third were with the nuclear family of wives (1221), sons (191) and daughters (102). Beyond this, 'kinsmen', brothers, brothers-in-law, fathers and sisters were all mentioned on more than fifty occasions, but the extended family as a whole accounted for only around one-eighth of links. This suggests that whilst the kinship relations were important in structuring the day-to-day social networks of urban-dwellers, their lives were focused very much around their own immediate families. Friends, though, were also important: over half the links recorded in the probates were with individuals apparently not related to the deceased. This latter figure may be artificially inflated by the pro-forma nature of the administration bonds which makes it more difficult to recognise kinship relations spelled out more explicitly in the wills by testators. That said, 46 per cent of executors were non-kin and only 38 per cent were wives or children. These figures are strikingly different from those recorded by Wrightson and Levine for rural Essex in the seventeenth century, where the totals were 13 per cent and 69 per cent respectively, and those for towns in the early nineteenth century, where about three-quarters of executors were closely related to the testator.[18] Moreover, these ratios were relatively stable through the sixty-year

---

[17] Levine and Wrightson, *Making of an Industrial Society*, p. 330; MacFarlane, *Family Life of Ralph Josselin*, p. 143. See also, Lane, 'Social and Business Networks'. Detailed family reconstitution offers a useful way of detecting a much fuller range of familial ties, but is impracticable for larger towns or regional analyses such as this.

[18] Wrightson and Levine, *Poverty and Piety*, pp. 99–100; chapters by Alastair Owens and David Green in this volume. They reflect more closely Lane's findings for Hinckley, where 24 per cent of executors were from the deceased's nuclear family and 52 per cent were

period, the proportion of related executors and administrators falling just slightly from around 44 per cent in the 1700s to 39 per cent by the 1750s.

Nonetheless, some longer-term changes in social networks are apparent. Even allowing for an element of under-counting of kin, it appears that townspeople in the early eighteenth century were more willing and/or able than either their rural counterparts or later urban-dwellers to draw on and trust a large number of friends and neighbours. Towns offered a far greater range of potential social contacts than did smaller rural settlements, giving the testator more choice when it came to naming executors. They effectively had less need to rely on family members to perform this task. At the same time, most towns were of moderate size in the early to mid-eighteenth century so that individuals remained part of a functioning if spatially ill-defined community. By the nineteenth century, it seems that urban growth had begun to undermine community sufficiently to refocus attention back onto the family when it came to personal matters and property.[19]

Table 5.1
The social nature of interpersonal linkages in southern
Lancashire and Cheshire

	All probates		Wills		Administration bonds	
	Total	%	Total	%	Total	%
Nuclear family	1514	29.7	932	37.9	582	22.1
Family of origin	341	6.7	180	7.3	161	6.1
Kin	310	6.1	202	8.2	108	4.1
Non-kin	2926	57.5	1143	46.5	1783	67.7
All	5091	100.0	2457	100.0	2635	100.0

Note: Nuclear family = wife, son, daughter; Family of origin = father, mother, brother, sister, uncle, aunt; Kin = brother-in-law, father-in-law, son-in-law, nephew, niece, cousin, kin.

Source: Wills and administration bonds proved 1701–60.

During this period at least, close family and neighbours formed the dominant element of individual life-worlds. Over three-quarters of the links identified were between people living in the same town and, as we shall see later, many people had close and trusted friends amongst their immediate neighbours. From this, it would appear that social networks were highly

unrelated - Lane, 'Social and Business Networks'. This highlights the need for parallel studies of towns and regions elsewhere in the country.

[19] See Dennis and Daniels, 'Community', pp. 7–23; Pooley, 'Residential Differentiation', pp. 133–44.

localised; perhaps, as King argues, due to the instability and uncertainty caused by migration and social exclusion.[20] However, analysis of links with people outside the 'home' town reveals very wide, if less dense, social networks. On average, the 1255 'outside' links took place over a distance of 24.5 miles, although distances ranged from less than a mile to over 380 miles. Unsurprisingly, these links became less numerous as distance increased, but this tendency was only marked for distances greater than 20 miles (Table 5.2). Indeed, almost one in ten outside links were between places more than 50 miles apart – a proportion which grew, but only slightly, during the period.[21]

Table 5.2
The spatial character of interpersonal linkages in southern Lancashire and Cheshire

	Wills		Administration bonds		All probates	
	Total	%	Total	%	Total	%
Under 5 miles	180	32.8	134	20.0	314	25.0
5–10 miles	108	19.7	160	22.6	268	21.3
10.1–20 miles	118	21.5	223	31.5	341	27.2
20.1–50 miles	77	14.1	143	20.2	220	17.5
Over 50 miles	65	11.9	47	6.6	112	8.9
Total	548		707		1255	

Source: Wills and administration bonds proved 1701–60.

Taken together, the outside contacts linked townspeople from north-west England into social networks which encompassed 450 settlements across the country. Whilst 352 of these, and 1045 of the 1255 outside links, lay within the region, the geographical extent of the collective social networks of particular towns could be considerable. For example, Cestrians had links with people in Holywell, Denbigh and Wrexham; Coventry, Hereford, Oxford and Nottingham; Dumfries, Edinburgh and Islay; London, Dublin and Cork; and seventy-one other places (Figure 5.1). Of course, no single individual enjoyed such extensive links, but it is evident that large and socially and geographically mixed networks were centred on the city. Also, whilst this picture is a composite of the social worlds of some 663 separate people, it is important to recognise the role which urban institutions (societies, guilds, newspapers, assemblies, courts of law and so on) played in shaping individuals' networks.

---

[20]   King, 'Migrants on the Margin?', p. 286.
[21]   Apart from this modest rise, from 7 per cent to 10 per cent, there were no changes of any note between the 1700s and the 1750s.

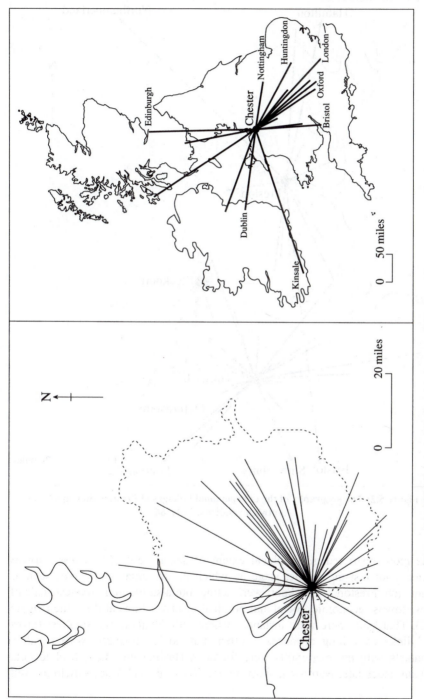

Figure 5.1: The geography of the interpersonal linkages of Chester residents, 1701–60

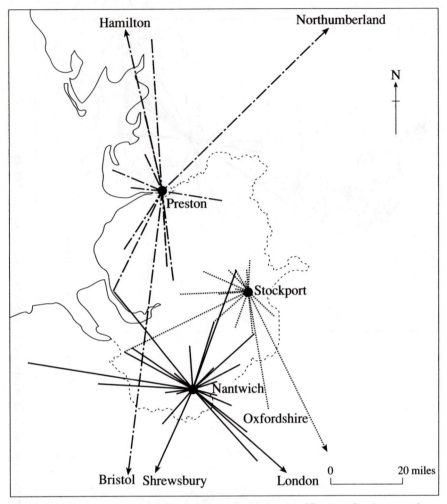

Figure 5.2: The geography of the interpersonal linkages of Preston, Stockport and Nantwich residents, 1701–60

The more restricted geographical extent of social networks in lesser towns reflects not just the smaller stage on which the inhabitants of towns such as Nantwich, Preston or Stockport were acting, but also the more modest scale of these towns' economic, social and political infrastructures at this time (Figure 5.2). That said, there were instances where individuals in the smallest towns had links over long distances – often, but not exclusively, with London. Contacts with the metropolis were found in Haslingden, Bury, Middlewich, Wigan, Rochdale, Nantwich, Warrington, Stockport and Macclesfield as well as Liverpool, Manchester and Chester. More unusually, Nathanial Forster, a vicar from Rochdale, named a gentleman and widow from Norwich as his executors; Richard Holland, a Macclesfield chapman, nominated a gentleman in Darlington in addition to his sister from Macclesfield and nephew from Doncaster, and a mariner from Hamilton was one of the co-signatories of the administration bond for the estate of John Edwards of Preston.[22] Notwithstanding these individuals, though, the geographical and, more arguably, the social range of a person's life-world was strongly moulded by the town in which he or she lived.[23]

Urban social networks were clearly varied in their geographical extent. Whilst notions of local country are a useful way of conceptualising these life-worlds, they were complicated by the overlaying of kinship, occupational, neighbourhood and other networks, and by the fact that friendship and kinship relations could remain close even over great distances. The bulk of inter-linkages may have taken place within the confined and often intra-urban spaces which defined the parameters of most individuals' everyday lives, but social networks were not collapsed into the insular and locality-centred webs described by King.[24] Proximity or frequency of contact were not the only underlying causes of social network formation. Despite, or perhaps because of, the highly mobile and transient nature of urban populations, their social networks incorporated geographically dispersed friends and family. This suggests that the lines of property transmission were not necessarily simple and direct; at least in their execution, they could involve complex and geographically widespread networks.

Property relationships and social networks

Given the wide social and geographical spread of networks, it is important to ask how such individuals were known to one another and how certain people were chosen or volunteered to be involved in the process of property transmission. In other words, what do the networks uncovered tell us about the significance of the relationships disclosed and how do they help us to understand the processes of property transmission?

The most obvious and numerous relationships were those within the nuclear family. Close family members were probably chosen because of their

---

[22] Lancashire Record Office (LRO)/WCW 1758 Nathanial Forster of Rochdale; Borthwick Institute York, Index of Wills, Richard Holland of Macclesfield; LRO/WCW 1760 John Edwards of Preston.

[23] This echoes Johnson's observation that the type of agriculture influenced the nature of the social networks in rural parishes – Johnson, 'Family, Kin and Community', pp. 186–7.

[24] King, 'Migrants on the Margin?', pp. 286, 292–4.

familiarity with the property being disposed, their trustworthiness and their knowledge of the locality. Indeed, the need to regulate and, if necessary, capitalise property locally was undoubtedly closely linked to the characteristic localism of petit-bourgeois property ownership and use.[25] Such tendencies were reinforced by the strong concentration of all probate linkages within the home town of the deceased. When testators looked beyond their own household for individuals capable of executing their wills, they turned most frequently to their immediate friends and neighbours. For example, Richard Parrot, a Chester draper, named a gentleman and a draper from Chester and his brother-in-law in nearby Plempstall as executors; Gerald Ford, a Wigan innholder, called on a maltster and a brazier from the town; and Joseph Herd, a tallow chandler in Manchester, named a chapman and a merchant also from Manchester.[26] The list could go on. What is apparent is that physical proximity was an important aspect in establishing friendships and cementing the type of trust needed between testator and executor. That said, even strongly-felt notions of friendship between inhabitants of the same town were often vaguely expressed. Richard Parrot was typical of scores of testators, describing fellow Cestrians Thomas Lloyd, John Holland and his daughters Abigail and Mary, John Yeoman and Edward Smith as 'good friends'.[27] What had made them so? Neighbourhood appears to have been important as a focus of friendship groupings. References to 'my neighbour' appear in a significant number of wills in relation to both executors and legatees, and clearly referred to friends living close to the testator. For example, when he died in 1715, John Holdford, gentleman, of Congleton left £10 to his 'opposite neighbour' a shoemaker called Thomas Thorley and a further £5 to Thorley's wife Elizabeth.[28]

Property relationships, as expressed through the probate records, were frequently very local and may, in turn, have been important in forming or bolstering notions and feelings of community in the growing towns of the eighteenth century.[29] Such feelings of neighbourliness and identity with the local community were also found in the bequeathing of small amounts to the

---

[25] See Crossick, G. and Haupt, H.-G., *The Petite Bourgeoisie in Europe 1780–1914: Enterprise, Family and Independence* (London: Routledge, 1995), pp. 198–204 and the chapter by Geoffrey Crossick in this volume.

[26] Cheshire Record Office (CRO)/WS 1717 Richard Parrott of Chester; LRO/WCW 1721 Gerald Ford of Wigan; LRO/WCW 1732 Joseph Herd of Manchester. None of the three wills made any mention of nuclear family.

[27] CRO/WS 1717 Richard Parrott of Chester. There are problems here of identifying precisely what was meant by 'friend' as it could be used to describe a range of social and even familial relationships.

[28] CRO/WS 1715 John Holdcroft of Congleton.

[29] Langton, J., 'Residential Patterns in Pre-industrial Cities: Some Case Studies from Seventeenth-century Britain', *Transactions, Institute of British Geographers* 65 (1975), pp. 8–23.

clergy or poor of the testator's 'home' parish. Whilst these gifts may have been suggested by those involved in advising testators and drawing up wills (lawyers and clergy, for example),[30] neighbourhood, religion and obligation came together in their sentiment and impact, and mutually reinforced the individual's links with particular people in particular places. Religious affiliation could also shape friendship patterns in a wider sense. Langton argues that Catholics in west Lancashire were intimately involved in regional and national Catholic networks which offered financial, political and emotional support in what was still an often hostile world.[31] Similar linkages were found amongst the Nonconformist communities of south-east Lancashire and east Cheshire, and certain individuals, such as Timothy Dean of Chester, left small legacies to the local Presbyterian minister.[32]

In this way and others, the probate records may be telling us less about the reality of social contacts and more about which individuals the testators wanted to be publicly seen and remembered as being associated with. In this way, will-making can be seen as an act of social envisioning – an idea that links closely with D'Cruze's notion of community brokers who formed the locus of a series of individual social networks and wielded significant social, political and economic influence in the town.[33] More broadly, she argues that 'your friends were those who supported your status in the public world', they were 'your landlord, your employer, the most affluent member of your parish vestry, the neighbourhood victualler, perhaps the local cleric'.[34] The idea that friendships, particularly those identified through the process of will-making, were at least partly defined by the status which they could bring to both testator and executor undoubtedly influenced the social networks of north-west England. A total of 580 gentlemen were named as executors or signed administration bonds in the probate records sampled. This represents 11.4 per cent of all links,[35] and included eighty-four contacts with merchants, eighty with mercers and drapers, fifty-four with innkeepers and thirty-three with grocers. Although questions of status are fraught with difficulty, not least because individuals who had retired from trade often styled themselves 'gentleman', it appears that these tradesmen enjoyed bonds of friendship with

---

[30] See the chapter by Alastair Owens in this volume; D'Cruze, 'Middling Sort', pp. 189–96.

[31] Langton, J., 'The Continuity of Regional Culture: Lancashire Catholicism from the Late-sixteenth to the Early-nineteenth Century', in E. Royle (ed.), *Issues of Regional Identity* (Manchester: Manchester University Press, 1997), pp. 82–101.

[32] CRO/WS 1729 Timothy Dean of Chester.

[33] D'Cruze, 'Middling Sort in Eighteenth-Century Colchester', pp. 189–96.

[34] D'Cruze, 'Middling Sort in Eighteenth-Century Colchester', p. 189. See also the chapter by Alastair Owens in this volume.

[35] This figure corresponds very closely with the ten per cent noted by Lane, 'Social and Business Networks'.

their social betters. Certainly, they were happy to use their wills to identify themselves as having such relationships. However, whilst the possibility of post-mortem social betterment is undoubtedly significant, it should not be forgotten that over half the probate records examined were administration bonds wherein the relationship was identified by the signatory to the bond, not the deceased. Naturally, betterment could work in both directions, but it seems more likely that the relationships recognised at death were, in the main, also significant life relations. In other words, the probate records represent a fair cross-section of genuine social relationships.

Such a view is strengthened by the fact that appointing executors or acting as an administrator was an act with important economic as well as social implications: the testator had to be confident that the named individuals had the commitment and necessary skills to carry out the instructions of the will. One vital attribute could be knowledge of or expertise in a particular trade,[36] and so we see many executors and administrators being drawn from similar trades to the deceased. For example, Richard Parrot appointed his 'good friend and master' John Holland as one of his executors; George Lingard, a Manchester innkeeper, left his affairs in the hands of two local maltsters, and George Royle from Stockport named two fellow grocers from the town as executors.[37] Overall, of the 2703 cases for which the occupation of both deceased and executor or administrator is known, 609 were in a similar trade and a further 71 were closely associated.[38] There was a slightly higher propensity towards this in commerce than in the professions (perhaps because of the need for specific expertise in post-mortem estate management, knowledge of debts and credits, and so on), and textiles dealers especially relied on each other to act as executors or administrators. Of 451 references to chapmen in the probate records, 114 involved links to other chapmen and a further 75 tied them to other textiles-related trades. In certain places these interconnections could be even closer; for example, the links of more than half of the Manchester chapmen lay within textiles manufacture and dealing. This occupational proximity became more important in the longer-distance links (Table 5.3). Those between individuals in similar occupations accounted for only 10 per cent of all 'outside' contacts, but formed 13 per cent of links over distances greater than 10 miles.

---

[36] Owens, A., 'Inheritance and the Life-Cycle of Family Firms in Early Nineteenth-Century England', unpublished paper. Lane, 'Social and Business Networks'.

[37] CRO/WS 1717 Richard Parrott of Chester; LRO/WCW 1704 George Lingard of Manchester; CRO/WS 1731 George Royle of Stockport.

[38] Close association is defined in terms of materials used or supplied rather than the actual trade of the individuals. Thus a brewer is seen as being 'closely associated' with an innkeeper, a grazier with a butcher, an ironmaster with an ironmonger, and so on. The problems of accurately identifying such associations are reflected in the low number of linked individuals enumerated.

Where geographical distance precluded the type of regular social contact of experienced between neighbours and within households, links cemented by commonalties of trade or business were evidently more significant. The latter, although less easy to identify, were especially important to longer-distance links with other towns and particularly with the metropolis. A total of fifty-six Londoners appeared as executors or administrators, forty-seven of whom were identified by their occupation: eleven were gentry, four were lawyers[39] and one was an undertaker, but the largest group (twenty-two individuals) were engaged in trade. As the main entrepôt and link to overseas supplies and markets, personal contact with business associates in London were essential for many manufacturers, merchants and retailers in the North West. These links provided reliable agents to transact business in the metropolis, important information on markets, prices and fashions, and supplies of raw materials, shop-goods and capital.[40] That personal friendship or family ties should be the cause or outcome of many of these contacts is unsurprising. As a result, economic and social networks were interrelated and intertwined.

Table 5.3
Occupation, kinship and the spatial characteristics of interpersonal linkages in southern Lancashire and Cheshire

		Similar occupation	Kin	Other	All
Under 5 miles	Total	26	53	235	314
	%	8.3	16.9	74.8	
5–10 miles	Total	18	58	192	268
	%	6.7	21.6	71.6	
10.1–20 miles	Total	43	83	215	341
	%	12.6	24.3	63.0	
20.1–50 miles	Total	27	63	130	220
	%	12.3	28.6	59.1	
Over 50 miles	Total	17	45	50	112
	%	15.2	40.1	44.6	
Total	Total	131	302	822	1255
	%	10.4	24.1	65.5	

Source: Wills and administration bonds proved 1701–60.

---

[39] Lawyers may have been chosen in these instances because of the complex or contested nature of the will.

[40] See, for example, Wadsworth, A. and Mann, J. de L., *The Cotton Trade in Lancashire, 1600–1780* (Manchester: Manchester University Press, 1931), pp. 29–36; Mass Observation, *Browns and Chester: Portrait of a Shop* (London: Lindsay Drummond Ltd., 1947), *passim*.

More important in terms of property and inheritance, these kinds of relationships linked the essentially local nexus of property ownership, use and transmission to much wider networks and much broader sets of social and economic influences.[41] The significance of the extended family in this geographical enlargement of the networks of property transmission was considerable. About one-third of the executors and administrators living more than 20 miles distant from the deceased, and over 40 per cent of those over 50 miles away, were drawn from members of the extended family (Table 5.3). Total numbers were quite small, but the relative importance of kin was significantly higher in the more distant links. Brothers (fifteen cases) and sons (eight) were most numerous amongst the longest links, but other members of the family of origin, including fathers, sisters and daughters were also called upon. So, too, was the extended family of brothers-in-law, nephews and sons-in-law, cousins and 'kinsmen', and even in one case a mother-in-law.

Here, at last, we have evidence of Levine and Wrightson's 'dispersed network' of relatives. Family ties were less affected by the friction of distance, not least because they did not necessarily need to be sustained by regular social or economic interaction: trust and knowledge of family affairs being based on kinship, not geography or economics. They were therefore critical in linking the townsfolk of north-west England into social networks which went beyond the spatially limited confines of nuclear family and immediate neighbours. Moreover, Cressy argues, they carried more meaning and were more resilient than bonds with only an economic, occupational or religious basis.[42] 'At issue is not propinquity, network density or frequency of involvement, but rather the potency and instrumentality of family ties'.[43] Thus, these dispersed networks of family, although they included comparatively few individuals, formed an important part of the social networks of the townsfolk of north-west England. By extending the trust and familiarity which existed within the immediate family over much wider areas, they helped to open up locally-focused concepts of and attitudes to property to broader influences. And they did so through a known and reliable set of personal relationships. At a more immediate level, they impinged directly on the actual processes of property transmission. The extended family was not merely an important channel for the transfer of property between individuals and generations, it was also a significant beneficiary of these transfers.

---

[41] See the chapters by W. D. Rubinstein and Geoffrey Crossick in this volume.
[42] Cressy, 'Kinship and kin interaction', p. 47.
[43] Cressy, 'Kinship and kin interaction', p. 49.

Social networks and property transmission

Eighteenth-century townspeople, like their rural counterparts, were primarily concerned in their wills to make provision for their immediate family: their wives and especially their children. Although inheritance strategies varied according to the amount and type of property to be disposed, the life-cycle stage of the testator and the composition of the immediate family, the testator's first concern was almost always his children.[44] Wives were provided for during the course of their lives, but – especially if the children were still in their minority – they frequently acted as effective trustees. If the wife had already died or if the nature of the business was especially complex or specialised, then formal trustees might be appointed until the children reached their majority. Naturally, arrangements varied in detail, but two examples serve to illustrate typical strategies.

Randle Wilbraham, a wealthy Nantwich gentleman from a family of considerable local important, died in 1732. He left £600, half his household goods and the majority of his real estate to his wife Mary with the instruction that, upon her death, the land would pass in equal share to his sons Roger and Randle. Whilst she had use of the land during her life, Mary had no power to dispose of it in her own right. Moreover, Randle senior had already given some land to Roger when he married, and gave further gifts of real estate and £1000 to his two other sons, Thomas and Henry, both fellows of Oxford colleges, and £2500 to his daughter Mary. Here was a man intent on providing well for his children and who saw comparatively few obligations beyond them. An unspecified number of grandchildren had £50 each, the local charity school was given £200 and each servant received small sums. In monetary terms alone, from a total of around £5500, more than 90 per cent was left to the immediate family and over 80 per cent directly to the children. The will of Thomas Williams, a Chester merchant, was rather smaller but more complex. His wife had already died so he placed his real estate in the hands of his executors and instructed them that all income was to be paid to his daughter Elizabeth. Having no other immediate relatives, Thomas apparently felt able and possibly obliged to leave bequests to a range of more distant relatives, and to friends and charities. His brother Robert got his clothing, £4 cash and 40 shillings per annum; two nephews received £20 and a niece £10; Thomas's executors were left £20 apiece, and his servant Lucretia £5; charities in Chester and Caernarfon were given a total of £60. The sums, though, were

---

[44] Wrightson and Levine, *Poverty and Piety*, pp. 95–9. See also Owens, 'Inheritance and the Life-cycle of Family Firms'; chapter by Ann McCrum in this volume.

comparatively small; Thomas was clearly intent on passing the bulk of his wealth directly to his daughter.[45]

Table 5.4

Kin and non-kin recognised in wills which contain no mention of children or wives

Legatee	Number of legatees	Monetary bequests (£)		
		Approximate total	Mean % of estate	Mean value
Nephew/niece	54	2849 + 5pa	31.4	52.8
Cousin/kinsman	43+	3080	17.2	71.6
Siblings (inc. in-laws)	25	1322 + 5pa	10.5	52.9
Godchildren	8	563	4.2	70.4
Great nephew/great niece	15+	475	2.5	31.3
Uncle/aunt	3	25 + 10pa	1.0	8.3
Total kin	*151*	*8664 + 70pa*	*66.8*	*56.2*
Servants	10+	100 + 10pa	6.3	9.5
Executors	11	156	2.2	14.2
Clergy	15	155	1.1	9.6
Other non-kin	95	1539 + 2.5pa	12.2	16.6
Total non-kin	*130*	*1900 + 12pa*	*21.8*	*15.0*
Poor	36	800 + 22pa	7.7	22.2
Schools	8	430	4.1	51.3
Total charity	*44*	*1230*	*11.8*	*27.5*
Total	**325**	**11794 + 104pa**	**100.0**	**35.9**

Notes: '+' in column two indicates an indeterminate plural number, as in 'my servants' or 'their children'. The mean percentage of the estate averages the proportion of each estate bequeathed to particular groups of legatees; the mean value of bequests is calculated by dividing the approximate total by the number of legatees in each group. In both cases, means exclude sums paid per annum.

Source: Wills and administration bonds proved 1701–60.

Such wills tell us much about the importance of the immediate family, and especially children, in the process of property transmission. They speak of lives centred very strongly around the closed nuclear family. However, we can learn more about the relationship between property and wider social networks if we examine wills of those without this central focus – to whom did such people leave their estates? There have been surprisingly few attempts in the past to address this question, although it is generally assumed that family

---

[45] CRO/WS 1732 Randle Wilbraham of Nantwich, CRO/WS 1736 Thomas Williams of Chester.

dominated legacies by the eighteenth century.[46] Detailed analysis of the small sample selected here (twenty-five wills)[47] suggests that family did indeed dominate even in the absence of wives and children, but that other influences were also strong (Table 5.4).

In all, these testators bequeathed around £12,000 as well as land, houses, shops, stock–in-trade, jewellery, books and so on to over 318 individuals or institutions. A little under half the recipients were family members and around 40 per cent were non-kin, including executors and servants.[48] A significant minority of wills also included gifts to charity, most often via church wardens, but also through blue-coat schools, infirmaries and even the guilds. Such largesse beyond the family circle has not previously been reported and is significant in terms of the recognisance of those who were socially and emotionally important to the testator. It hints at lives centred on local communities and confirms that processes of property transmission need to be seen in the context of all the various social networks outlined above. At the same time, it is clear that a distinction should be drawn between the generally larger legacies left to family, for their financial security, and the often very small token bequests made to friends. Within family (whether nuclear or extended), the emphasis was on obligation and provision; for friends, volition and gifting was more prevalent.

Looking at these bequests in more detail, a range of non-kin were recognised in the wills. One obvious group of beneficiaries was executors, the testator acknowledging the commitment shown and the work to be carried out. Their appearance as legatees would give them extra significance in property transmission, but only a handful of executors received gifts and just eleven were not related to the testator through (higher-order) kinship ties. With two exceptions, these people received tokens rather than substantial sums: most were in the range of 3–10 guineas and, on average, such gifts accounted for just 2.2 per cent of the value of the estates examined. Servants, too, were sometimes thanked for their loyalty with legacies, although the amounts were again modest. Zachary Turnpenny of Nantwich was typical, leaving 10 shillings to each of his servants and half a year's wages to whoever was attending him at his death. His gift of a hat band and pair of gloves for each of the men 'that usually have assisted in carrying me to and from my room' was

---

[46] Johnson, 'Family, Kin and Community', p. 186; Cressy, 'Kinship and Kin Interaction', p. 55.

[47] These formed a random sample of wills where no mention was made of a nuclear family. It includes men from across the region and represents a range of 'occupations' from gentleman to innkeeper.

[48] This figure is considerably in excess of the c. 10 per cent reported by Cressy and Johnson.

more unusual.[49] Bequests were also made to fifteen clergymen, often by name, but occasionally in a more generalized gift to the work of a particular church or denomination. Thus, Henry Antrobus gave £10 to the minister of the Church of England in Knutsford, whilst Timothy Dean put £30 in the hands of his trustees, the interest on which was to be paid to a Protestant minister in Chester.[50] Always, though, the amounts were little more than tokens in terms of the total estate value. On average, these three groups together received less than 10 per cent of the monetary bequests, reinforcing the idea that legacies to non-kin were gifts, perhaps recognising services rendered or enhancing the testator's status through largesse, rather than mechanisms for providing future financial security.

The clear majority of non-kin bequests were made to friends, who alone accounted for an average of one-eighth of the estate values. The average sum was around £16, but the range was enormous: Richard Wild, a Chester schoolmaster, made no fewer than eighteen gifts of 20 shillings, whereas William Bagnall of Macclesfield gave £500 to one Mary Chantell, the widow of a local maltster.[51] Most testators gave variable amounts, presumably adjusting the sum in accordance with the level of attachment felt to the legatee. Richard Parrot left gold rings worth 20 shillings to sixteen of his friends, but made gifts of £5, 20 guineas, 30 guineas and £60 to his particular friends.[52] Again, then, we have a picture of the layers of social relationships which enveloped individuals and informed the process of property transmission. These were people with whom Richard Parrot did not have links of family obligation, but to whom he clearly shared close, if varied, emotional ties. These networks of friends were important enough for him to leave over half of his money to non-kin. Many, but by no means all, were local, underlining once more the importance of neighbourhood and, more arguably, community in shaping attitudes to property transmission.

This sense of place-identity emerges again in gifts to charity. In all, the twenty-five testators gave a total of about £1250 to various charitable bodies, with particularly large sums being earmarked for the infirmary in Chester and blue coat schools in a number of towns. The widespread nature and relatively high level of giving to these good works (11.8 per cent of the estate on average) is in marked contrast to the steady decline recorded for rural Lincolnshire.[53] The generalised explanations offered by Johnson – the rise of

---

[49]   CRO/WS 1741, Zachary Turnpenny of Nantwich.
[50]   CRO/WS 1716, Henry Antrobus of Knutsford; CRO/WS 1729 Timothy Dean of Chester.
[51]   CRO/WS 1732 Richard Wild of Chester, CRO/WS 1727 William Bagnall of Macclesfield.
[52]   CRO/WS 1717 Richard Parrott of Chester.
[53]   Johnson, 'Family, Kin and Community', pp. 189–90.

Protestantism and the falling-off of community awareness – may need to be reviewed for towns. Whilst status could be posthumously enhanced by supporting the work of a prominent civic institution such as an infirmary,[54] the regular appearance of bequests to the poor of the parish or the education of its children suggests an attachment to community and an awareness of its needs. This idea is reinforced by the fact that gifts were always place-specific; they generally referred to the town where the testator was or had been resident, and were often very local or specific in terms of the actual beneficiaries. In Chester, for example, Timothy Dean left £50 to the city's blue coat school; £25 each to the parishes of St Mary's and St Peter's, but £50 to the parish of St Michael's, and £100 to the 'Aldermen, Stewards and Company of Mercers and Ironmongers' for the relief of its six poorest members.

Notwithstanding these numerous and varied bequests, it was to their wider families that these apparently childless testators left the majority of their estates. Around £8400 plus land, shops, houses, stock-in-trade, heirlooms, household goods, plate, books and a range of personal effects were bequeathed to relatives from brothers and sisters to second cousins. On average, kin accounted for over two-thirds of the estates' monetary values and they featured prominently amongst the residual beneficiaries (Table 5.4). Sometimes the sums were very small: John Dale, a Macclesfield innholder, was by no means exceptional in leaving just 20 shillings each to his two sisters-in-law and five nephews and nieces.[55] The average was around £56, however, and single bequests could be very large indeed. Excluding real estate, the largest single legacy was £1000 given by William Whitfield, a Chester merchant, to his unmarried sister Hannah,[56] but there were ten other gifts of £200 or more made to cousins, nephews, godchildren and kinsmen. Across all the wills examined, the obligation to family was clearly strongly felt, if sometimes grudgingly met. Alexander Haughton of Stockport left £10, £15 and one shilling to three sisters to whom he was related, but appears to have done this solely to discharge any claims which they might make on the basis of their grandfather's will.[57] More commonly, there was clearly a feeling that kin should be recognised with bequests: that part of what it meant to be a family member was to provide, wherever possible or necessary, for kinsfolk. For example, Timothy Dean left £234 to a total of thirty-two relatives including his brother, sister-in-law, cousins and second cousins, and Peter Cotton made gifts ranging from one

---

[54] Porter, R., 'The gift relation: philanthropy and provincial hospitals in eighteenth-century England', in G. Lindsay and R. Porter (eds), *The Hospital in History* (London: Routledge, 1989), pp. 158–61.

[55] CRO/WS 1736 John Dale of Macclesfield.

[56] CRO/WS 1758 William Whitfield of Chester.

[57] CRO/WS 1731 Alexander Haughton of Stockport. One shilling was normally seen as a 'cut-off legacy' – a calculated insult to an out-of-favour relative.

guinea to £400 to twenty kinsfolk. His feelings of familial obligation were evidently strong, as he even gave £100 to the wife of a cousin, 'whose name I have forgot'.[58] The general impression, though, is of testators leaving bequests to relatives with whom they had real emotional ties.

Siblings and cousins often received significant sums, but it was nephews and nieces who dominated these family bequests, receiving on average about one-third of the estates. As with nuclear families, then, property transmission was characterised by inter-generational transfers. Inheritance was therefore important to social reproduction even in the absence of wives and children: money was still used to support the next generation or establish them well in the world. Without children of their own, testators retained this important function of property transmission and refocused its benefits onto the offspring of their siblings and cousins. Richard Leversage was clearly anxious to assist his brother's two sons. He stipulated that 6 shillings should be paid each week to his niece Mary Cook and her husband William 'for and during the life of my indiscreet nephew Thomas Leversage'. The money was to be passed on to Thomas or spent by Mary for her brother's support and maintenance, but not to service his debts. Whilst attempting to rescue one nephew from distress, Richard was also anxious to reward the fidelity of another nephew, also called Richard Leversage, who was then his apprentice. He gave the young man £600 with the 'hope that he will continue in business with credit and reputation'.[59] In this way, monetary support and social reproduction through property transmission remained centred on the family, but the definition of that family was broadened considerably. When linked to the previous discussion of social networks, this reinforces the impression that the relationships and linkages which shaped and were expressed through property transmission were geographically complex. As the extended family was often not locally resident, localised worlds and interactions were overlain by much broader linkages of friendship and, above all when it came to property, of kinship.

Conclusions

This chapter has explored the social and geographical dimensions of the inter-personal networks which framed the individual and collective life-worlds of testators and thus informed their decisions on property transmission. In focusing on essentially rural and often agricultural areas, previous studies have emphasised the importance of local country in shaping these networks. The townspeople studied here had rather different social networks which

---

[58] CRO/WS 1729 Timothy Dean of Chester, CRO/WS 1716 Peter Cotton of Chester.
[59] CRO/WS 1760 Richard Leversage of Nantwich.

incorporated family and friends from wide geographical areas as well as the immediate vicinity. Most bonds were very local, linking inhabitants of the same town or even the same house, but a significant number were much more widely dispersed, tying the townsfolk of north-west England to family and friends in towns and villages across the country. Kinship ties were strongest with the immediate family, with wives and children most frequently being named as executors. They were most familiar with the property to be disposed; they were local (and thus had first-hand knowledge of the trade and social networks of their husbands and fathers), and, above all, they were trustworthy and reliable. As the major legatees of most estates, the nuclear family had a strong interest in the property transfers detailed in the wills: they were, in effect, both the operatives and objects of property transmission.

Friends were most readily found amongst neighbours, re-emphasising the localism of the networks and customs which informed property ownership, use and transmission. However, broader occupation, trade and business networks as well as the extended family were also incorporated into these property relationships as particular skills, knowledge or expertise was required. In many ways, this sparse and dispersed network may have been as emotionally, socially and economically important to the testators as their more dense localised social networks. These were friendships which could be sustained without regular personal contact and yet were sufficiently close to form the basis of some of the most intimate and financially significant relationships an individual might experience. They meant that townspeople, and thus towns and the region in general, were in touch with and influenced by the values of a diversity of places, not least the metropolis. Most telling in the present context, they were important in linking the often localised nexus of property ownership and relationships to wider social and economic influences.

Ultimately, we must ask what these social networks can tell us about the transmission of property in early eighteenth-century England: how did the two interrelate? First, basic spatial analysis of these networks has demonstrated the geographical complexity of the individual social worlds in which decisions concerning property were to be made. The life-worlds of townspeople were multi-layered and incorporated many overlapping communities of interest, amongst which the family was pre-eminent. Second, the status of those identified as executors and administrators tells us much about the social significance of property and its post-mortem transmission. Individuals were chosen for good if multifaceted reasons, and the relationships thus signalled were clearly close in emotional, social or economic terms. On top of this, the process of being an executor or administrator served to cement those relationships by declaring them publicly and extending into the circle of family and friends who had an interest in the estate. Third, and arising from this, these relationships were an important part of social reproduction. At one level, effective executors and administrators were essential to the successful and smooth transmission of property which, above all, aimed to secure or establish the next generation of the family.[60] This made them direct conduits in the reproduction of the family unit or, at least, family fortunes. At a second level, the mutual trust and familiarity which linked testator and executor were, through the process of transferring property, themselves transmitted to or reinforced in the testator's family and legatees. Through this mechanism, property transmission served to tie families into local and wider communities and may thus have played a significant role in the formation of communities in and the social cohesion of eighteenth-century towns.

---

[60] See the chapter by Ann McCrum in this volume.

Chapter 6

The role of London in Britain's wealth structure, 1809–99: further evidence

W. D. Rubinstein

This chapter has a number of separate purposes. The first and most important is to present the major findings of a very comprehensive study concerning everyone leaving an estate of £100,000 or more in Britain between 1809 (when the probate sources first can be used for this purpose) and 1899, especially with regard to the geographical distribution of the business venues or source of fortune of these top wealth holders, in particular emphasising the role of London in the nineteenth-century wealth structure. The second main purpose is to draw attention to some hitherto overlooked aspects of London's role as the main British centre of wealth holding and its importance in attracting wealthy non-British investors seeking an absolutely secure place to deposit their fortunes. Finally, this essay will examine some aspects of the probate process itself for the important effects these were likely to have had upon British investment patterns and upon the British economy.

My work *Men of Property: The Very Wealthy in Britain Since the Industrial Revolution* comprised a study of everyone leaving £500,000 or more in Britain between 1809 and 1939.[1] It examined this group of approximately 1,350 persons in order to draw broad conclusions about a range of their economic and social characteristics including, the occupations or sources of wealth, geographical venue, social origins, education, religion and political connections of Britain's top wealth holders. Perhaps the main conclusion of this study is that the plurality of non-landed wealth holders in Britain earned their fortunes in the City of London, as merchants, bankers, and the like, rather than as manufacturers and industrialists. This conclusion provided some of the factual bases of the so-called 'gentlemanly capitalism' school associated with Peter Cain and Tony Hopkins, with which I am broadly in agreement. It also led to several 'spin-off' debates in articles, especially on the propensity of businessmen to purchase land during the nineteenth century.[2]

---

[1]   Rubinstein, W. D., *Men of Property: The Very Wealthy in Britain Since the Industrial Revolution* (London: Croom Helm, 1981).

[2]   See Cain, P. J. and Hopkins, A. G., *British Imperialism: Innovation and Expansion 1688–1914* (London: Longman, 1993); Cain, P. J. and Hopkins, A. G., *British Imperialism:*

The very wealthy and the wealthy

A detailed study of the wealthy in particular locales, especially urban areas, serves many useful functions. Most obviously, it can identify much of the locale's economic elite and business notables in a precise and objective way, including many men who would otherwise be unlikely to become known to the historian. Many wealthy persons were well-known in their cities and towns, often serving as a local member of parliament, mayor, member of the town council, justice of the peace, or the like. On the other hand, many others adopted no obvious public role and were significant simply as major participants in the local economy. Historians of local elites in the nineteenth century ordinarily focus on the careers of office-holders such as members of the town council, or on the leaders of one or two very major businesses, often ignoring those local wealth holders without a significant public face to their careers. Identifying this stratum of the local elite is one of the most important benefits of this approach to the subject. This is particularly true in the case of London, whose local government was skeletal until 1889 and where (apart from the very limited group of aldermen of the City of London) very few wealthy men played any role whatever in the governmental affairs of London (as opposed to the Westminster Parliament). London's wealth holders are, in fact, more difficult to identify than any others. Given the vast number of wealthy and middle-class people in London, and the fact that many London wealth holders were involved in financial, commercial and service pursuits with meagre premises and few employees, or were idle rentiers, identifying London's richest men is a much more hazardous pursuit than for most provincial towns.

These difficulties were compounded by other factors as well. The scale of wealth was considerably higher in London than in any provincial city. A fortune of £200,000 in 1880 would have marked its holder as one of the very richest men in Wolverhampton, Norwich, Sunderland or even Birmingham or Leeds, but would hardly have been noticed in London and was certainly nothing extraordinary. Nineteenth-century London directories contain the names of literally tens of thousands of active merchants and other businessmen and professional persons in the capital. Because so many rich men lived in London, and because the recognised local-governmental and other routes leading to a title of some kind were, for businessmen, fewer in London than in

Crisis and Deconstruction: 1914–1990 (London: Longman, 1993). On landowning see, for example, Thompson, F. M. L., 'Business and Landed Elites in the Nineteenth Century', in *idem*, (ed.), *Landowners, Capitalists and Entrepreneurs* (Oxford: Clarendon Press, 1994); Rubinstein, W. D., 'Businessmen into Landowners: The Question Revisited', in N. Harte and R. Quinault (eds), *Land and Society in Britain, 1700–1914* (Manchester: Manchester University Press, 1996); Nicholas, T., 'Businessmen and Land Ownership in the Late Nineteenth Century', *Economic History Review* LII (1999), pp. 27–44.

the provinces, it was probably the case that fewer London businessmen actually achieved a peerage, baronetcy or knighthood than in many provincial cities (the City's civic elite being the obvious exception), notwithstanding the greater opportunities enjoyed by Londoners for forging links with the government and their greater wealth. Finally, one fact which is easy to overlook is that London had no local newspapers. Whereas a prominent cotton manufacturer in Bolton, worth perhaps £175,000 at his death in 1890, was virtually certain to be accorded a lengthy obituary in Bolton's local newspaper (or newspapers), with innumerable details on his biography, career and family, a London stockbroker or important merchant with a fortune just as large was most unlikely to have an obituary in any newspaper or be listed in any published source, unless he had also produced some notable achievements in another field, one which was likely to be publicly noticed.

For all these reasons, it is much more difficult to identify the wealthy economic elite of London or for the historian to learn much about that person's career. This has been an important factor in the almost universal predilection by economic historians not to focus on London but on the provinces, especially the great manufacturing towns of the industrial revolution, a tendency which has only been reversed since the 1970s with the growth of the so-called 'gentlemanly capitalism' school. Nevertheless, it seems to me that much about London's economic elite since 1780 still remains a near-total blank, particularly when one moves away from the very famous City dynasties. The bewilderingly large number of wealthy Londoners, together with the relative absence of biographical sources equivalent to those available for the provincial wealthy, means that this blank is unlikely ever to be satisfactorily filled in.

Over the past ten years or so I have been undertaking a much wider study of everyone leaving £100,000 or more during the nineteenth century, which is now nearing completion.[3] This chapter is, in fact, the first essay in print which attempts to summarise some of the major findings of this second project – a study which, it must be emphasised, is very significantly larger than my previous project, entailing the study of the biographies of no less than 7,471 persons who left £100,000 or more between 1809 and 1899.

There are many reasons for undertaking this much larger study, but three stand out. First, a much larger sample allows the historian to derive conclusions about both the characteristics of the group, and changes within it, with a much greater degree of confidence. Very few, if any, studies of elite groups have comprised nearly 7,500 persons, and the sheer size of the sample inspires considerable confidence in its conclusions. Secondly, the list of names

        [3]   Whilst in Australia (where I lived until September 1995), I was fortunate to be funded by the Australian Research Council for most of the period in which I was engaged in this second project, and was able to employ a full-time research assistant in London, Dr Carole M. Taylor, for whose help I am most grateful.

in this study, and the biographical information gathered on each person, is in itself an important reference tool for economic, social and even political historians allowing, for instance, the compilation of comprehensive lists of local economic elites, including those wealthy local men who were not necessarily famous, either in their own time or amongst historians. An analysis of the 372 wealth holders in this study associated with Manchester, or the 110 from Newcastle upon Tyne, would themselves be obviously important for ascertaining the nature of the economic elite of these two cities (or any others). Finally, the social and economic characteristics of the large sample of nearly 7,500 persons worth £100,000 or more differs in significant ways from the characteristics of the smaller sample of those worth £500,000 or more, and it is important to be able to identify these differences in an accurate way.

The sources

Before proceeding, some basic points about the nature of the probate records ought to be made clear. Cash figures for the value of all estates left at death (including intestacies) in Britain may be found in the probate calendars available at the Public Record Office, at First Avenue House on High Holborn (to which the records formerly held at Somerset House were transferred in 1998), and elsewhere. Prior to 1858, probate was the responsibility of the many ecclesiastical courts; to make a long story short, most very large estates left in England and Wales were probated in the Prerogative Courts of Canterbury or of York. From 1858, all probate was centralised in the (secular) Principal Probate Registry, long at Somerset House. There were separate probate courts in Scotland and Ireland.[4] This study commences in 1809 because only then was a valuation figure given to estates worth over £100,000 (rather than being described as 'upper value'. Many years ago, in 1972–73, I went through all relevant probate calendars and copied out the names, valuation figures and other relevant information about everyone leaving £100,000 or more from 1809–1899, although only estates of £500,000 or more were used as the statistical base of my previous studies. For the present study, some years at the end of the nineteenth century were also rechecked comprehensively to identify estates missed previously. It should be strongly emphasised that there are no official lists of large estates in any source, and anyone seeking to identify wealthy persons from the probate records in a comprehensive way must abstract their names by hand, as I did.

---

[4]   For further details, see Rubinstein, *Men of Property*, pp. 12–19.

During the nineteenth century, the valuation figure consisted of the gross value of the unsettled estate left by the testator. Its chief omission was the capital value of the land left by the testator.[5] Up to a point, the size and annual rental of the land owned by deceased persons can (outside of London) be ascertained for the period 1873–75 from the *Return of Owners of Land* undertaken by Parliament, whilst revised figures from the *Return* were compiled for all significant owners in John Bateman's *Great Landowners of Great Britain and Ireland* (1884). Nevertheless, the number of wealthy landowners in this study is consistently underestimated. Those who did leave £100,000 or more and are classified as 'landowners' are included because they left £100,000 or more in personalty. Most assets held overseas are excluded from the valuation figures, as, of course, are *inter vivos* gifts to relatives of the deceased. Apart from these omissions, there is no reason to suppose that the valuation figures are anything but accurate. Inventories of the estates of deceased persons may be consulted in the case of Scottish estates, but not in the case of estates probated in England and Wales.

Having compiled a list of wealth holders, the researcher must then begin the process of identifying each person. The probate calendars list only the name, date and place of death, and address of the testator; the probate valuation, and the names of the executors. Occasionally – perhaps one case in three – an occupation is listed as well. This was taken from the will or probate document and may or may not be accurate. In this study (and in my previous one of top wealth holders) I sought a wide variety of biographical information, as noted above, on every person. Where relevant, dozens of sources were consulted on every single person, especially sources held at the Institute of Historical Research and the Society of Genealogists in London, particularly local directories and genealogical works. Currently, more remains to be done, especially in the compilation of local newspaper obituaries and other local biographical sources and in the reading of wills, but the broad conclusions of the large project, investigating everyone leaving £100,000 or more from 1808 to 1899, are now fairly clear, at least for certain facets of the biographies of each wealth holder. In terms of the occupations and geographical venue of the business or professional activities of persons in this project, less than 10 per cent remain completely unknown. (Of course, for other biographical categories, for instance the father's occupation or the education of the wealth holder, the percentage of unknowns is very significantly higher and, in many cases, will probably never be ascertained in a lifetime of searching. This project, like other studies of business leaders, inevitably suffers from the fact that enormous amounts of information are available on a minority of those included, but virtually no information at all may be obtained on many others.)

---

[5]   See the discussion in the chapter by Alastair Owens in this volume.

The geography of the wealthy

According to the probate records, a total of 7,471 persons left £100,000 or more in Britain between 1809 and 1899.[6] This part of the discussion in this paper will examine the overall numbers and the main geographical venue of the business or professional activities of each person in the study. Table 6.1 sets out the general findings of these headings.

This table records the total number of estates of £100,000 or more, by five-year period; the number in each five-year period which could be assigned to a particular geographical venue; the number of estates whose business or professional wealth was earned in London; and the London percentage amongst all estates which could be assigned to a specific venue. Two points should be strongly emphasised in considering this table. First, the venue to which a wealth holder was assigned is that where the fortune was earned, not where the wealth holder lived. (If the criterion of residency were employed, rural Wiltshire, Bournemouth, and Brighton would appear to be centres of wealth-making.) This identification could, naturally, only be made after elaborate research, often into the career of the father, grandfather or other antecedent relatives. In most cases, however, an assignment to a particular venue is clear and straightforward: a London stockbroker to the City of London, a Bradford woollen manufacturer to Bradford, and so on. Secondly, the group of 1,931 wealth holders (25.8 per cent of the total sample) who could not be assigned to a particular venue fall into a number of very distinct and separate categories. The three largest were landowners (who were not assigned to a specific venue, for the purposes of this essay, which was limited to business and professional wealth holders), wealth holders (both British and foreign) whose fortunes were earned abroad, and unknowns. As well, many military officers (generals and admirals) and many Church of England clerics who left £100,000 could not accurately be assigned to a specific venue; the same applies to some civil engineers and some miscellaneous figures such as diplomats whose main source of wealth appeared to be the salaries from their diplomatic posts.

---

[6] Actually, the total figure must be higher than this. Not all pre-1858 ecclesiastical court records were researched, only the three most important ones (the Prerogative Courts of Canterbury and York and the Consistory Court of Chester [Lancashire records at Preston]), and it is possible that some estates of £100,000 or more were missed. Scottish probate records began in a usable form in 1825, Irish records in 1858. Ireland was researched through 1895, but not for the period 1896–99. Additionally, some listings of large estates were simply missed by me through human error. It is thus likely that the actual number of estates of £100,000 or more is about 5–10 per cent higher than this figure. As noted, too, inclusion of the capital value of land would raise the total figures considerably.

Table 6.1

Wealth holders leaving £100,000 or more, 1809–99, by five-year periods, with geographically assigned and London totals

Venue period	N	Assigned	London	% London
1809–14	120	75	63	84.0
1815–19	117	77	61	79.2
1820–24	153	97	67	69.1
1825–29	156	99	66	66.7
1830–34	174	110	80	72.7
1835–39	163	125	90	72.0
1840–44	191	114	59	51.8
1845–49	187	123	68	55.3
1850–54	203	131	73	55.7
1855–59	241	173	74	42.8
1860–64	332	237	119	50.2
1865–69	444	336	156	46.4
1870–74	644	502	211	42.0
1875–79	692	527	227	43.1
1880–84	773	571	242	42.4
1885–89	806	635	243	38.3
1890–94	981	758	298	39.3
1895–99	1094	850	349	41.1
	7471	5540	2546	46.0

Source: See text.

It will be seen from Table 6.1 that the number of wealth holders increases in regular progression (with a plateau in the 1820s and a decline in the late 1830s and late 1840s), so that ten times as many estates of £100,000 or more were left at the end of the nineteenth century as in the period 1810–1820. This rise in the number of top fortunes appears to have outstripped the overall increase in British gross national income (which is, of course, not the same thing as wealth, and might in any case be distributed quite differently), which rose from an estimated £301 million in 1811 to £1,643 million in 1901.[7]

The table also shows that top fortunes earned in London comprised the great majority of all probated fortunes of £100,000 or more early in the century, but

[7]   Mitchell, B. R. and Deane, P., 'National Income and Expenditure I: The Industrial Distribution of the National Income, 1688–1955', in *idem*, *Abstract of British Historical Statistics* (Cambridge: Cambridge University Press, 1971), p. 366.

then, from the 1840s onwards, shared a steady decline before rising slightly again at the end of the century. Nevertheless, fortunes earned in London never comprised less than 38 per cent of all large estates which could be assigned to a specific venue, and constituted 46 per cent of all such estates for the nineteenth century as a whole. Until 1840, London was completely dominant as the centre of wealth-generation in Britain, and always remained the most important single centre, whose importance always far exceeded its share of the population (in 1901 Greater London was estimated to have a population of 6,586,000 or 15.9 per cent of the United Kingdom's population of 41,459,000).

Nevertheless, London's overall percentage in the British wealth structure did diminish after about 1840 and then remained broadly steady for the last third of the century. This trend is only to be expected: London was categorically the largest pre-existing centre of business and professional life prior to the nineteenth century. Even if both the City of London and London's manifold other centres of wealth-generation kept pace with Britain's overall rates of economic growth, clearly the new centres of trade, industry and commerce were also growing, perhaps just as rapidly, and from a much lower base level. London's role as a centre of the generation of middle-class incomes also showed something of the same movement (although in a more extreme form). Of all incomes in Britain which were liable to pay income tax (those of £100 or £150 or more, a lower limit which varied throughout the nineteenth century), just under 50 per cent were generated in London and the Home Counties in 1811–12, but only 35 per cent in 1851–52.[8] Thereafter, however, London's portion of all taxable incomes continued to grow, and (together with Home County incomes) had reached about 45 per cent of the British total by 1900–1901.[9]

This is not the pattern we observed in Table 6.1. Why the discrepancy? A number of reasons may be advanced. First, of course, income and wealth are conceptually different concepts. Wealth is income which has been saved and invested in commodities which have a market value. There is, therefore, a time-lag between income-earning and wealth-accumulation, especially at the level of wealth discussed in this paper and particularly in view of the generally age-specific nature of probate (age-specific to the elderly). It is likely that London's regional wealth percentage in the last decades of the nineteenth century reflected the regional income percentages (for very high incomes) of several decades before, when London had relatively declined. Secondly, the distribution of estates of £100,000 or more resembles a pyramid, with many more at the lower end of the wealth scale than the higher end. The great rise in

---

[8]   Rubinstein, W. D., *Elites and the Wealthy in Modern British History* (Brighton: Harvester, 1987), p. 81.
[9]   Ibid.

the number of large estates in the course of the nineteenth century thus brought into the criteria adopted in this study very many additional fortunes in the £100,000–£200,000 range than larger ones. This level of wealth holding appears to have been typical, in particular, of factory owners and other industrialists in the North of England and other manufacturing areas who, by the late nineteenth century, had accumulated sufficient capital to make a marked impact upon the statistics of this study. In other words, the fastest-growing group amongst Britain's top wealth holders during the period c. 1860–1899 as measured by the probate records appear to have been northern industrialists, especially because they appeared heavily at the lower end of the class of wealth holders examined here. My analysis of middle-class income-earners noted a distinct swing back to London, away from the northern industrial areas, in the late nineteenth century and the Edwardian periods.[10] It may just be possible to see the beginnings of a similar trend in the probate data examined here, and it would be useful to extend this study into the inter-war period, when the high income-earners of the late-Victorian and Edwardian eras would be dying off in numbers.

London's role in Britain's wealth structure comprised many different functions. The most important component of London's economic role was the City of London, the historic 'square mile' of financial and mercantile activities which was at the very heart of the British economy during the nineteenth century. Because this essay is primarily concerned with the geographical venues of the activities of the wealth holders rather than their occupations, only a cursory examination can be made here of the role of the City. Comparing four decadal periods, one finds that the wealth holders classified as earning their fortunes in the City of London comprised 63.2 per cent of all London-generated fortunes in the decade 1820–29; 62.4 per cent in the decade 1850–59; 57.1 per cent in the decade 1870–70; and 56.7 per cent in the decade 1890–99. There was thus a small but steady increase in the percentage of fortunes generated in London outside of the City. The overall percentage of the City's wealth holders amongst all deceased British wealth holders does show a considerable decline (in line with the decline of London in the overall picture) from 55.3 per cent of all estates assigned a venue in the period 1820–99, to 33.9 per cent in 1850–59, 24.3 per cent in 1870–79, and 22.8 per cent in 1890–99. This was, of course, emphatically a relative rather than an absolute decline: the number of probated estates which originated in City fortunes rose from 84 to 103 to 250 to 366 in these four decades. The reasons for the relative failure of the City to keep pace with the number of British fortunes as a whole are difficult readily to identify, but probably relate to the very sharp relative growth of estates at the lower end of the wealth scale, and perhaps to an

---

[10]   Ibid., pp. 97–8.

increasing concentration of City fortunes compared with other parts of the economy. Again, it would be interesting to see if there was a swing back to the City after 1900. To be sure, the importance of the City in the British economy is only partly indicated by these figures. Increasingly, it became the venue of investment from all parts of Britain and overseas, a matter which will be further explained below.

The remainder of London's large estates ranged very widely in their natures. Apart from businesses in other parts of London – retailing, manufacturing, brewing, shipping and transport, amongst others – London was home to the Bar and to a considerable portion of Britain's most successful solicitors, to society physicians, to the press, publishing, and entertainment, and to the civil service – that is, to most of the most successful members of the professions and the higher administrative classes. Indeed, London's centrality for the British wealth structure flowed in large part from the fact that its economy was not exclusively oriented around business life (and still less around one or two particular industrial activities, as was the case in many manufacturing towns) but was the most diverse and wide-ranging of any place in Britain, if not in the world. It is not easy to think of another great city, even Paris, which dominated so many different economic activities and which was also so populous in relation to the country of which it was the capital. Within Britain, London's importance also flowed from the fact that no other city had the ancillary, non-economic professional and administrative structure which was so much a part of metropolitan life. As regional centres, Manchester and Glasgow had many solicitors, successful barristers and fashionable physicians, as well as their own press, but this was simply not on the scale of London. Nor did they have the apparatus of central and imperial government and administration which London uniquely possessed. Smaller, but still important, manufacturing centres and trading towns had even less in the way of this diversity. In industrial cities dominated by one or two economic activities the wealthy elite was over-whelmingly centred amongst the most successful entrepreneurs in those trades.

As important as London was in the British wealth structure, its importance is certainly underestimated in these statistics. The statistics presented here exclude from any venue a number of categories of wealth holders, most of whom had salient London connections. As noted, landowners are not included in these statistics, yet most large landowners had London residences and spent a major fraction of the year in London, the acknowledged social and political centre of the landed upper classes. Foreign fortune-holders (who will be discussed in more detail below), also excluded from these figures, almost certainly had the bulk of their wealth invested in London banks and other forms of security, whilst British-born businessmen who made their fortunes overseas often lived in the West End or the Home Counties when they retired. About two-thirds of the 'unknown' category, those wealth holders whose source of wealth and its geographical venue could not be traced, also lived in London or the Home Counties. Many, almost certainly, were little-known London businessmen or professionals or their relatives who were not listed in any London directory which I consulted. There was, as well, a constant drift of residency from the north to the south, so that many children and grandchildren of northern manufacturers, even when still engaged in the family firm as partners or directors, and certainly as shareholders, lived chiefly in London and the South of England, associational networks strengthened by public school and Oxbridge education, marriage into old wealthy families, Pall Mall club membership, election to Parliament, membership on City boards, and the like. Inter-generational associational networks seldom ran the other way, especially in the long term. Finally, it should be remembered that wealth holders in this study cover, equally, the City merchant banker worth £3 million and the Burnley manufacturer worth £150,000. Setting a higher minimum level of wealth, as was done in my previous studies, shows a greatly increased percentage of top wealth holders in London, especially in the City.

London's place in the national wealth structure will become clearer if it is compared with other leading geographical centres of the British economy during the nineteenth century. Therefore, the number of wealth holders in this study are shown, in Tables 6.2 and 6.3, by five-year period for many of the leading economic focal points outside of London. Table 6.2 examines the number of wealth holders whose fortunes are earned in three places, Manchester, Liverpool, and the remainder of Lancashire and Cheshire, with their overall percentages amongst all wealth holders in this study who can be assigned to a specific venue (tht is, omitting landowners, foreign fortunes, smaller categories like military officers, and unknowns). Table 6.3 produces similar data for Birmingham, Bristol, Glasgow, Leeds and Newcastle upon Tyne, five of the leading cities in Britain.[11] Obviously, many other leading cities – Bradford, Leicester, Nottingham, Wolverhampton, Edinburgh and Dublin, to name six obvious candidates – are not included here, but will appear in a fuller study of this subject.

Table 6.2 details the totals of wealth holders for Lancashire and Cheshire. Some points are clear. Manchester produced somewhat more wealth holders than Liverpool, whilst the number located elsewhere in Lancashire and Cheshire was also very substantial. In total, wealth holders from Lancashire and Cheshire amounted to just under one-fifth of the British total for the whole nineteenth century, about 38.9 per cent of London's total. Despite the key importance of Lancashire's trade and industry for the nineteenth-century British economy, and despite, too, the levelling-off in the percentage of

---

[11]   In the case of Glasgow and Newcastle upon Tyne, colliery owners, ironmasters and steel manufacturers in the immediate environs of each city were also included in these totals.

London estates, London always retained a very substantial lead over
Lancashire (plus Cheshire). Many of the small industrial towns in these two
counties were also highly productive of substantial fortunes, with fortunes
widely dispersed amongst local centres. The fifty-four wealth holders in
Lancashire and Cheshire outside of Manchester and Liverpool in the five-year
period 1890–94, for instance, were distributed amongst no less than twenty-six
local centres, with Bolton producing eight wealth holders in this period,
Oldham seven, Accrington, Bacup, Preston and Rochdale three each, and
others from towns such as Blackburn, Bury, Stockport and Wigan.

Table 6.2
Wealth holders in Lancashire and Cheshire, with percentages of assigned British totals

Period	Manchester		Liverpool		Lancs./Ches.		Total	
	No.	%	No.	%	No.	%	No.	%
1809–14	0	0.0	0	0.0	1	1.3	1	1.3
1815–19	0	0.0	0	0.0	1	1.3	1	1.3
1820–24	2	2.1	3	3.1	0	0.0	5	5.2
1825–29	4	4.0	3	3.0	0	0.0	7	7.1
1830–34	1	0.9	2	1.8	1	0.9	4	3.6
1835–39	0	0.0	6	4.8	2	1.6	8	6.4
1840–44	5	4.4	4	3.5	6	5.3	15	13.2
1845–49	4	3.3	7	5.7	4	3.3	15	12.2
1850–54	12	9.2	5	3.8	6	4.6	23	17.6
1855–59	8	4.6	5	2.9	8	4.6	21	12.1
1860–64	15	6.3	10	4.2	10	4.2	35	14.8
1865–69	24	7.1	18	5.4	18	5.4	60	17.9
1870–74	35	7.0	33	6.6	38	7.6	106	21.1
1875–79	44	8.3	43	8.2	46	8.7	133	25.2
1880–84	37	6.5	41	7.2	27	4.7	105	18.4
1885–89	55	8.9	58	9.1	37	5.8	150	23.6
1890–94	59	7.8	58	7.7	54	7.1	171	22.6
1895–99	67	7.9	61	7.2	59	6.9	187	22.0
	372	6.7	307	5.5	318	5.7	997	18.0

Source: See text.

Table 6.3
Wealth holders in five major cities, with percentages of
assigned British totals

Period	Birmingham		Bristol		Newcastle upon Tyne		Leeds		Glasgow	
	No.	%	No.	%	No.	%	No.	%	No.	%
1809–14	2	2.7	2	2.7	0	0	0	0	0	0
1815–19	0	0	5	6.5	1	1.3	0	0	0	0
1820–24	0	0	1	1.0	1	1.0	0	0	0	1.0
1825–29	0	0	2	2.0	1	1.0	0	0	0	3.0
1830–34	1	0.9	1	0.9	3	3.0	0	0	0	0
1835–39	2	1.6	7	5.6	1	0.8	0	0	0	0
1840–44	1	0.9	1	0.9	2	1.8	3	2.6	3	2.6
1845–49	3	2.4	4	3.3	0	0	5	4.1	1	0.8
1850–54	0	0	3	2.3	3	2.3	1	0.8	2	1.5
1855–59	2	1.2	3	1.7	3	1.7	5	2.9	8	4.6
1860–64	3	1.3	7	3.0	5	2.1	7	3.0	11	4.6
1865–69	7	2.1	9	2.7	8	2.4	7	2.1	9	2.7
1870–74	13	2.6	13	2.6	8	1.6	10	2.0	22	4.4
1875–79	4	0.8	8	1.5	11	2.1	10	1.9	19	3.6
1880–84	9	1.6	7	1.2	14	2.5	8	1.4	33	5.8
1885–89	7	1.1	5	0.8	12	1.9	8	1.3	34	5.4
1890–94	14	1.8	16	2.1	19	2.5	17	2.2	34	4.5
1895–99	25	2.9	15	1.8	18	2.1	11	1.3	33	3.9
	93	1.7	109	2.0	110	2.0	92	1.7	213	3.8

Source: See text.

Table 6.3 details the numbers of wealth holders in Birmingham, Bristol, Newcastle upon Tyne, Leeds and Glasgow. From these figures, Glasgow clearly emerges as the most important of these five cities, with nearly twice as many as the runners-up, Newcastle and Bristol. (Bristol's surprising total reflected its importance as a pre-industrial commercial and shipping centre, and the growth there of new industries, such as tobacco, after the mid-nineteenth century.) Despite its size, Birmingham produced only ninety-three fortunes of £100,000 or more during the nineteenth century, barely one-quarter of Manchester's total, thus conforming to its well-known image as a centre of relatively small-scale engineering industries and workshops. The percentage of many of these cities in the national British total also levelled off in the late nineteenth century, following the same pattern as London in a less pronounced way, as fortunes of £100,000 or more became more common throughout the entire country, including cities and towns not explicitly discussed here.

The wealthy with fortunes earned abroad

One of the most interesting categories of wealth holders revealed by this study consists of persons whose fortunes were earned abroad. Because so little is known about this class of wealth holders, especially foreigners who left enormous estates in Britain, it is worth examining them in more detail. This category actually comprises two distinct types of person: genuine foreigners, often with no discernible previous connection with Britain, and British entrepreneurs or professionals who made a fortune overseas and then retired to Britain. In between these two categories one might point to another group, British émigrés (in particular to Australia, Canada and South Africa) who often fully took part in the public life of their adopted country for many years, but who retired to Britain. Foreigners leaving fortunes in Britain appear to be much more numerous in the latter half of the century than in the first half. Although not numerically very significant in the overall wealth structure, these groups of foreigners left disproportionately more than British wealth holders and, it seems clear, represented a significant addition to Britain's stock of wealth. Indeed, the old quasi-Marxist theory that Britain industrialised in part because of 'super-profits' (those earned by naked expropriation from the natives or slaves) repatriated from the early British Empire may well have an element of truth, and such repatriation may well have continued as an important part of the British economy throughout the nineteenth century. It might be most useful to look at this type of wealth holder during two time-periods in order to ascertain something of the nature and dimensions of this group, and I would therefore like to examine these groups at fifty-year intervals, those deceased in 1820–29 and 1870–79.

The former group comprised thirty wealth holders, or nearly 10 per cent of the total of 309 estates of £100,000 or more left during this decade. (It was probably true that foreign fortunes, especially the wealth of East India and West Indies merchants, was relatively more important to the British wealth structure earlier in the century than later on; this was also true of the occupational backgrounds of British members of parliament in pre-1830 parliaments compared with those later in the century.) Nearly all of the 1820–29 group were British merchants and planters overseas who returned to Britain, often with very large fortunes indeed. Amongst the thirty foreign wealth holders deceased in this decade were eleven East India merchants; nine West Indies planters and merchants; two each from Canada, France, Portugal and the

United States, and one each from China and the Netherlands. One, Edward Lascelles (1740–1820), a major sugar-planter in Barbados, became a member of parliament and was eventually created Earl of Harewood; he left £250,000 in personalty. Several others also left very large fortunes, including the Jamaica planter David Lyon (c. 1754–1827), who left £600,000; Edward John Hollond (d. 1821) of the East India Company at Madras, who left £600,000; and the Bombay merchant John Forbes (c. 1743–1821), who left £350,000. The East India Company featured very prominently amongst this group, for instance Robert Nicholson (d. 1821), a Lieutenant-General in the company's service, who left £100,000; Thomas Bridges (c. 1743–1823), another of the company's lieutenant-generals (at Madras), who left £120,000; and Samuel Gardner (1755–1827), 'for many years Military Secretary to the East India Company's Government at Calcutta, under the Marquess of Hastings' (in the words of *Burke's Landed Gentry* for 1914), who left £140,000.

The 1870–79 foreign cohort numbered seventy-four individuals out of 1,336 persons leaving £100,000 or more in the decade, or 5.5 per cent of the total. This cohort was much more geographically diverse than its predecessor fifty years earlier, with fifteen earning their fortunes in India and four in the West Indies, but also no less than ten in France, four in America, three in Australia, Italy and Mexico, two in China, Egypt and Portugal, and others in Belgium, Brazil, Germany, Peru and Russia. A notable feature of this group was the significant number of foreigners, with little or no obvious attachment to Britain, who left large estates here. The £120,000 left in England by Napoleon III, who died in exile in Kent in January 1873, does not seem hard to explain, nor, perhaps, the fortune of £1,880,000 left in Britain by Baron Nathaniel de Rothschild (1812–70), head of the Paris branch of the family (and purchaser of the Chateau Mouton vineyards), who was born in England and educated at University College, London. More difficult to explain, however, was the £500,000 fortune left in Britain by Count Urbain Greffulhe (d. 1879), an enormously wealth Paris merchant banker, or the £140,000 fortune of General Casimir de Rochechouart, Duc de Mortemart, a French general who died in Paris in 1875, or the £500,000 estate left in London by Raphael de Ferrari, Duc de Galliera, a Genoese nobleman who lived in Paris. It would seem that London became the preferred place of security for a wide variety of foreign wealth holders, in so far as motivation may be inferred from the presence of their fortunes in Britain. This was especially so for wealth holders from countries in Europe and places like Latin American which were frequently rocked by revolutions and mob violence. Apart from those wealthy foreigners noted above, many other such persons left significant fortunes in Britain, amongst them numerous aristocrats from the Continent (especially France, Spain and Portugal) and Latin America. As well, wealthy persons from more stable countries such as the United States left large estates in Britain even though they had no obvious connections here. For instance, Samuel J. Tilden (1814–84), a wealthy New York lawyer and philanthropist, and the Democratic Party's presidential candidate in 1876 (who was actually elected President over Rutherford B. Hayes, only to have his election 'stolen' from him as a result of a corrupt deal in the United States Congress), left £138,000 in London. Similarly, Isaac M. Singer (1811–75), the American inventor of the sewing machine, left a £200,000 estate at his death. (Singer, however, lived in Paignton, Devon, at the time of his death, although his chief business interests remained in America).

In addition to these types of foreign wealth holders, there were also, as noted, many instances of British-born persons who had emigrated to the newly-developing areas of the empire, often for many years, only to return to Britain as wealthy men in their retirement. Many had started life poor, and clearly felt a sense of triumph in returning, decades later, as wealthy squires or Mayfair gentlemen. Australians, in particular, had a penchant for this. Amongst those who died leaving substantial British estates in the decade 1870–79, for instance, were John Peter (1812–78), the son of a farmer near Glasgow, who emigrated to Sydney in 1832 with £50 and his fare; he accumulated 'vast properties' of Australian grazing land, totalling 740,000 acres, and lived at 30 Park Lane after about 1870, leaving £350,000 in Britain and another £126,000 in Australia.

Together, these foreign groups made a notable impact upon the structure of wealth holding in Britain, but in ways which remain to be determined. Whilst one often hears of British investment overseas and its possible effect upon the British economy, one hears of the opposite – inward immigration or large-scale investment by already wealthy foreigners – much less often. Yet the latter appears to have been one of the more notable benefits of the rock-like stability enjoyed by Britain's political and economic institutions during the nineteenth century, as well as by London's pre-existing financial and equities structure, which facilitated large-scale inward investment. Whilst some of the groups which were notable for this, such as rich American émigrés, are well known, others, especially the Hispanic and Latin American contingent, are apparently unknown, and form no part of our image of the wealth structure of nineteenth-century Britain.

Probate, wealth and investment

The third matter I would like to address briefly here is the effect of the probate process itself upon the nature of wealth and investment in nineteenth-century Britain. Anyone familiar with the wills of affluent and wealthy persons throughout the nineteenth-century will be aware that, almost invariably, these contained a clause, apparently standard, which gave wide-ranging powers to the executors of the estate. In the words of one such wealth holder's will, probated in 1880, and very like many others:

> upon trust ... the said Trustees [executors] shall sell my real estate and convert my personal estate into money and shall out of the monies so arising ... invest the same in any of the Public Stocks or funds or Government securities of the United Kingdom or India or any Colony or Dependency of the United Kingdom or upon real securities in England and Wales ... or upon the debentures or mortgages of any Railway Company or other Corporation, Company, or Public body municipal or otherwise in the United Kingdom or India

Other wills which I have read sometimes varied these provisions to include the United States as a permissible place of investment. This clause was purely an enabling one, giving the executors the right to sell the testator's estate and invest the proceeds, within certain clearly-defined boundaries, as they wished, but it must have had very important consequences, which remain unexplored. For instance, this provision clearly gave the executors the right to sell the testator's share in his own firm. Executors often (although not always) included the sons or other close relatives of the testator, who presumably had the major say in how the estate was to be treated. It may well be the case that many sons or other close relatives used this clause as the occasion to disengage from the family firm and to reinvest the proceeds into British equities or government securities. Quite often, too, the testator's solicitor was an executor of the estate. In all likelihood, solicitors invested the proceeds from assets disposed of from the estates of wealthy testators in the most conservative possible manner.

In any case, the fact that a wealthy testator customarily had several executors also probably mitigated against any speculative investments, or those which could not be fully justified at a conference of executors who had responsibilities for the widow and other relatives of the deceased. The probable effects of this clause were thus, firstly, to end many a family's connections with their original business and to invest the proceeds, whatever the geographical locale of the family, in the well-established component of the London equities market; and, secondly, to continuously reorientate investments in more conservative directions. It is reasonable to assume (although there is no direct evidence for this) that this common provision in many wills was disproportionately likely to enable the heirs of wealthy testators with factories or other industrial enterprises in the North of England to disengage from their family firms and become rentiers in the South East. Something like this must, indeed, have occurred amongst the lesser heirs of a wealth holder (nephews and nieces, daughters and so on) who were often paid a specified annuity, which was presumably met from a capital sum set aside for this purpose. One imagines, too, that many public-school and Oxbridge-educated sons or grandsons of northern industrialists would not have been averse to severing direct ties with northern industrial towns, or to taking their legacy in a much more liquid, near-cash form rather than depending upon the ancestral business. If so, these must have had profound effects upon the nature of nineteenth-century British investment patterns and, indeed, upon the evolution of the British economy, but in ways which remain to be fully explored.

Chapter 7

Inheritance and the family: the Scottish urban experience in the 1820s

Ann McCrum

The family has been central to the study of post-mortem property transmission. Across time and over space immediate kin have, almost without exception, been identified as the main recipients of testamentary gifts.[1] However, within Britain research has tended to concentrate on the issue of aristocratic inheritance, exploring the transmission of land from one generation to the next and examining how this affected family formation and the economic and social reproduction of rural society.[2] This particular study is concerned with urban families, who differed from rural families in their inheritance practices.[3] The estates of urban families were more likely to consist of a higher level of moveable assets than those of rural testators. This was linked to a pattern of inheritance characterised by an even division of estate rather than one based upon the principle of primogeniture. This chapter aims to explore in more detail the inheritance strategies of urban property owners in order to cast light on the ways in which inheritance reproduced the social structures of middle-class families.

It is necessary to situate this discussion of inheritance within the context of patterns of household formation in Scottish towns in the early nineteenth

---

[1] See *inter alia*: Ditz, T., *Property and Kinship: Inheritance in Early Connecticut, 1750–1820* (Princeton: Princeton University Press, 1986); Finch, J., Mason, J., Masson, J., Wallis, L. and Hayes, L., *Wills, Inheritance and Families* (Oxford: Clarendon Press, 1996); Goody, J., Thirsk, J., and Thompson, E. P. (eds), *Family and Inheritance: Rural Society in Western Europe, 1200–1800* (Cambridge: Cambridge University Press, 1976); Sabean, D., *Property, Production and the Family in Neckarhausen, 1700–1870* (Cambridge: Cambridge University Press, 1990).

[2] See, for example, Spring, E., *Law, Land and Family: Aristocratic Inheritance in England, 1300–1800* (Chapel Hill: University of North Carolina Press, 1990).

[3] This chapter is based on research carried out for a forthcoming PhD thesis by Ann McCrum, Department of Economic and Social History, University of Edinburgh. Special thanks are due to Professor R. J. Morris for his comments and help.

century. The nuclear family was the defining hallmark of most urban households and its reproduction was ensured by the dynamics of the middle-class life cycle. As children grew older, marriage and employment provided opportunities for leaving the family home, setting up their own household and securing economic independence. This notion of securing independence and setting up home was significant in informing partible inheritance strategies. As R. J. Morris has observed, the equal division of estates provided children with the means to enter the adult phases of the middle-class property cycle.[4] However, property transmission strategies were also powerfully shaped by patterns of household dependency. The first priority of many testators was to ensure the well-being of dependants such as unmarried daughters, widows and young children. Indeed, the provision of a home and an income for such dependants was central to the inheritance practices of urban people and often resulted in deferred inheritance for other nuclear family members. In short, satisfying the needs of dependants came before supplying economic independence.

Nevertheless, evidence suggests that households devised ways of supporting offspring whose own advancement was hindered by a delayed system of inheritance. Unmarried women, for example, often helped their married siblings with housekeeping, child care and nursing. In addition, they frequently provided care for ageing family members, especially their parents, or kept house for unmarried or widowed brothers or uncles. There are also instances recorded where they lent money to ailing family businesses or helped younger members of the family to start out in business.[5] Therefore, although the presence of unmarried women in urban families often resulted in a delay in the final settling of an estate, it also provided a reservoir of service for the extended family to tap into. The importance of this larger family circle is an enduring feature of the patterns of inheritance amongst urban families and points to the need to situate nuclear households within their extended inter-generational context.

The social reproduction of families and households was thus at the heart of the inheritance strategies of the Scottish urban middling sort. Many of the inheritance practices pursued by testators had ambitious social goals. For example, married men who left young children followed strategies that prioritised the education of sons and their future placement in a suitable occupation, and the provision of marriage portions for daughters. The requirements of the family governed the transmission of property and informed

---

[4]   Morris, R. J., 'The Middle Class and the Property Cycle During the Industrial Revolution' in T. C. Smout (ed.), *The Search for Wealth and Stability: Essays in Social and Economic History Presented to M. W. Flinn* (Basingstoke: Macmillan, 1979), pp. 108–10.

[5]   See the chapter by Penelope Lane in this volume which examines the role of women as money-lenders in eighteenth- and early nineteenth-century English towns.

the investment practices of the urban middling sort. As the family members entered business or the professions, or dispersed due to marriage, property was dispersed too. Therefore, although death was usually the occasion of the largest transfer of property, it was only the last in a series of property transmissions which had been negotiated over the life cycle of the family.[6] Inheritance practices were aimed at the continuation of family strategies after death. To this end, investment strategies were normally based on secure investments in order to safeguard the income of dependants. The social standing of many of the middling sorts was not only very modest but, on many occasions, was also extremely fragile. Thus, the reduction of risk and the provision of a stable income for the family was a priority for these people when they contemplated inheritance strategies.[7]

Although inheritance practices can be viewed in terms of strategies for family and household reproduction, these topics must be considered within the framework of Scottish urban culture and the distinctive legal context of Scotland at that time. This chapter therefore begins with a discussion of the primary source material – testaments from Glasgow and Edinburgh from the early 1820s – and the legal system which shaped their creation, their format and, to a lesser extent, their content. It then goes on to examine the themes of family reproduction through analysis of the distinctive, but related, inheritance practices of men and women in early industrial Scotland.[8]

The source and its legal context

Testamentary information for Glasgow and Edinburgh was obtained from the Sheriff Court and Commissary Court records.[9] The sample consists of every testate case leaving more than £40 entered in the records for Glasgow for the years 1822, 1823 and 1824; and for Edinburgh and Leith for the last month of 1822, all of the year 1823 and the first seven months of 1824. There were 254 cases in total: ninety-four from Glasgow and 160 from Edinburgh and Leith (Table 7.1).

---

[6]   Morris, 'The Middle Class and the Property Cycle'.

[7]   On the subject of secure investments, see the chapter by Geoffrey Crossick in this volume.

[8]   For a more detailed discussion of the socio-economic make-up of Scotland at this time, see Devine, T. M. and Mitchinson, R. (eds), *People and Society in Scotland*, vol. 1 (Edinburgh: John Donald in association with the Economic and Social History Society of Scotland, 1988); Michie, R. C., *Money, Mania and Markets* (Edinburgh: John Donald, 1981).

[9]   The status and function of these courts was being revised in the early nineteenth century and there is some overlap between the jurisdiction of the two, particularly in Glasgow. The records of these courts are now held at the Scottish Record Office in Edinburgh.

Table 7.1
Testators in Glasgow and Edinburgh, 1822–24

	Glasgow	Edinburgh	Total
Testate men	67	93	160
Testate women	29	65	94
All testate	96	158	254

Note: Totals for Edinburgh include Leith.
Source: Scottish Record Office (SRO) Sheriff Court and Commissary Court Volumes.

The larger number of women in Edinburgh and Leith is probably not the result of a greater proportion of women making wills in the capital. In both cities the testacy rate for women was approximately 70 per cent. There were simply more women in Edinburgh than in Glasgow. In the early-nineteenth century, Edinburgh held attractions for middle-class ladies: it was a centre of consumption, had plenty of middle-class housing, and no shortage of servants.[10] There was also an inherent age bias in the source. Although there are young people's estates present in the sample, the total group is inevitably skewed towards those approaching the end of the life cycle. As the records did not include age at death, attention is focused on life-cycle stage at death. Thus, whether their children were minors or adults, whether a person was widowed or still married or had parents, are important indicators of their responsibilities at the time of death. In addition, the documents recorded assets as gross values; the use of the wills as sources exhibits similar weaknesses to those described by David Green elsewhere in this volume.

Although there are many similarities in inheritance practice between the urban middle class in Scotland and their counterparts in England, one area of considerable difference was the legal framework within which post-mortem transfer was accomplished. The principal differences between the Scottish and English systems in the early nineteenth century was that in Scotland there was less individual freedom to gift the entire estate; certain rights for the immediate issue had to be met. To understand these differences, something of the broader legal context of marriage and inheritance must be known.[11] From 1563 until the 1820s, succession was part of the jurisdiction of the Commissary Court. After this period, it fell within the remit of the Sheriff Court. Despite these shifts in the spheres of responsibility, there was surprisingly little change to the statutes

---

[10]   At the end of the eighteenth century there was one servant for every eight families in Edinburgh compared with one for every fourteen in Glasgow – see Nenadic, S., 'The Rise of the Urban Middle Class', in Devine and Mitchison, *People and Society in Scotland*, p. 112

[11]   Discussion of the English context can be found in the chapter by Alastair Owens elsewhere in this volume.

which ruled succession until after 1830.[12] Throughout the period the Scottish legal framework for the post-mortem transfer of property not only differentiated between testate and intestate estates but also between moveable property, known as personal property in England, and heritable property, known as real property in England. In addition to the four major divisions of testate moveable, intestate moveable, testate heritable and intestate heritable, matrimonial property law was an important component of the laws of succession.

Scotland resembled its Continental neighbours until 1855, in that it had a bilateral system of inheritance whereby a woman's property was part of a common fund although her husband administered it. The most important aspect of matrimonial property law in Scotland was the legal supremacy of the husband. On marriage, the administration of a woman's moveable property was taken over by her husband. When a couple married, their moveable property was said to form a common fund known as the *communio bonorum*. Scottish law in the form of *jus mariti* gave the husband complete power of administration over the *communio bonorum* and therefore the wife's moveable property was in effect the husband's absolute property for the duration of the marriage.[13] The rents of the wife's heritable property or interest on personal loans were treated as moveable estate and fell within the husband's jurisdiction also. The actual heritable property, however, was not available for him to dispose of.[14] Nevertheless, on the wife's death if she had made a proper will her legatees would receive her share of the *communio bonorum*: that is, one-half of all moveables if there were no children or one-third if there was live issue. If the wife died intestate with no issue, her half of the fund was due to her next of kin.

There had always been a certain portion of property which was excluded from the common fund and so did not fall within the husband's rights of administration. The most common category was those goods classed as paraphernalia comprising the wife's clothing, her jewellery and the receptacles which contained them.[15] In addition, there were also means by which the husband's *jus mariti* and rights of administration could be excluded. In the first place, any maintenance provisions made to the wife by any person, including the husband, did not fall within the legal boundaries of *jus mariti* and the right

[12]   Clive, E., *The Law of Husband and Wife* (Edinburgh: W. Green, 1982), pp. 1–7.

[13]   Watson, J., *A Treatise on the Law of Scotland Respecting Succession Depending on Deeds of Settlement* (Edinburgh: Bell and Bradfute, 1826), p. 282.

[14]   Duff, A., *Treatise on Deeds Chiefly Affecting Moveables* (Edinburgh: Bell and Bradfute, 1840), p. 225.

[15]   Fraser, P., *Treatise on Husband and Wife According to the Law of Scotland* (Edinburgh: T. and T. Clark, 1840), p. 770.

of administration of the husband or any of his creditors.[16] Another way in which a married woman's moveable property could be removed from the jurisdiction of her husband was by the express renunciation of the *jus mariti* by the husband in an antenuptial contract. In addition, a third party was also able to convey moveable property to single or married women exclusive of *jus mariti* and curatorial powers or rights of administration of any husband.[17] A further means of excluding a husband's rights over his wife's moveable property was by use of a trust. The trustees held the estate and used it to produce interest which was paid to the woman. The exclusion of *jus mariti* or the use of trusts were both common practices in the inheritance strategy of men leaving moveable property to their female relatives.[18]

These various measures resulted in the evolution of a bilateral inheritance system in Scotland, where children often inherited from both parents. In comparison, English property laws had resulted in the development of a unilateral inheritance practice with children mostly inheriting from their fathers. Laws passed at the end of the seventeenth century gave almost total testamentary freedom in England.[19] In contrast, Scottish law stated that the widow was entitled to an interest in one-third of her husband's heritable property, provided the marriage had lasted a year and a day, and that the husband was entitled to the liferent of all his late wife's heritable property, as long as a child which had been heard to cry had been born to their union.[20] It also entitled children to claim one-third of their father's moveable estate if there was a widow or one-half if there was no widow. The children's share or *legitim* was divided equally amongst them.

Although a man with legitimate children did not have the right to completely disinherit his children, there were various calculations which were made before the division of the *legitim* of which the most important was the identification of *inter vivos* gifts. These gifts by the father were treated in law as having been advances against their *legitim* unless they had been used to feed, clothe and educate the child before they reached the age of majority or were a reward for services which the child had rendered.[21] This process of calculating advances in life against the *legitim* was known as collation. The rules which limited fathers' freedom to settle their estates did not apply to

---

[16]   Ibid., p. 764.

[17]   Duff, *Treatise on Deeds*, pp. 226–7.

[18]   *Bell's Principles of the Law of Scotland*, 4th edn (Edinburgh: T. and T. Clark, 1839), p. 725.

[19]   Blackstone, W. *Commentaries on the Laws of England* (London: T. Tegg, 1850), ff. 492–3.

[20]   McLaren, J., *The Law of Scotland in Relation to Wills and Succession*, vol. 1 (Edinburgh: Bell and Bradfute, 1868), p. 106.

[21]   Ibid., pp. 133–4.

single men and women, or widows and widowers without children, who had complete freedom to do as they pleased with their estates. Married women with separate estates which were excluded from the *jus mariti* also had greater freedom in their testamentary practice than their husbands. In addition, the post-mortem transfer of property had to meet certain criteria. These included a definitive form of disposition and settlement, the use of both maiden and married names for married women, proven sanity and a certain level of health, particularly if a will was made shortly before death. Despite all the restrictions described, all Scots had at least one-third of their moveable property to settle as they wished and their entire heritable estate subject to any burdens such as terce or courtesy.

The rules for intestate estates in the first half of the nineteenth century differed for men and women. As has already been described, a married woman's heritable estate was subject to courtesy and half or one-third of the *communio bonorum* was due to her next of kin. When a man died intestate his heritable property was directed to the eldest son or that son's issue by the rule of primogeniture.[22] His moveable estate was divided equally amongst the nearest kin. There was no preference of male heirs and the issue of predeceased kin were not promoted to their parents' rank in the line of succession.[23] If there were no issue, the estate was divided amongst the deceased's siblings or their issue. As with testate estates, collation was required to return any payments made to the descendants during the intestate's life.

In summary, the legal framework within which post-mortem transfer was managed in Scotland until the middle of the nineteenth century had much in common with the system in England in the early modern period. However, whereas England had moved towards greater freedom and more individual rights for testators, Scotland retained a system which protected the rights of widows and children. Furthermore, various measures were available to protect women's property, particularly from a husband's creditors, and these were widely used. It can thus be determined that Scottish laws of succession in the first half of the nineteenth century assumed a cultural background where the rights of the family were paramount. As we shall see, this had a great bearing on the inheritance strategies followed by the urban middle class of Glasgow and Edinburgh. It also encouraged the use of professional legal expertise in drawing up wills. Indeed, the sample only contains seven wills which appear to have been produced without professional input of some kind.[24]

---

[22] McLaren, vol. 1, *Law of Scotland*, pp. 61–5.

[23] Ibid., pp. 111–14.

[24] For the use of legal expertise in will making in an English context see the chapter by Alastair Owens in this volume.

Men and inheritance

The principal subdivision within the total group of men was between those who had children and those who did not, although the existence of a widow was also an important factor. As can be seen from Table 7.2, eighty-nine of the 160 men in the sample had legitimate children to provide for and a further five had illegitimate offspring. Moreover, there were sixty-three married men who needed to make provision for their wives. This means that the sample contains a variety of familial circumstances and allows some conclusions to be drawn about the inheritance strategies of these various groups.

Table 7.2
Marital and family status of testate men in
Glasgow and Edinburgh, 1822–24

Marital status	With legitimate issue	With illegitimate issue	Without children	Total
Unknown	13	4	31	48
Unmarried	0	0	4	4
Married	63	1	29	93
Widowed	13	0	2	15
Total	89	5	66	160

Source: Scottish Record Office (SRO) Sheriff Court and Commissary Court Volumes.

Table 7.3
Total moveable estate values of testate men in
Glasgow and Edinburgh, 1822–24

Total values of estates	Absolute numbers
Under £1000	55
£1001–£5000	64
£5001–£15,000	26
£15,001–£30,000	7
Over £30,000	8

Source: Scottish Record Office (SRO) Sheriff Court and Commissary Court Volumes.

Inheritance strategy was also influenced by the level of wealth. The total values of men's moveable estates ranged from £94 to £76,002.[25] Within this range, fifty-five estates were under £1,000 in value and 105 were over £1,000 in value (Table 7.3), indicating that the group as a whole were fairly wealthy. Indeed, if all the estates are added together, their total value was £928,718 – a large sum of capital to be dispersed on death and one which held real social and economic implications for the testators and their families. Although differences in marital status, the presence or otherwise of children and the size of the estates caused some variation in the way an estate was dealt with, the main destination of this inheritance was to members of the deceased's family.

Fathers

As in England, the major element of the inheritance strategy of fathers was provision for wives and children with equal division for children as the norm.[26] There were very few fathers who tried to control their children's behaviour by means of their testaments and very few who bequeathed estate to any but their immediate family. The majority of married men and fathers in Glasgow and Edinburgh who died in the early 1820s leaving more than £40 in moveable assets not only fulfilled their legal obligations but also left more property to their wives and children than the law demanded of them. Indeed, there were only two cases where the bare legal minimum was adhered to. The normal practice for these men was to liferent house, furnishings and a substantial income to the wife for her widowhood in lieu of *jus mariti* and then to leave the estate in various portions amongst the children. The way in which this practice was realised was connected to the size of the estate. In the case of small estates, both heritable and moveable property were usually liferented to the wife and only after her death or remarriage would the estate have been divided up for the issue. In contrast, if the estate was large, only part of the property was liferented to the wife and therefore the children received portions on their father's death and the rest when their mother's share fell to them on her death or remarriage.

In addition, most fathers were careful to divide their estates equally amongst their children. Ensuring that children received equal shares was a task which required care and attention, and the wills reflect this. For example, George Kinnear, a banker of Queen Street Edinburgh, left a large moveable estate worth approximately £47,000 and made complex provisions for his wife and eleven children. The central tenet of his will was that his six sons were to receive £4000 each to set them up in business and his five daughters were to

---

[25] All sterling amounts are in 1820s values.
[26] See the chapter by Alastair Owens in this volume.

receive the same amounts. The married daughters, however, had been given £2000 each for their marriage portions and therefore this sum was to be deducted from their inheritance.[27] George Kinnear's disposition and settlement set out his wishes in a businesslike fashion with no hint of sentiment and was typical of the wills in general. In contrast, there were some documents which not only displayed the deceased's desire to be even-handed but also real chagrin at the behaviour of some family members. In one instance, John Clarkson, a wright in Glasgow, left a moveable estate of £130 and heritable property which provided an income of £45 per annum. He instructed that the proceeds of one-third of the entire estate should go in the first place to his wife in liferent and at her death to two of his daughters share and share alike. The remaining two-thirds was to be divided equally between these same two daughters and thus, exceptionally, a third daughter was excluded from any share in his estate. His reasons for doing this were clearly stated in the will:

> I hereby provide and declare that as my daughter Anna Clarkson, wife of Richard Montgomerie, threadmaker in Philadelphia, America, and her said husband have already received from me upwards of £100 and in regard they left this country about five years ago in a clandestine manner taking with them by stealth a bill on which they received £106, which I had to repay, I hereby expressly exclude, debar them and their heirs.[28]

The careful reckoning of gifts made voluntarily or otherwise during life and deducted from the final inheritance is a common feature of the dispositions and settlements. In most cases, these provisions took the form of simple collation and there is very little evidence of inheritance practice being used to punish misdemeanours. The few fathers who used their wills to introduce sanctions for past behaviour seem to have been particularly worried about their children's marriages. An example of this rare behaviour is that of James Neilson. He had five sons and five daughters by his second wife. Their marriage contract allowed each child £500 capital on their father's death. For all his sons and four of his daughters this sum was increased to £1500 each on which the interest was payable to them until they reached the age of twenty-three years, when they would receive the capital absolutely. One daughter, however, was excluded from these arrangements and was left the £500 capital and a further £25 per annum for life. James Neilson stated his reasons for this very clearly as follows:

> Whereas my said daughter Ann not only without my consent but against all my advice and remonstrances was married in Edinburgh the twenty-

---

[27] Scottish Record Office (SRO), SC70/1/31.

[28] SRO, SC36/51/2.

sixth day of April last to Alexander Iranovitch Julian Katte Ghery Krim Ghery and intends soon to accompany her husband to live in Tartary or some part of the Russian Empire and whereas by the contract of marriage settlement aforesaid the sum of five hundred pounds therein secured to each of my children is the whole that they or any of them can demand or claim from me or my representatives for Bairns part of gear legitim portion natural executry and any thing else that they or any of them can ask or claim from my estate real or personal as herein before mentioned excepting what I might think fit to bestow upon any or either of my children of my said good will only. And although my said daughter Ann has no right or claim to more than the legal interest being twenty five pounds sterling until the principal sum of the aforesaid five hundred pounds is paid and although she has married a foreigner contrary to my will yet I am desirous from natural affection as the interest of the said five hundred pounds may be found insufficient to support her abroad to make some addition to her income. I therefore give grant and bequeath unto my said Daughter Ann the annual sum of twenty five pounds sterling to be paid to her every year during her natural life. [29]

James Neilson still made handsome provision for his daughter but apart from the £500 pledged to each child in his marriage contract, Ann would have had much less control over her income than her sisters and would also have had a smaller income. A further example shows the reluctance that these men had to take punitive action against their issue. George Winton, architect in Edinburgh, notes in his will that his son William had lately gone to the East Indies taking a wife, Mary Clark, with him much against George's 'inclination'. Despite his annoyance with William, the equal terms of George's disposition and settlement were not changed.[30]

Although most fathers left their estates divided equally amongst their children there was one small but significant group who behaved differently. These were men who had small businesses.[31] As the businesses were too small to divide up and still provide a livelihood it was usual to leave the shop or firm to one son. In order to fulfil the conditions of *legitim* and *jus mariti* this son, who was often the eldest, was burdened with the care of the widow and his unmarried sisters. In the case of larger businesses, complex provisions were often made to give the son or sons taking over the firm time to pay the other members of the family their share of the capital. This sometimes ran into many years and in two cases, the sisters' share of the capital was to remain in the business and they were to receive a liferent of the interest. Clearly, the form in which property was held influenced the adoption of a certain type of

---

[29] SRO, SC70/1/28.
[30] SRO, SC70/1/28.
[31] See the chapters by Penelope Lane and Geoffrey Crossick in this volume.

inheritance practice. Wills made by men who owned the family home and had unmarried daughters displayed similar behaviour in the short term. Normal practice was for the house and contents to be liferented by the unmarried daughters in much the same way as a widow. On the marriage or death of the last daughter the house would be sold and the capital divided amongst the entire sibling group in equal portions. Thus, in the long term, it became an even division of property.

Most fathers instructed that all property, heritable and moveable, should be converted into money and the capital equally divided amongst their children, subject to collation and any burdens for the widow. Men with children fulfilled their legal obligations to their offspring and also mirrored the intestate provisions for moveable property. In the case of heritable property their practice differed from the intestate procedure where the heir, who was the eldest son, inherited all. In fact, most of them also divided the heritable property 'share and share alike'. However, although property was evenly divided, there was some difference in the manner in which it was to be held. Some men left property to their sons absolutely but their daughters received their shares in liferent. In fact, 60 per cent of fathers with daughters left it to them absolutely. Most women who received property absolutely were disponed and settled exclusive of *jus mariti*. Even in cases where the estate was settled in liferent, the ultimate destination of the property was usually the legatees' respective issue who would receive it absolutely but exclusive of *jus mariti* if they were women.

At all times the wife and children had priority, but some larger estates also included gifts to siblings or provision for parents. One particular example which illustrates the priority of the wife and children is that of John Kidd, a Glasgow merchant, who, having made provision for his wife and two children, also left £500 in liferent to his sister Margaret Kidd and then in fee to his children in a testament drawn up in 1818. However, in a codicil published in 1822 he states that: 'in respect of the heavy losses which I have sustained in trade and the great fall which has taken place, in the value of kind of property since the said Disposition and Deed of Settlement was executed by me, I do hereby revoke ... the legacy of £500 to Margaret Kidd or Anderson'.[32] Thus, it can be seen that John Kidd's provision for his sister was made when he considered that he had disposable wealth, but that below a certain level only wives and children could be provided for. The type of calculations that had to be made to take these types of decisions depended not only on the level of wealth held by people but also on the standard of living deemed necessary within families. Furthermore, the fluctuations in the fortunes of these middling types of people, particularly the Glasgow merchants, meant that these were not

---

[32]   SRO, SC36/51/4, p. 281.

isolated decisions. Immediate family came first and, by and large, these men could not afford, or saw no reason, to provide for much more. Thus, men with children left the bulk of their estates to those children (after making provision for any wife) and the majority were informed by an ideal of equality in dealing with the disposal of their property.

Men without children

Men with no children had much greater freedom to bequeath their estates as they pleased. They were able to make decisions about post-mortem transfer based on different criteria from fathers and could be regarded as having had the opportunity to choose their 'family'. Of these men, 86 per cent bequeathed their estates to members of their legitimate kin after provisions for any spouse had been made. Therefore, the interpretation of family in the context of inheritance was still immediate kin, usually siblings and their children, but a variety of criteria were used in defining a hierarchy of family.[33]

Within this group there were a number of men who left gifts to those termed as 'namesake' children. In one example, William Calderhead, merchant in Glasgow, had a moveable estate at death of over £20,000. He arranged for incomes for his brother, sister and cousins, and their children. He also left some fairly large amounts to charity, £100 to a friend, and the residue was liferented to his sister, then to his brother and, after their deaths, was left in fee amongst the issue of his five cousins with the exclusion of John Marshall, eldest son of his cousin Jean Calderhead as he 'has behaved excessive ill'. Three of his cousins each had a son called William and he made gifts to these three 'Williams' of 1000 guineas each, over and above their share in his residue. Thus it can be seen that William Calderhead, with freedom to dispose and settle his estate as he pleased, gave gifts to various individuals and groups, but especially rewarded those in the next generation who had his name.[34] In such cases the individuals had held the name of the deceased since birth, but another possible strategy which was adopted occasionally involved the legatee changing his name to that of the legator. One such case was that of Robert Carrick, banker in Glasgow, who left moveable estate in excess of £43,000 and also a considerable amount of heritable estate which was entailed to George Carrick, junior. In a codicil the entail was cancelled and the estate disposed and settled on David Carrick Buchanan, formerly David Buchanan.[35] In this case the testator effectively disinherited the heir, who was his nephew, and replaced

---

[33] This reflects practices apparent in eighteenth-century Lancashire and Cheshire. See the chapter by Jon Stobart in this volume.

[34] SRO, SC36/51/3.

[35] SRO, SC36/51/3.

him with another person provided that person changed his name to include the testator's surname. This tactic illustrates the notion of choice in gifting an estate but also the desire to perpetuate a family name.

In view of the importance of kinship in their inheritance practice, services to these people may have been an important part of family strategy. Reciprocity is certainly present in some of the testaments, including several where one niece or sister received more than the other members of the family because she was living with or keeping house for her uncle or brother. One example of this kind of testament is the trust disposition and settlement of Hay Donaldson, Writer to the Signet, who left his estate equally divided amongst his nine siblings except that a double share was bequeathed 'to the said Anne Donaldson as a testimony of my gratitude to her for the charge she has taken of my family and for the comfort I have derived from her society'.[36]

Reciprocity was also present in the wills of those with legitimate issue, albeit less frequently. The testament of William Bannerman provides an example of one of these few reciprocal gestures. After providing for his wife and family the only other gift made in this testament was to a niece who was to receive £100 on her wedding day, 'in consideration of the friendly aid I received from her mother at the time I commenced business'.[37] This particular case illustrates the length of time which may have been involved in repayment of past favours or services rendered, as the reciprocal measure benefited the next generation rather than the person who had performed the service originally. It also indicates the informal methods used within families to calculate debts. In this case there may have been no expectation of any actual repayment but the transaction was expressed in terms of a debt of gratitude and ties of affection. Help from family members may not appear on the balance sheet of many businesses but was obviously a factor in the lives of some of the legators.

Those without issue also used a mixture of liferent and absolute gifts, and were more likely than fathers to leave gifts of varying sizes to family members, but the majority still left their estates evenly divided amongst their nearest kin and if the legacies were left in liferent, they were usually left ultimately as an absolute gift to the legatees' respective issue. Therefore, despite the greater freedom available to those without legitimate issue, most of them also disposed and settled their estates on their nearest kin. One particular example illustrates the strength of blood ties as the central tenet of inheritance strategy within this group. In this case, small tokens were left to friends and a large amount to a niece, but a significant part of the estate was gifted to children of cousins where the addresses were not known and the names of the legatees had been

---

[36]   SRO, SC70/1/29, p. 69.
[37]   SRO, SC36/51/3.

forgotten. This was a writer who knew he could leave more to his friends if he wished but who chose to leave the bulk of his estate to blood-relations, most of whom had not been in contact with him for a long time.[38]

Overall, men left most of their estates to their nearest kin and usually left it in equal shares. Although some women received their share of the estate absolutely, many were liferented their portions. In the long run, however, most estates were left in fee absolutely so that granddaughters or great-nieces would inherit their part of the estate absolutely. The middle ranks of urban-dwellers in the 1820s represented an extremely varied group both in social and economic terms. Nevertheless, differentiation in inheritance practice, although affected by levels of wealth in the short term, appears in the long term to have been more strongly connected to marital status and the question of whether there were children. Men sometimes left gifts to friends, but these tended to be tokens rather than any substantial bequests. The wills clearly reveal that these people had a lot of friends and contacts amongst the inhabitants of Scotland's two largest urban centres – a fact borne out by the choice of executors. Members of the family are present in most dispositions and settlements as well as professionals such as Writers to the Signet, but, as other chapters in this volume have indicated, most testators also appointed friends, colleagues or business partners as executors or trustees. In spite of the importance of this group as executors, very few received more than small token gifts. The emphasis of all inheritance practice was very much on the family, the aim being the successful reproduction of the middle-class family unit.

Women and inheritance

In contrast to the male testators examined above, very few of the women studied were married: all but two were widows or spinsters (Table 7.4). Moreover, only 30 per cent of the women had children, compared with 59 per cent of men. The level of women's wealth also differed greatly from that of the men in the sample. The values of the women's moveable estates ranged from £41 to £12,439, the overall total being £112,003. There are less women than men in the sample but this is still a considerably smaller level of wealth than that held by men on average (just £1192 compared with £5804). As can be seen in Table 7.5, sixty-three women died with less than £1000's-worth of moveable assets and only thirty-one with more than £1000 in personal property.[39]

---

[38] SRO, SC70/1/30. See also the discussion of Peter Cotton in the chapter by Jon Stobart elsewhere in this volume.

[39] For the situation in London, see the chapter by David R. Green in this volume.

Table 7.4
Marital and family status of testate women in
Glasgow and Edinburgh, 1822–24

Marital status	With legitimate children	With illegitimate children	Without children	Totals
Unknown	1	0	6	7
Unmarried	0	0	38	38
Married	0	1	1	2
Widowed	26	0	21	47
Totals	27	1	66	94

Source: Scottish Record Office (SRO) Sheriff Court and Commissary Court Volumes.

Table 7.5
Total moveable estate values of testate women in
Glasgow and Edinburgh, 1822–24

Total values of estates	Absolute numbers
Under £1000	63
£1001–£5000	29
Over £5000	2

Source: Scottish Record Office (SRO) Sheriff Court and Commissary Court Volumes.

Despite the lower level of wealth exhibited by women, they had a high level of testacy and distinct agendas for post-mortem transfer of their estates. The important division within the group was similar to that found with men in that the presence of children was the decisive factor in shaping a woman's inheritance strategy. There were, nevertheless, differences in the way women left their property which resulted in a gendered pattern of post-mortem transfer.[40]

Mothers

In general, women with children behaved in much the same manner towards their offspring as did fathers, and so require little further discussion. Unmarried daughters were often favoured in the wills of both fathers and mothers. Elizabeth Miller or Machen was typical of many mothers in that she

---

[40]   See the chapters by Penelope Lane and David R. Green in this volume.

apportioned in her will, 'Use of whole household possessions until she marries or dies to daughter Elizabeth Machen ... Interest on the heritable subjects to Elizabeth all the days of her life she shall remain unmarried'. The residue was to be divided equally amongst all six children including Elizabeth.[41] This last stipulation was more unusual, however, in that whereas most fathers left their estates to their children share and share alike, only 45 per cent of mothers adopted this pattern, the majority leaving unequal shares. A typical example of this behaviour can be seen in Ann Gordon or Maitland's instructions. She left all of her estate equally between her four daughters and nothing to her son Pelham Maitland as he 'has already been placed by me in a situation in which he may be well-provided for' and nothing to her son Robert Maitland as he 'has prospects of being provided for better than any of his sisters'. Furthermore, she stated that an advance of £200 to Pelham was not intended as a gift and must be repaid to his sisters.[42] In another similar case, Rachael Barclay or Playfair, widow of James Playfair, architect in London, bequeathed all her estate, except for some small legacies, to her daughter Jessie 'because of the great service to family particularly me and my youngest daughter during illness'. In contrast, she did not leave legacies to her two sons because 'they are independent', not because she 'love[s] them less'.[43] These wills betray the concern that mothers felt over independence for their daughters.

These examples are typical of the preoccupations mothers displayed when arranging their affairs, and if they displayed bias it was towards their daughters rather than their sons. In common with fathers they rewarded services, and provided homes and incomes in liferent for unmarried daughters. In contrast, however, they often chose to exclude sons who were independent in order to increase legacies to daughters whom they perceived as lacking independence. This equates well with the findings of David Green in this volume, who noted that women were anxious to provide an independent life for other women. Furthermore, as he observes of London, if there were no daughters to provide for – and in the Glasgow and Edinburgh sample many female testators apparently did not have children (Table 7.5) – then other women would benefit from this largesse.

Women without children

Women without children again exhibited similar behaviour to men without issue in that all but two of them left the majority of their estates to family members. However, in contrast to childless men but in line with mothers, only

---

[41] SRO, SC36/51/4.

[42] SRO, SC70/1/28.

[43] SRO, SC70/1/28.

one-third of these women left their estates equally divided amongst their nearest kin. Those leaving unequal amounts appear to have been motivated by similar concerns to mothers. In particular, they shared the same concerns over unmarried female relatives and they generally left more to nieces than nephews. In common with some men, a number of women favoured namesake children. The child was usually a niece bearing the same name. In the case of Rachel Marjoribanks, a great-niece who was also called Rachel Marjoribanks was referred to as a 'name daughter' and bequeathed a considerable sum of money.[44] The naming of a child after a sister or brother, particularly an unmarried sibling, would appear to have often resulted in a special relationship.

It was also amongst childless women that mutual dispositions and settlements were most frequently used. This was a common practice for unmarried siblings. For example, Miss Graeme Hepburn had a mutual disposition and settlement with her two sisters Anne and Christian who had the same address as her. They made everything over in favour of each other as long as they remained unmarried and, after the death of the last surviving one, the estate was to go to a nephew and a niece, who were the younger children of their brother.[45] This example is typical of this form of will, particularly the fact that the three sisters lived together.

Although the major part of women's estates, whether childless or not, was bequeathed to family members, small gifts to others were a feature of some settlements. Approximately a quarter of all the women left some bequests to charity in comparison to just 2 per cent of men. In both cases all charitable gifts came from testators without children. A typical example of this type of giving was the disposition and settlement of Mary Black, a spinster of Glasgow, who died in March 1822 and left her estate in liferent to her brother and after his death to their nieces. After the death of the nieces the estate was to be realised for 'behoof' of the Royal Infirmary of the City of Glasgow with the exception of £10 per annum for the Corporation of Cordiners in the Burgh of Glasgow.[46] Other recipients of legacies from women were servants. Once more this type of giving was mostly confined to women without children and the sums gifted were usually quite small.

A further distinguishing factor between men's and women's wills was the fact that in general, women's and especially childless women's dispositions and settlements were more detailed. Some appear to have enumerated every possession and given small things to a huge number of individuals. Typical of this kind of testament was that of Miss Catherine Baird, who bequeathed all

---

[44]   SRO, SC70/1/28.
[45]   SRO, SC70/1/28.
[46]   SRO, SC36/48/17.

who bequeathed all household goods and personal effects to her sister, Mrs Rachel Baird, widow of Dr Patrick Cumin, Professor of Oriental Languages at the University of Glasgow, with the exception of a full set of tea china, which she left to her grand-niece, Christian Gibson or Anderson, and 'the largest of my china punch bowls to Mrs Helen Gray or Woddrop, widow of William Woddrop as a token of respect'. Miss Baird also left £30 over and above her share in the residue to a niece, Miss Jean Cumin, 'for the valuable services she has rendered me'. A gold reading-glass was bequeathed to another niece, Janet Wightman or Gibson, and the 'china mugs and chrystal candlesticks' were left to her nephew William Cumin, a surgeon in Glasgow. In addition, £5 was given to her servant and the residue was left equally amongst a nephew, five nieces and two grand-nieces.[47]

Post-mortem transfer of property obviously provided an opportunity for repayment of past kindnesses or care and gave the legator a chance to express affection in a material way. Many of the women needed all of their property to provide an income and there may not have been much left over for gifts whilst they were alive, and therefore the ability to divide up their estates after death may have been very important to them. Due to their own experience of life they may have favoured those in need or in a similar situation to themselves.

The Honourable Barbara Rollo, youngest daughter of the deceased Lord Rollo, died in March 1824 and left a moveable estate of £489. She was living in her deceased mother's house in Albany Street, Edinburgh in which she had a share. Barbara had drawn up a general disposition and settlement in 1798 which gave the liferent use of all her estate to her two sisters, the Honourable Isabella Rollo and the Honourable Elizabeth Cecilia Rollo, as long as they remained unmarried. After their marriages or deaths the estate was left in fee to all surviving brothers and sisters 'share and share alike' or their share divided equally amongst any legitimate issue if they predeceased Barbara. However, in 1823 the provisions of the testament were altered in response to changed circumstances. Her brother James, was dead; Elizabeth Cecilia, her sister, had married and was 'now Mrs Bruce and well cared for'; another sister, Jane Rollo or Hunter and her family were 'in affluent conditions', and Roger Rollo was 'in good circumstances'. As a result, Barbara decided to leave her estate in liferent to her sisters Isabella and Mary and in fee to the younger children of her brother John, Lord Rollo, excluding his eldest son 'as he will be provided for by his father'. In addition she settled the liferent of her 'share of my mother's house in Albany Street' on the unmarried daughters of John, Lord Rollo 'as long as they are unmarried'. After the liferents had expired the residue was divided amongst the remaining sisters and the children of Roger Rollo.[48] Barbara was the

---

[47]   SRO, SC36/51/4.
[48]   SRO, SC70/1/31.

youngest daughter of Lord Rollo and unmarried. In her testament she appears to have favoured younger children and unmarried daughters after the liferent of her less affluent sisters expired, which hints at the relevance of women's own experience of life to their inheritance practice.

Not least because of the generally smaller size of the women's estates, their intended legatees were not rich heirs or heiresses. Their legacies were more likely to have been tokens, albeit a few of them large ones, of love and respect or perceived duty. Grace Campbell or Buchanan made her will in 1819. It is a complex document in which she left both her heritable and moveable estate to her nieces and nephews in varying amounts and in both absolute gifts and liferents. She also left some money to charity. In 1822 Grace added a codicil in which the major instruction was to bequeath 100 guineas to her niece Annette Montgomery Hamilton, stating that she 'did not put her in originally as she has married well and has a large fortune as a married woman' but that she 'felt bad about leaving her out'.[49] In this example, an original strategy based on provision for those in the family who were most in need was superseded by sentiment or perhaps by ideas of fairness or duty.

In summary, it is clear that despite the differences women exhibited in the terms of their dispositions and settlements, they conformed to the normal pattern of settling most of their estates on family members. However, they were more likely to take the circumstances of their relatives and their own personal dealings with them into account when drawing up their wills. The portions which they bequeathed reflected this strategy. As Vickery maintains, men and women appear to have had very different attitudes to moveable assets.[50] Women would appear to have had a greater emotional investment in personal effects and thus, for them, the transfer of this property was more than a material calculation. For some women, each commodity was imbued with a certain significance and this was included symbolically as part of the gifting process. In fact, many of the wills are highly detailed documents with complex provisions which illustrate a number of practices and motives, both material and emotional.

Conclusion

The reproduction of the urban middle-class family is the context within which this work has approached inheritance. Urban families rarely held large amounts

---

[49] SRO, SC70/1/28.

[50] Vickery, A., 'Women and the World of goods: a Lancashire Consumer and her Possessions, 1751–81', in J. Brewer and R. Porter (eds), *Consumption and the World of Goods* (London: Routledge, 1993), p. 294.

of land and moveable assets were usually the main components of their estates. This facilitated partible inheritance. It would appear that with the exception of some businesses, the actual heritable or moveable assets were of little importance. The deceased expected most of the property to be sold and converted into money which could then be reinvested by the legatees in a form suitable for them.[51] The exceptions to this were household furniture if there was a widow or an unmarried relative to be provided for, and some keepsakes such as jewellery which were often left specifically as mementoes. This overall flexibility allowed exact divisions of the property and made for considerable ease in administration for the executors. This adaptable approach to property by most testators, and particularly men, suggests a familiarity with the manipulation of assets to provide an income rather than the investment of property with emotional and sentimental value. This highlights the nature of urban life in the 1820s where most of these middling sorts relied on incomes based on their ability to earn a living or on moveable assets to produce an income. Even those who derived incomes from heritable property were rarely totally dependent on such payments and did not value the specific property. To this end, they were happy to sell heritage and buy other houses or land, or convert it into moveable assets. Thus, in general, the urban family appears to have relied on the ability of fathers, sons and sons-in-law to participate successfully in the workplace for an adequate length of time during their adult lives.[52]

Middle-class family reproduction in early nineteenth-century Edinburgh and Glasgow was achieved by the education and subsequent placement of sons in suitable occupations, the provision of marriage portions for daughters and the maintenance of unmarried women within the home. Thus, inheritance practice, especially that of men, can be seen as an extension of family strategies adopted in life and continued after the death of the testator. If, however, the testators were old when they died, the next generation were often parents themselves and thus the legacies they received would not have been needed to supply their own marriage portions or settle them in an occupation. Receiving their inheritance at a later stage in the life cycle meant it could be used for different purposes. This suggests that businesses could have been expanded with the extra capital, their own children provided with capital, or perhaps retirement could have been made possible with the extra assets. This emphasises the generational aspect of inheritance which is central to understanding the dispersion of capital and its uses within the family.

---

[51] See Morris, R. J., 'Reading the Will: Cash Economy Capitalists and Urban Peasants in the 1830s', in A. Kidd and D. Nicholls (eds), *The Making of the British Middle Class? Studies of Regional and Cultural Diversity since the Eighteenth Century* (Stroud: Sutton, 1998), pp. 126–7.

[52] See the chapter by Geoffrey Crossick in this volume.

The family in the 1820s was based on gendered notions of domesticity. Only two wives, in the sample, were expected to run their late husband's businesses: one was a flesher's and the other a saddler's. Furthermore, only two women without husbands, a widow and a spinster, had businesses of their own. One reason for this may have been that many of the sample were retired; certainly, the sample group was, on average, older than the population at large. Nevertheless, it would appear that women's role in the 1820s was based on the concept of women in the domestic sphere. The majority of all the women who were mentioned in wills or left dispositions and settlements of their own, required maintenance within a household. This was the ideal and is reflected in the wills, which assumed that at least the widow could be maintained by the post-mortem estate. This may not always have been the reality but it was central to the middling sorts' perception of the desirable norm and conveys a strong impression of women functioning in the domestic sphere.

Women making wills were less likely than men to use equal shares in the division of their estates. Although they were similar to men in their desire to provide for unmarried women and reward services rendered to them, they also wished to promote independence for other women in the family. As they had smaller amounts to leave it is possible they needed to target their bequests and therefore gave to those most in need or in similar positions to themselves.

Urban families were reproduced in the form of nuclear households, and marriage usually necessitated the setting up of a separate household. The unmarried siblings who lived together were often remnants of nuclear households who had been left behind when parents died and other siblings married. There are instances, however, of spinsters living with married or widowed siblings and unmarried men living with widowed sisters. In the reconstruction of ideas of the family which explore the early formation of the nuclear family in England and the emergence of individualism, stress has been laid on the disappearance or non-existence of the extended household.[53] This has led to the privileging of the individual and the nuclear household as the locus of family ties. There is no doubt that the middling ranks of Glasgow and Edinburgh in the 1820s inhabited nuclear households. Their wills, though, reveal a society where support for the elderly, the care of children, the running of households and companionship for each other was often met within the extended family. Siblings, cousins, nieces and nephews were all important in these roles, and contacts within the extended family remained an important element in the survival of the urban middle class. In addition, the provision of maintenance by fathers, sons and brothers to other family members was central

---

[53] Macfarlane, A., *The Origins of English Individualism: The Family, Property and Social Transition* (Oxford: Basil Blackwell, 1978); Laslett, P., *The World We Have Lost – Further Explored* (London: Methuen, 1983).

to investment strategy. The moveable property alone of the male testators in the sample was valued at a total of nearly £1 million sterling. Many men left instructions that the estate which should be used to support women was to be invested in heritable property or government funds. In fact, Scottish law at this time limited trustees to investment in safe funds. Therefore, it may be concluded that the meaning of property in urban contexts was powerfully shaped by the priorities of the family and gendered notions of domesticity.

In conclusion, the larger family circle was particularly important for the unmarried and their inheritance practice reflected this. Those with issue had their children as their priority but it must be noted that these same children were frequently included in the wills of unmarried aunts, uncles and cousins or the cousins of their parents. Furthermore, the needs of the family were paramount in shaping investment. The considerable moveable assets of the group plus heritable assets were mainly put to work to support the family. The emerging middle class in Edinburgh and Glasgow saw the reproduction of the family as central to their existence and this was reflected strongly in their inheritance practice.

Chapter 8

Women, property and inheritance: wealth creation and income generation in small English towns, 1750–1835

Penelope Lane

Studies of women's property holding in early modern England have shown that contrary to the prescription of common law, women owned and inherited property on a relatively equal basis with men.[1] Women's status and rights regarding property holding, however, appear to have declined during the course of the eighteenth and early-nineteenth centuries. Davidoff and Hall have argued that women's property became tightly controlled by their male relatives. Whilst men would manage and deploy their assets in economic endeavour, women were not expected to be 'active economic agents or even care for their own property'. Thus women's property held in personal trusts, a device mainly associated with the upper middle class, became a resource for male enterprise whilst women received only income.[2] Moreover, some historians contend that women had a greater 'emotional investment' in household and personal goods because they were unlikely to own or bequeath real estate.[3] Maxine Berg's research on the industrial towns of Birmingham and Sheffield in the eighteenth century questions these perspectives on women's property rights. She argues that trusts were set up by people of varying degrees of wealth and for different reasons. More often than not, personal trusts were created to provide for children rather than wives. Indeed, Berg contends that the provincial industrial classes in fact used trusts as a device for protecting women's property. Indeed, her research suggests that the women of these

[1] Erickson, A. L., *Women and Property in Early Modern England* (London: Routledge, 1997); Churches, C., 'Women and Property in Early Modern England: A Case Study', *Social History* 23 (1998), pp. 165–80.

[2] Staves, S., *Married Women's Separate Property in England, 1660–1833* (Cambridge Mass.: Harvard University Press, 1990); Davidoff, L. and Hall, C., *Family Fortunes: Men and Women of the English Middle Class 1780–1850* (London: Hutchinson, 1987), p. 209.

[3] Ibid., p. 211; Vickery, A., 'Women and the World of Goods: A Lancashire Consumer and Her Possessions, 1751–81', in J. Brewer and R. Porter (eds), *Consumption and the World of Goods* (London: Routledge, 1993), p. 294.

industrialising communities enjoyed a remarkable degree of proprietorial autonomy. Importantly, she found that women owned considerable amounts of real property and in general 'disposed of it as they wished'.[4]

Women's ability to own and exercise control of their property is central to our understanding of women's participation in the wider economy during the eighteenth and early nineteenth centuries, since this perception of a marginalisation in women's property rights is paralleled by their exclusion from sectors of commercial enterprise.[5] Davidoff and Hall have further argued that, despite limited control and ownership of property, and a perceived retreat from trade (promoted largely from the increasing identification of middling women with the domestic sphere, and the difficulties of engaging in a market based on large-scale enterprise), women were in private the 'hidden investment' of the family business. Women continued to perform a wide variety of tasks such as caring for family members, supplying small sums of money with which to generate new businesses and earning money in the 'interstices of household management'. All this whilst simultaneously trying to maintain rank by the 'appearance of a non-working lifestyle'. Women would only openly enter the public world of trade if they had no income of their own or no man to support them.[6] Therefore, in reality, women continued to work in both the public and private sphere.

David Green has correctly highlighted the need to consider the different experiences of wives, widows and spinsters in the processes of wealth creation. With some optimism, he sees the early nineteenth-century 'independent' women of London's middle class in a superior position to that of their working-class sisters. As Green states, 'whilst for working-class women widowhood, and to a lesser extent, spinsterhood, were often steps towards dependence and poverty, for their middle class counterparts such status could and frequently did bring personal autonomy as well as legal and financial

---

[4] Berg, M., 'Women's Property and the Industrial Revolution', *Journal of Interdisciplinary History* 24 (1993), pp. 240–43.

[5] Clark, A., *Working Life in the Seventeenth Century* (London, 1919, reprinted Routledge, 1992); Pinchbeck, I., *Women Workers and the Industrial Revolution* (London, 1930, reprinted Routledge, 1969); Hill, B., *Women, Work and Sexual Politics in Eighteenth Century England* (Oxford: Basil Blackwell, 1994); Davidoff and Hall, *Family Fortunes*.

[6] Davidoff and Hall, *Family Fortunes*, pp. 272–315. Given the lack of reliable quantifiable evidence there is no firm foundation for accepting the view of a decline in women's participation in business over the course of the late eighteenth and early nineteenth centuries. See Hunt, M., *The Middling Sort: Commerce, Gender and the Family in England 1680–1780* (London: University of California Press, 1996), p. 145; Barker, H., 'Women, Work and the Industrial Revolution: Female Involvement in the English Printing Trades, c. 1700–1840', and Sked, S., 'Women Teachers and the Expansion of Girls' Schooling in England, c. 1760–1820', both in H. Barker and E. Chalus (eds), *Gender in the Eighteenth Century* (London: Longman, 1997), pp. 81–100; Davidoff and Hall, *Family Fortunes*, pp. 293–304.

independence'.[7] However, he also notes that female testators often made provision for other women, suggesting that there were some amongst the middle class who needed additional forms of economic support.

Alastair Owens has recently pointed to the lack of research undertaken on informal welfare strategies amongst the middle class, particularly those that relate to post-mortem inter-generational estate provision. He has suggested that in order for the interests of some family members to be promoted, this often came at the expense of others, particularly women.[8] He concludes from his recent study of property transmission amongst Stockport's middle class between the years 1800 to 1857, and in line with the Davidoff and Hall thesis, that 'inheritance did more to constrain the married women of industrialising urban communities than it did to socially or economically empower them'.[9] Is this generally true for all industrial towns of the early nineteenth century? Did inheritance practices really contrive to exclude women from economic activity? How far were widows and spinsters able, or content, to live off a rentier income? Could our views be altered by examining the differences that existed outside of larger industrial centres and the metropolis, by looking at smaller towns in the context of regional industrial development? The prevailing economic environment in which women lived, and died, is as important for our understanding of their economic participation as any religious and social discourse exhorting middle-class women to their proper role in life. It is likely, moreover, that if women were pushed to the periphery when it came to property holding or engaging in business, as some historians have argued, it would become an even greater necessity for women to protect themselves from economic insecurity. This was especially important for those women inhabiting the fringes or lower ranks of the middle class.[10] Indeed, the paradoxical elements that linked women's economic activity and their middle-class status ensured that they continued to figure large in the economy of the late eighteenth and early nineteenth centuries.

This chapter will begin first by exploring patterns of inheritance as they relate to widows in a small industrial town in the East Midlands. It will be

---

[7]   See the chapter by David R. Green in this volume.

[8]   I am grateful to Alastair Owens for providing me with a copy of his paper, '"The Duty and Paramount Obligation of Every Considerate and Rational Man": Will-Making, Inheritance and Middle-Class Welfare Provision in an Industrial Town'. Paper prepared for the Social History Society of the United Kingdom Annual Conference, University of York, 2–4 January 1999.

[9]   Ibid.

[10]   The 'fringes' of the middle class would include those Earle has described as 'petty capitalists' whose 'activities not only fed and clothed them but also enabled them to accumulate on a regular basis and improve themselves'. Earle, P., *The Making of the English Middle Class* (London: Methuen, 1989), pp. 4–5. For a discussion of the distinguishing features of the lower ranks, see Davidoff and Hall, *Family Fortunes*, p. 24.

argued that the provision men made for wives, family members and other kin frequently obviated any idea that their widows would become economically inactive. Secondly, the examination of wills left by widows and spinsters from two very different towns suggests that industrial development created opportunities for women's property holding and wealth creation.

Background

Before discussing the findings of the study in detail, it first must be placed in context. In the eighteenth century, England was undergoing a continuing process of regional specialisation.[11] Trends with their origins in previous centuries saw the economic landscape of the East Midlands transformed as pastoral farming came to dominate agriculture, and framework knitting the industrial sector.[12] Nowhere were these changes felt more than in the county of Leicestershire. Towns were deeply interconnected with the processes of economic change. Urban areas functioned as important centres of exchange and distribution, promoters of industrial development, providers of specialist services and sources of capital investment.[13] However, it is only in relatively recent times that the economic, social and cultural role of small towns (that is, those of a few thousand people) has claimed the attention of historians.[14] The economic diversity within and between towns in the region is important, since this had the propensity to determine types of property, affect levels of wealth and inform patterns of inheritance.

Two Leicestershire towns were selected for this study: Ashby de la Zouch and Hinckley. Towards the end of our period, in 1831, Hinckley's population

---

[11] Hudson, P. (ed.), *Regions and Industries: A Perspective on the Industrial Revolution* (Cambridge, Cambridge University Press, 1989).

[12] Thirsk, J., 'Agrarian History 1540–1950', in W. G. Hoskins and R. M. McKinley (eds), *The Victoria County History of Leicestershire*, II (Oxford: Oxford University Press, 1954); Broad, J., 'Alternate Husbandry and Permanent Pasture in the Midlands, 1650–1800', *Agricultural History Review* 28 (1980), pp. 77–89; Felkin, W., *History of the Machine-Wrought Hosiery and Lace Manufacturers* (1867, reprinted Newton Abbot: David and Charles, 1967); Wells, F. W., *The British Hosiery and Knitwear Industry* (Newton Abbot: David and Charles, 1972), Chapman, S. D., 'The Genesis of the British Hosiery Industry, 1600–1750', *Textile History* 3 (1972), pp. 7–49 and 'Enterprise and Innovation in the British Hosiery Industry, 1750–1850', *Textile History* 5 (1974), pp. 14–37.

[13] Corfield, P., *The Impact of Towns 1700–1800* (Oxford: Oxford University Press, 1982); Clark, P. and Corfield, P. (eds), *Industry and Urbanisation in Eighteenth Century England*, Centre for Urban History, University of Leicester, Working Paper 6 (Leicester, 1994).

[14] Clark, P., 'Small Towns in England 1550–1850: National and Regional Population Trends', in P. Clark (ed.), *Small Towns in Early Modern Europe* (Cambridge: Cambridge University Press, 1995), pp. 90–92.

had risen to nearly 6,500, whilst Ashby's stood at 4,400.[15] Ashby, located in north-west Leicestershire, had a typical market-town economy. At the end of the eighteenth century, it was said to be inhabited by 'shopkeepers, innkeepers, manufacturers of woollen and cotton stockings and hats, farmers and labourers'.[16] Significantly, as local antiquarian John Nichols could record, 'the town is the Earl of Huntingdon's ... The inhabitants especially the better sort, are generous and sociable beyond those of most towns ... This place has long been famed for convivial musical meetings'.[17] In keeping with the prevailing ambience of the town, the discovery of a spring in a coal-pit in the nearby village of Moira led to the building of the Ivanhoe Baths in the early 1820s. In this period hotels were erected to accommodate visitors, and a theatre was built in 1828.[18] By 1830, Ashby stood in sharp contrast to the industrial centres of the region, and one commentator described the people of the town as 'chiefly engaged in general trade, and as there is but one small ribbon manufactory in the town, it is consequently free from the noise and the unwholesome effluvia of a populous manufacturing place'.[19]

Hinckley, on the other hand, could probably be described in these latter terms. This town, situated in the extreme west of the county close to Warwickshire, became an organising centre for the hosiery industry. The stocking frame made its first appearance at Hinckley in 1640 and by 1778 an estimate suggests there were some 764 frames in operation.[20] In 1782 Nichols wrote, 'the introduction of stocking-manufactory has considerably augmented the traffick of the town, which is supposed to contain 750 houses and 4,500 inhabitants.[21] However, it suffered in the general regional decline of the early-nineteenth century. By the 1840s poverty was rife and nearly 40 per cent of the town's population received poor relief.[22] On the basis of these descriptions we might consider that Ashby offered a pleasanter, more 'genteel' environment for

---

[15] 1831 Census Abstract.

[16] Hillier, D., *The Story of Ashby de la Zouch* (Buckingham, Barracuda, 1984), p. 93.

[17] Nichols, J., *The History and Antiquities of Leicester*, III, ii (London, John Nichols, 1804), pp. 612–13.

[18] Scott, W., *The Story of Ashby de la Zouch* (London: George Brown, 1907), pp. 231, 245.

[19] Quoted in Royle, S., 'Functional Divergence: Urban Development in Eighteenth and Nineteenth Century Leicestershire', Leicester University Geography Department Occasional Paper, 3 (1981), p. 10.

[20] Nichols, J., *The History and Antiquities of Leicester*, IV, ii (London, John Nichols, 1811), p. 679.

[21] Nichols, J., *The History and Antiquities of Hinckley* (London, John Nichols, 1782), p. 22.

[22] Francis, H. J., *A History of Hinckley* (Hinckley: W. Pickering and Sons, 1930), p. 64; Royle, S., '"The Spiritual Destitution is Excessive – the Poverty Overwhelming": Hinckley in the Mid-Nineteenth Century', *Transactions of the Leicestershire Archaeological and Historical Society* (1978–9), pp. 51–60.

the widow or spinster, but when it came to money-making and property holding, it was Hinckley that seems to have offered the greatest opportunity.

Wills: a source for examining women's economic activity

The lack of probate inventories in this period places heavy reliance on the information in wills.[23] These only document some of those occupations and interests in which men were involved, and record less information still when it comes to those of women. Moreover, the evidence also tends to be weighted towards financial activity rather than business concerns. However, wills have the advantage that they describe a person's real as well as personal property, and also disclose the detailed social and economic relationships of inheritance. Indeed, systems of inheritance, especially those aimed at wives, are particularly revealing since they illustrate that women not only continued in their husbands' businesses, but sometimes began their own. The information in wills also suggests that the provision made for wives was not always adequate.

In order to explore the themes outlined above, three sets of wills have been selected for these towns. Two data-sets, one from each town, includes information from all the wills left by women and proved in the Archdeaconry Court of Leicester between 1750 and 1835. This amounts to about one-fifth of the several hundred which remain extant.[24] The third data-set has been constructed by taking a random sample of eighty-eight men's wills, that is, some 26 per cent of all those for Hinckley covering the same years and proved in the Archdeaconry Court.[25] Unfortunately, many of the elite members of these towns, especially those dying after 1800, were more likely to have their wills proved at the Prerogative Court of Canterbury, and are thus excluded from the sample.[26] Additionally, the concentration on small towns inevitably means that insufficient data is generated in some cases with which to determine trends

---

[23] See Spufford, M., 'The Limitations of the Probate Inventory', in J. Chartres and D. Hey (eds), *English Rural Society, 1500–1800* (Cambridge: Cambridge University Press, 1990).

[24] Berg notes that, whilst women in various parts of the country left around 10 per cent of all wills, women in Birmingham and Sheffield left 22.8 per cent and 18.1 per cent respectively: 'Women's Property', p. 237. These proportions are also commensurate with those found by Alastair Owens, however, David R. Green's study of London shows that the proportion of wills left by women was much higher. See their respective chapters in this volume.

[25] The data acquired from men's wills forms part of that generated by the Leverhulme Funded Project, 'Urban and Industrial Change in the Midlands 1700–1840', co-ordinated by the Centre for Urban History, University of Leicester.

[26] As there is no comprehensive index of wills proved in the Prerogative Court of Canterbury existing for the county for the eighteenth and nineteenth centuries identifying those for a specific place would be extremely difficult. See Wykes, D., 'Sources for a Study of Leicester Trade and Industry, 1660–1835', *Business Archives* 45 (1979), p. 11.

over time or between categories. Identifying the boundaries of the middle class in any urban population is problematic and it is equivocal how far women could, by their own enterprise and property holding, claim middling status. As this study includes only individuals whose wills were proven locally, we are, for the most part, dealing with the less wealthy members of the urban middle class,[27] those who we might expect would need to engage in trade and who would have been very mindful of the welfare systems of inheritance.

Married women and inheritance

Patterns of inheritance as they relate to married women, set out in men's wills for the town of Hinckley, are presented in Table 8.1. When a man died, his widow was likely to become less economically secure as his estate was dissipated by the payment of debts, legacies, testamentary expenses and funeral costs. The severity of this decline depended on a number of factors. As we might expect, very few women were the sole beneficiary of their husband's will. Just nine widows were bequeathed all their spouse's real and personal estate. The necessity of providing for dependants immediately brought into play a different set of inheritance strategies. Widows in these circumstances were less likely to inherit real estate outright, but would enjoy a life interest. However, this is not inconsistent with earlier periods.[28] The proportion of married women (29.4 per cent) inheriting real estate 'for their own use' contrasts with the widows and spinsters from Hinckley and Ashby who bequeathed real estate (see Table 8.2). This contrast is significant, highlighting the differences between the towns, and between groups of women. It further illustrates that women could, and did in sufficient numbers, own this form of property. Only in a minority of cases did men liquidate all their real estate in order to provide an income for their wives and younger children. As the holding of real property took the form of a few cottages or tenements, rents already provided a steady source of income for families. This type of inheritance ensured continuity. Nonetheless, it cannot be ignored that over half the widows would have inherited their deceased husband's real estate for the term of their natural life only. The importance of real estate in the process of wealth creation and as a method of generating income for women will be discussed further below.

Given the desire to preserve real property for heirs, and provide a life income for widows, the finding that 56.7 per cent of widows inherited personal

---

[27] The value of personal estate (see Figure 8.1) does, however, indicate that the samples cover a broad cross-section of the population of each town.
[28] Erickson, *Women and Property*, p. 216.

estate is not surprising. It was, of course, common for married women to inherit household goods.[29] However, in all but seven of the thirty-four cases, widows received the residue of their husbands' personal estates, once debts and legacies had been paid. Although, again, if we exclude those widows who were bequeathed household goods alone with gifts of cash, held a life interest in their deceased partner's estate or were supported by an annuity, then less than 50 per cent received a legacy of personal estate for their own use. The patterns of inheritance as they relate to married women in Hinckley in the late eighteenth and early nineteenth centuries can be said to support both the orthodox and revisionist perspectives on women's property holding.

Table 8.1

The characteristics of inheritance as they relate to widows in Hinckley, 1750–1835

	No.	%
Men who predeceased their wives†	60	68.2
Men who made their widows the sole beneficiary of their will	9	15.0
Number of married men bequeathing real estate	51	85.0
Real estate:		
Widows inheriting all/part of their husband's real estate	15	29.4
Widows with a life interest only in their husband's real estate	26	51.0
Other: real estate liquidated, none to bequeath, etc.	20	19.6
Personal estate:		
Widows inheriting all/part of their husband's personal estate	34	56.7
Widows with a life interest only in husband's personal estate	15	25.0
Widows maintained by annuities, or at son's discretion, etc.	11	18.3
Widows inheriting businesses (specifically stated)	12	20.7
Proviso of remaining 'my widow'	17 (58)	29.3
Men with widows recorded as executors	34	56.6
Men with widows recorded as trustees	5	8.3

Note: † Includes two women who lived with men as if married to them.
Source: Wills proved at the Archdeaconary Court Leicester, Leicester Record Office.

---

[29] In early nineteenth-century Stockport, for example, household goods were the item wives were most often bequeathed: see Owens, 'Will-making, Inheritance and Middle-Class Welfare Provision'.

Whilst it can be argued that inheritance strategies conspired to marginalise large numbers of married women, it is clear that there were others who could personally control and dispose of property. But whatever form inheritance strategies took, many wives became economically disadvantaged at the onset of widowhood. It is worth considering the contents of men's wills in more detail because it cannot always be assumed that a rentier income was sufficient to maintain women or that they became less inclined to participate in their husbands' businesses or trades. Indeed, some inheritance strategies aimed to keep women in business.

Widows and business

Widows inheriting unconditionally or controlling personal estate during their lifetime is indicative of many widows continuing to engage in enterprise. In Hinckley, of those testators that left specific instructions that their spouses were to carry on in business, or where widows could be located in trades directories, 20 per cent of widows continued to do so. In Stockport in the early nineteenth century, wives inheriting businesses appear to have been rare, with less than 9 per cent documented.[30] In some of those cases where widows were entrusted with the management of businesses they were maintaining them for a son to take over when they reached the age of twenty-one. Mary Wale, for example, was bequeathed the grocery shop and real estate but only until her son George came of age.[31] William Ward, a blacksmith, left his personal estate to his 'wife and son to enable them to carry on in business'.[32] Similarly, the will of John Lockton recorded in 1824 that 'I do hereby direct that my wife shall carry on and follow the trade of framesmith and shall leave the stock tools and implements of trade for her own use and benefit until my son shall attain the age of twenty-one years and when he shall have attained that age ... the said trade shall be carried on for their mutual benefit and advantage'.[33] However, unlike the first of these examples, the wives of William Ward and John Lockton have their role affirmed even after their sons have reached the age of twenty-one. Sometimes widows were given the choice of whether to liquidate estate or not, and this again shows that in some instances wives rather than sons were given primary responsibility for the family business. William Moore made a bequest to his wife Elizabeth of 'all my household goods, furniture, brewing vessels, stock in trade, money debts, which may be due to me at the time of my decease and all my other personal estate and effects'. She was to

---

[30] Owens, 'Will-making, Inheritance and Middle Class Welfare Provision'.
[31] John Wale, Broker, 1811/234, Leicestershire Records Office, hereafter L.R.O.
[32] Will of William Ward, Blacksmith, 1762/267, L.R.O.
[33] Will of John Lockton, Framesmith, 1824/129, L.R.O.

make 'a true and perfect inventory thereof' and after paying his just debts and testamentary expenses, 'either carry on my businesses of a butcher and victualler with the assistance of my son William Moore or sell and convert into money my said personal estate and effects as may be advantageous'. In either case, Elizabeth was to maintain herself and bring up the younger children.[34]

The business acumen demonstrated by women undoubtedly differed as widely as it did amongst men. But husbands would not have instructed their wives to carry on in trade, support their children and hold together an important part of the estate, if these women had not first been active within the business or capable of preserving it. Although numerous women provided the linkage that connected the businesses and trades of one generation of males with another, and their part can certainly be viewed as 'carers' or 'custodians' of property, there was often a more public and responsible role for widows. Moreover, as the woman was capable of looking after the business in her husband's absence,[35] we must question how far her new role may have departed from her previous one. How, then, did this affect a woman's social status? A strict interpretation of the evidence in wills can be misleading. As we have seen, a significant number of Hinckley widows inherited most of their spouse's personal estate, and we should not discount the possibility that they kept businesses intact, even when it is not expressly stated that they should do so. Given women's strong association with the food and drink trades particularly,[36] we would expect this. Indeed, in 1821 William Boyer, victualler, bequeathed half of his household goods, stock-in-trade, casks, book and other debts, sums of money to Ann Pulsford 'who lives with me'.[37] The following year Ann could be found running the board in the borough of Hinckley.[38]

We cannot infer from wills that the bequests made to wives in the form of rents from real estate and annuities were sufficient to support a widow or that they were their only sources of wealth and income. Daniel Greatrex, a carrier, made provision for his widow in this way, but the following clause written in his will does not suggest that he expected her, or necessarily believed that she would be able, to live off this income alone. Thus, 'if Elizabeth Greatrex, my

---

[34] Will of William Moore, Butcher and Victualler, 1827/134, L.R.O.

[35] Pinchbeck, *Women Workers*, p. 282.

[36] Prior, M., 'Women and the Urban Economy of Oxford 1500–1800', in Prior, M. (ed.), *Women in English Society 1500–1800* (London: Methuen, 1985), p. 106; Wright, S., 'Holding Up Half the Sky: Women and their Occupations in Eighteenth Ludlow', *Midland History* 14 (1989), p. 63.

[37] Will of William Boyer, Victualler, 1821/19, L.R.O.

[38] Pigot's *Commercial Directory*, 1822/3. The term 'who lives with me' may imply that Ann was a servant or a female relative. However, usually, if women fell into these categories they were identified as such. In this, and in another woman's case, Ann inherited this legacy from a man who had no children and no close relatives, although the other half of the estate provided legacies for distant kin. Whatever the nature of the relationship, she obviously performed the duties within the business normally associated with a wife.

wife through affliction or infirmity shall stand in need of more support than the profits from the rents and interest will allow they [his trustees] shall take a sufficiency from the principal for her comfortable support during the term of her natural life'.[39] It was also recognised that some women might actually want to keep businesses going on their own account. Robert Goode, a pawnbroker and hosier, recognised that his wife Lydia may survive him and had entered in his will that if she 'chooses to carry on the pawnbroking business or any other business' she must pay his six children 'their equal portions of one half of the residue of my personal estate over and above the legacies of £60 each'. Robert Goode's personal estate was valued at £3,500: a considerable sum of money.[40] These legacies to his children would have depleted the estate and Lydia would have to work hard to recoup this wealth. Lydia was, however, no stranger to enterprise and business activity. Upon the death of her first husband George Ball, she had been charged with continuing 'my business as a framesmith in my now accustomed manner'.[41]

The use of trustees grew over the period. Between 1750 and 1799, the mean number of trustees per will across the sample of male wills as a whole was 1.0. From 1800 to 1835, however, the mean increases to 1.26. The men who acted as trustees were often friends and business associates of the deceased. Many of the trusts set up by male testators in the Hinckley sample focused on the care of children and, for example, ensuring the payment of legacies, as well as for the maintenance of wives. In only eight cases did women act as trustees and just five of these were wives. This is in marked contrast to the 54 per cent of women who were executors. Davidoff and Hall have argued that since women were increasingly viewed as dependent, they had to rely on males to operate trusts or act as financial agents.[42] But just how much control trustees had over women when it came to using 'their discretion to the best of their judgement and ability' to carry on a business for the benefit of a testator's wife and children is unclear. In 1835 John Holt instructed his friends to 'permit my wife and son to carry on my business as a Grocer so long as they can agree to manage the same with profit and advantage and not otherwise and not without the consent and approbation of my trustees'.[43] Edward Dawson specified these terms in his will.[44] However, his wife Mary is listed as a bookseller and stationer in Pigot's directory for 1822/23, and had obviously continued in this branch of her husband's business over a decade after his death.[45]

---

[39]   Will of Daniel Greatrex, Carrier, 1820/68, L.R.O.
[40]   Will of Robert Goode, Pawnbroker and Hosier, 1835/86, L.R.O.
[41]   Will of George Ball, Framesmith, 1822/6, L.R.O.
[42]   Davidoff and Hall, *Family Fortunes*, pp. 277–8.
[43]   Will of John Holt, Grocer, 1835/105, L.R.O.
[44]   Will of Eliott Dawson, Hosier and Stationer, 1809/65, L.R.O.
[45]   Hannah Barker has shown that women continued to engage in this trade well into the nineteenth century. See Barker, 'Women, Work and the Industrial Revolution'.

In an age when women were likely to have more than one husband, some men were obviously greatly concerned that their property did not find its way into some other family, especially if that might be at the expense of their children. In 29.3 per cent of cases men ordered that their widow's interest in the estate would not continue if they chose to remarry.[46] John Orton's will included the clause if 'my wife shall happen to marry again and take a second husband' she would receive 20 shillings and 'she shall not have the benefit or advantage' of his personal and real estate.[47] The use of this clause appears to have increased in Hinckley over the period, and only three wills include it before 1780. Whilst, again, this practice can be seen as helping to lock wives into widowhood, it could as much promote economic activity as well as prevent it. The provision made for a widow could well be insufficient on its own, but its importance might not be worth losing by entering another marriage. As we shall see, widows may well have chosen to rely on their own efforts and keep their independence.

A widow's life interest in estate was not just about preserving family property for children. In 1784 Thomas Parsons, a hosier, bequeathed his wife four messuages which after her death would pass to his two daughters as tenants-in-common. However, if these girls died before reaching the age of twenty-one years or left no issue, the beneficiary of Thomas' real estate would be his cousin, Robert Baines, for the term of his natural life, after which the estate would pass to Robert's children.[48] Similarly, Thomas Smith left all his household goods, all his stock plus his horses, gigs and carriages with money, credits and all other personal estate in trust to his two 'friends'. He directed they should 'suffer and permit my wife Ann' to have the 'use and enjoyment' for her natural life or until she remarried. At this point, Thomas's estate would be liquidated and shared between his brother and sister. Ann's efforts would not go entirely unrewarded, however, as she was to receive 'a third to dispose of as she wishes',[49] although it might well have aggrieved Ann that it was her work that would maintain her in-laws' legacies. This discussion has shown that inheritance practices did as much to encourage the economic participation of wives as they did to exclude it. Historians need to give much more emphasis to those determinants embodied in the processes of property transmission that pushed women into the economy.

---

[46] This is higher than the 20 per cent found by Alastair Owens for Stockport. See Owens, 'Will-Making, Inheritance and Middle Class Welfare Provision'.

[47] Will of John Orton, Carpenter and Joiner, 1754/160, L.R.O.

[48] Will of Thomas Parsons, Hosier, 1784/144, L.R.O.

[49] Will of Thomas Smith, Victualler, 1831/159, L.R.O.

Widows and spinsters: wealth creation and income generation

Having seen how inheritance strategies could promote a widow's economic activity, we turn in the second part of this chapter to the ways in which women exploited opportunities in the urban environment. Historians have identified the preponderance of female legatees in the wills made by widows and spinsters. Personal preference, friendship, motives of equity and concerns about the relative economic position of women encouraged testators to commonly bestow cash gifts, household goods, wearing apparel, but also real estate, shares, stocks and bank deposits.[50] Bequests also demonstrate the sources of business and financial activity. Mary Alt of Ashby, for example, ran the post office and had a millinery business. Her will dated 3 March 1808 revealed that she also had money out at interest to a gentleman in Ravenstone, and had shares in the Ashby canal.[51] Regional and local economies impacted on the ability of women to create wealth and earn a living. Figure 8.1 suggests that women in the industrial town of Hinckley were better off in this respect.

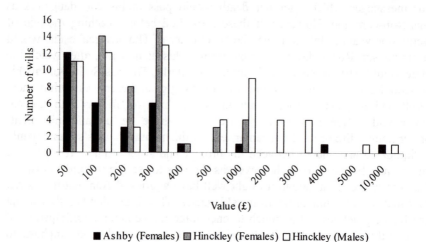

■ Ashby (Females) ▨ Hinckley (Females) ▢ Hinckley (Males)

Figure 8.1: Value of personal estate, Ashby de la Zouch and Hinckley, 1750–1835

Altogether, eighty-nine of the 141 wills left by women in both towns documented the value of a woman's personal estate during the probate process,

---

[50] Erickson, *Women and Property*, pp. 212–16; the chapter by David R. Green in this volume.

[51] *Universal British Directory* (1790–1798); Will of Mary Alt, Widow, 1826/6, L.R.O.

and this enables some distinctions to be made between the levels of wealth of these groups of women. These values do not record exactly how much the goods were worth, only that their value was less than, for example, £100.[52] Women leaving wills in Hinckley appear, on the whole, to have been wealthier than those in Ashby, although most women in either town left a personal estate valued at £200 or below. In both cases, spinsters did not rank amongst the highest values, but the worth of their personal estates was not noticeably lower than the average overall. Most of these values relate to the early nineteenth century, and they show that between the years 1799 and 1835 the average amount of personal estate left by women in Hinckley was £219 compared with the £164 left by women from Ashby.[53] A more detailed examination of this evidence revealed that the largest amounts were left by Ashby women: no woman from Hinckley, for which information remains, had her goods valued at more than £1,000. At the other end of the spectrum, where we find the least wealthy, Ashby women again occurred most frequently, with 23.3 per cent of them leaving personal estates of £20 or below compared to Hinckley's 18.9 per cent. When we include those of sixty-three men, we find that men were generally wealthier than both sets of women. This confirms, not unsurprisingly, that lone women were in a weaker position economically. However, a substantial proportion of males (41.3 per cent) left personalty valued at less than £200.[54] The wide range of values and the limited number of observations do not allow an adequate discussion of the changes in relative values of these personal estates.[55] But, given the rise in prices from the third quarter of the eighteenth century, this must have bitten hard into the incomes of many women and men in both towns.

Displayed in Table 8.2 are the various methods recorded in wills that were the sources of women's wealth and income. At first sight these data may seem to support the view of those historians who believe that economic change and women's growing dependence on men disinclined them to participate or have an interest in business, since the emphasis is clearly on financial activity. Precisely what dealings lay behind such terms as 'credits', 'security or securities for money' is often not clear, but given the previous discussion, this

---

[52] These figures neither take account of a testator's debts. However, it is assumed that women in Hinckley were no more debt-ridden than those in Ashby. Of Ashby wills, 55 per cent recorded a personal estate value compared to 68 per cent of those for Hinckley.

[53] In order to give a more realistic picture of women's wealth in Ashby the mean excludes two large personal estates of £3500 and £9000.

[54] It is, of course, possible that these figures are distorted by the exclusion of wills proved at the Prerogative Court of Canterbury.

[55] This is especially true for Ashby where there are only thirty observations for the entire period. Moreover, as wealthier individuals were more likely to have their wills proved at the Prerogative Court of Canterbury after 1800, this makes comparisons over time with this data even more unsatisfactory.

is more likely to be a consequence of the bias within the source rather than the reality.

Table 8.2
Evidence of income-earning activities appearing in women's wills, Ashby de la Zouch and Hinckley, 1750–1835

	Ashby de la Zouch		Hinckley	
	No.	%	No.	%
Women leaving wills	59	100.0	82	100
Women leaving real estate‡	14	23.7	35	38
Type of real estate where known:				
Buildings†	5	8.5	16	19.5
Land	5	8.5	17	20.7
Women referring to the following in their wills:				
Security or securities for money	10	16.9	21	25.6
Money at interest	9	15.3	1	1.2
Money-lending: bonds, etc.	8	13.6	9	11.0
Credits	7	11.9	12	14.6
Book debts or other debts	2	3.4	4	4.9
Ready money	12	20.3	25	30.5
Frames	0	0.0	9	11.0
Women involved in agriculture and bequeathing animal stock:				
	4	6.8	7	8.5

Source: See Table 8.1.
Notes: ‡ Real estate (other than for own use).
         † Includes messuages which, in some cases, incorporated land as well as a garden.

Real estate

Historians believe that men and women chose to deal in investments and real estate because there was less risk attached to this method of earning income. This is especially true for women since their resources were often smaller than those of men.[56] It seems that from the early years of the eighteenth century more people, and especially widows and spinsters, began to live completely or partly from investments.[57] However, whilst women may have had a greater

---

[56]   Jordan, *Women and Credit*, pp. 77–8.
[57]   Hunt, *The Middling Sort*, p. 146.

opportunity to make 'safe' investments we cannot assume they became less likely to participate in business. Real estate, as noted earlier, is often documented in wills and it was found that 29.4 per cent of married women from Hinckley were bequeathed real estate. When this is compared with that left by women leaving wills in Ashby and Hinckley, we find that some 23.7 per cent of those from Ashby and 38 per cent of women from Hinckley did so. However, whilst the data confirms that women owned and controlled real estate, these proportions are less than the 48 per cent left by women in the large industrial towns of Sheffield and Birmingham during the eighteenth century.[58] These distinctions are also notable when compared with London, where this form of wealth played only a very minor role in the bequests of female testators in the first part of the nineteenth century.[59] When it came to disposing of real estate, women from Ashby and Hinckley most frequently favoured females, although significant numbers of males also received similar legacies.

The higher proportion of women bequeathing real estate in Hinckley rather than inheriting it, is indicative of unmarried women owning real property, but also results from widows and spinsters adding to their holdings. We know from the Hinckley Poor Rate Book of 1790 that Susannah Nutt, the widow of Joseph Nutt, apothecary, had at least thirty-five houses, a malt kiln, two shop premises, stables, a barn, an orchard and two lots of land within the town itself. Her will of 1799 also refers to a tripe house and 'a lately erected messuage' situated in the area of Stockwell Head. This suggests that she had bought property since her husband's death and not relied on rents from her current holdings to provide her maintenance. In addition, she also received income from monies owing on mortgages, bonds and contracts. Susannah appears to have had no relatives, or none she cared to leave her real property and personal wealth to. She stipulated that her entire estate was to be sold to satisfy her own debts, and importantly, the unsatisfied legacies bequeathed by her sister, with the residue to be shared amongst her executors.[60] Unpaid debts or legacies, as well as providing for relatives, must have given women a further incentive to create additional wealth as well as live off the rents and interest payments from inherited property.

That more women from Hinckley bequeathed real property illustrates how some towns could provide greater scope for investment in real estate. The growth in the population of the town on the back of the expansion of the hosiery industry created the need for living accommodation and workshops. Framework-knitters' cottages from the early part of the eighteenth century became a popular investment for 'all classes of people' in Leicestershire and

---

[58]   Berg, 'Women's Property', p. 241.
[59]   See the chapter by David R. Green in this volume.
[60]   Will of Susannah Nutt, Widow, 1799/34; Hinckley Poor Rate Book 1790, 1243/218, L.R.O.

Nottinghamshire.[61] Of those women from Hinckley who mentioned real property in their wills, nearly two-thirds held messuages, tenements, cottages and land within the town itself, whereas less than half of Ashby women did so. Whilst it is possible that women had migrated to the town from elsewhere, which may account for this contrast, it seems more probable that differences in landownership, and more specifically industrial enterprise in Hinckley, produced the potential for opportunities in real estate. This is further indicated by direct references to real property. Unfortunately, it is not possible to determine the exact amount owned, but the wills made by women from Hinckley describe 'several' or two or three messuages or tenements, which suggests that the rents from these buildings combined well with other forms of income. This also partly explains why women from the town had more ready money at their disposal. Women from Ashby, on the other hand, were less fortunate. As much of the property in and around the town was owned by the earls of Huntingdon and later the Earl of Moira, building ownership and landownership would have been much more circumscribed. This is the most probable reason why the majority of real estate held by Ashby women was located elsewhere in other counties of the Midlands, principally Staffordshire, Derbyshire and Nottinghamshire. Hinckley women also owned real estate in the first two counties and also Warwickshire.

Money-lending and investments

Women's role in money-lending in the early modern period has been well documented by historians. Women functioned in this business at every level of society, from those with quite meagre resources to the very wealthy women who supported the elite.[62] It has been argued that, in English rural society for the 400 years following 1500, money-lending was 'the most prominent economic function of the widow'.[63] Women within towns also served in this capacity. As the system of credit was so ubiquitous, evidence of financial activity regularly occurs in probate records. Although the figures are small, money-lending as a form of income was probably more important to women living in Ashby, as they seem to have had greater emphasis on lending, with

---

[61] Chapman, 'The Genesis of the British Hosiery Industry', p. 38.

[62] See Chester Jordan, W., *Women and Credit in Pre-Industrial and Developing Societies* (Philadelphia: Princeton University Press, 1993); Tittler, R., 'Money-Lending in the West Midlands: the Activities of Joyce Jeffries 1638–49, *Historical Research* 67 (1994); Holderness, B. A., 'Widows in Pre-Industrial Society: An Essay Upon Their Economic Functions', in R. M. Smith (ed.), *Land, Kinship and Lifecycle* (Cambridge, Cambridge University Press, 1984); Holderness, B. A., 'Credit in a Rural Community, 1660–1800', *Midland History* 3 (1975).

[63] Holderness, 'Widows in Pre-industrial Society', p. 435.

money out at interest, for example, on bonds and notes. Women from Hinckley, on the other hand, appear to have left more ready money and security or securities for money. The expansion of the hosiery industry was in part supported by people wanting to extend their interests.[64] Wills occasionally record to whom money was lent and list a variety of tradespeople, and individuals connected to the hosiery industry. One of the few surviving probate inventories for this period shows that spinster Mary Taylor of Hinckley in 1781 had money secured on bonds, notes and a mortgage to a bricklayer, two framework knitters and a gentleman.[65] Money-lending could sometimes lead to the acquisition of a client's property. Alice Drought, for example, came 'into the peaceable possession' of two tenements when a borrower failed to keep up payments on a mortgage.[66]

Developments in the regional infrastructure also provided further avenues for women to invest their money. Turnpike trusts were a popular investment in the latter part of the eighteenth century and much of the money raised by trusts came from people making small loans. Spinster Mary Birch of Ashby, for example, received the interest of £30 'secured upon the tolls from the Tamworth and Sawley Ferry Road' which she then bequeathed to Ann Shepherd for the term of her natural life; thereafter the principal sum with any arrears of interest went to Ann's son.[67] Canals also became an important avenue of investment as the profitability of the early waterways and the possibilities for trade that this form of transportation could bring were realised. Investments, however, did not always yield the expected return. The Ashby canal, for example, was opened in 1804, but dividends were not paid out to investors until 1828, and the original shares of £100 had dropped in value to £10.[68] The bequest Mary Alt made her sister Frances Hextall in 1808 included 'everything else I may be entitled from the Ashby canal'.[69]

Provision in the form of annuities for female relatives and friends was more common. Women in both towns arranged for mothers, sisters, nieces and female friends to have the interest from a principal sum during their lifetime. However, concern for a relation and family obligations occasionally only lasted as long as the legatee remained unmarried.[70] Analogous to those provisos made by husbands restricting their wives' interest in real and personal estate until they remarried, some female testators felt compelled to add a similar clause in

---

[64]   Chapman, 'The Genesis of the British Hosiery Industry', p. 40.
[65]   Probate inventory of Mary Taylor, Spinster, 1781/73, L.R.O.
[66]   Will of Alice Drought, Wife, 1788/57, L.R.O.
[67]   Will of Mary Birch, Spinster, 1808/20, L.R.O.
[68]   Hadfield, C., *The Canals of the East Midlands* (Newton Abbot: David and Charles, 1976), p. 152.
[69]   Will of Mary Alt, Widow, 1826/6, L.R.O.
[70]   See the chapter by Ann McCrum in this volume.

their wills. In 1765 Susannah Milward stipulated that her sister-in-law would lose the interest from £200 should she marry again.[71] Brothers and nephews were also chosen as the beneficiaries of annuities, and whilst they did not figure so often as recipients, their presence suggests that these legacies should not just be seen as a means of supporting economically inactive women.

Women's strong involvement in money-lending helps explain why cash gifts and income generated from investments were so common. These bequests reflected women's own wealth and areas of expertise, and some widows were keen to protect these interests from sons-in-law or their daughters' prospective husbands. Elizabeth Pullin, for example, left her daughter the Bulls Head and outbuildings with her money on notes and bonds, and all other personal estate on the understanding that these were for Rebecca's 'sole and separate use ... and shall not be liable to the debts, control or engagement of her present or future husband'.[72] Likewise, Elizabeth Richards stipulated in her will that each of her two daughters 'shall have the free and entire disposal each of their own share by deed and will as fully as if she or they were unmarried and in default of such appointment the same shall go and belong to the child or children of them'.[73] Clauses protecting women's property and concerns about husbands 'intermeddling' can be regularly found in both men's and women's wills. This is something that Maxine Berg found in her study of the industrialising communities of Birmingham and Sheffield.[74]

Frame rents

Property in the form of stocking frames gave women an alternative method of income-earning that blended well and reflected their role as money-lenders. Whilst the renting out of machines occurred in other textile industries it never became as widespread as in the hosiery trade.[75] Women in the East Midlands region had, if not a unique opportunity, then certainly one that benefited women in the region. Women who were situated in or close to one of the putting-out centres could take advantage of an industrial structure that, by the fourth decade of the eighteenth century, had made it less usual to find a knitter who owned their own frame. By 1800 it was rare to find one that did.[76] Most of

---

[71] Will of Susannah Milward, Widow, 1765/142, L.R.O.
[72] Will of Elizabeth Pullin, Widow, 1799/152, L.R.O.
[73] Will of Elizabeth Richards, Widow, 1779/171, L.R.O.
[74] Berg, 'Women's Property', p. 248.
[75] Wells, *The British Hosiery and Knitwear Industry*, p. 75.
[76] Ibid., p. 64. A useful investment for the widow or spinster but a source of unceasing hardship for workers in the industry. One of the major complaints made at the 1845 enquiry into the condition of the framework knitters was that as wages had declined frame rents remained static. See Minutes of Evidence, PP, 1845, XV.

the frames were located within villages and small towns and situated roughly within a 6 mile radius of the three main organising centres of which Hinckley was one.[77] Nine women's wills document bequests of stocking frames, all of them from Hinckley. Women also made bequests of money to buy frames. Sarah Seller, a spinster, set aside £10 for her brother to buy his son a stocking frame.[78] This form of legacy is similar to those that provided for the purchase of craft tools or for the funding of an apprenticeship.

Chapman has argued that in the early decades of the eighteenth century this type of investment was popular with 'a large group of widows' who acquired a 'small income' from the ownership of a few frames, and in so doing, avoided a visit to the overseer of the poor.[79] The importance of the rent to widows and spinsters of a small number of frames is demonstrated in wills. Mary Towers in 1823 bequeathed two stocking frames to her niece Mary Ann Wallin as well as all her household goods.[80] In men's wills this type of legacy is even more noticeable. However, whilst two of the frame-owning women left personal estates of below £20, three others had theirs valued at less than £200, £300 and £600. This suggests that frame-letting could be sufficiently profitable to interest all types of women, not only the least wealthy. Much of the capital for the industry came from individuals in the drink trades, although people from most occupations also invested heavily in frames.[81] The will of Elizabeth Jee, proved in 1806, illustrates that she operated as a victualler, owned stocking frames and held real estate.[82] In a number of cases it is clear that that the rents from stocking frames were part of a wider portfolio of money-lending activities. Ann Smith lent money on bonds and notes in addition to profiting from frame rents, as did Mary Towers, who entrusted £140 to her brother, a framesmith.[83] Investment in stocking frames, annuities and real estate all formed part of those combinations of income-earning and wealth-creating activities that helped women spread financial risks. These women, as Churches has pointed out for the economically active widows in the town of Whitehaven in the late seventeenth and early eighteenth centuries, were 'not just a backwater through which property made its sluggish way before finally returning to the mainstream in the hands of a male heir'.[84]

---

[77] Mills, D., 'Rural Industries and Social Structure: Framework Knitters in Leicestershire, 1670–1851', *Textile History* 13 (1982), p. 185.

[78] Will of Sarah Seller, Spinster, 1812/183, L.R.O.

[79] Chapman, 'The Genesis of the British Hosiery Industry', pp. 39–40.

[80] Will of Mary Towers, Widow, 1823/95, L.R.O.

[81] Chapman, *The Genesis of the British Hosiery Industry*, p. 39.

[82] Will of Elizabeth Jee, Victualler, 1806/20, L.R.O.

[83] Will of Ann Smith, Spinster, 1827/168; Will of Mary Towers, Widow, 1823/95, L.R.O.

[84] Churches, 'Women and Property', p. 178.

Executors: relatives and 'friends'

We saw in the earlier part of this chapter that the majority of men chose their wives to act as executors. Whilst female testators favoured female legatees, their preference when it came to executors, as other historians have found, was usually for men.[85] Over three-quarters of women from Hinckley entrusted males to act as executors. For Ashby it was lower at 67.8 per cent (see Table 8.3). This is a reflection of the larger number of spinsters in the Ashby data that selected women to oversee their wills. As this role carried with it great responsibility, the majority of executors were close male and female relatives, for example sons and daughters, sisters and brothers. However, women also chose 'friends', although some of these were probably also distant kin. D'Cruze has identified the existence of a significant minority of men in the middling sort who had a 'heightened public role' in the community of early eighteenth-century Colchester. These men functioned at the core of the political, business and social networks of the town. Importantly, it was via such individuals that others within the middling ranks had to operate since the 'community brokers', as they have been described, were the conduits to credit, political status and office. These men were powerful allies and would be sought out to act, for example, as trustees, executors and witnesses.[86] Jon Stobart, however, offers a different perspective from these hierarchical social links. In the towns of early-eighteenth century Cheshire and south Lancashire, a testator's executors were generally found to be of the same social status.[87]

Bonds of friendship and neighbourliness amongst men bound up with associated business interests make it easier to determine what might have informed these relationships. For women, on the other hand, this is not as straightforward. Of course, the friends of a widow were very likely to be those of her dead husband. These men acted as executors and trustees and assisted with the care and maintenance of children and wives. Male relatives, we know, were frequently called upon on this regard. The appointment of executors and trustees, and the legacies made to 'friends' and relatives, help demonstrate a number of different aspects of business, community and economic change. Davidoff and Hall have argued that women's growing dependence meant greater recourse to financial agents. The manner in which women conducted business and their financial affairs was probably not very different from the

---

[85] Erickson, *Women and Property*, p. 220; see also the chapters by David R. Green and Alastair Owens in this volume.

[86] D'Cruze, S., 'The Middling Sort in Eighteenth Century Colchester: Independence, Social Relations and the Community Broker', in J. Barry and C. Brooks (eds), *The Middling Sort of People: Culture, Society and Politics in England, 1550–1800* (London: Macmillan, 1994), pp. 190–99.

[87] See the chapter by Jon Stobart in this volume.

ways in which men did. However, this would be dependent on the activity. As we have seen, some widows took over and ran businesses after their husbands' demise: women in the victualling trade, for example, appear to have had little trouble in this regard. Nonetheless, other businesses and economic activity required male assistance.

Table 8.3
The appointment of executors, Ashby de la Zouch and Hinckley, 1750–1835

	Females		Males		Females and males	
	No.	%	No.	%	No.	%
Ashby de la Zouch	14	23.7	40	67.8	5	8.5
Hinckley	13	15.9	63	76.8	6	7.3

Source: Wills at Leicester County Record Office.

The rapid development of the hosiery industry in the second half of the eighteenth century was accompanied by structural change with the emergence of middlemen and the extension of frame-letting.[88] Some women may have rented out their frames directly but it is likely that this function was performed by a member of their family or kin. Sarah Bolesworth, for example, bequeathed to her second cousin from nearby Burbage her 'stocking frames or machines now in his possession'.[89] Sarah Hurst, spinster, made hosier John Basford the sole executor of her will and left him 'securities for money, stocking frames, book and other debts ... for his own use and benefit'.[90] Whilst assisting women to buy and rent out frames or conduct other aspects of business can be seen as a means of helping women to secure an income, there could be less altruistic motives behind these actions. The networks engendered by family ties or friendship had a fundamental relationship at their core: manufacturers, masters and middlemen needed money to invest in their businesses or stocks of frames to sub-let and run their work. Middlemen did not operate to any degree within the town of Hinckley but appear to have commonly let frames in the surrounding village areas, and this is where many of the 'independent' frames owned by widows and spinsters went.[91] Erickson contends that 'women made

---

[88]   Many of the 'independent' frames, as they were known, were sub-let to knitters by middlemen.

[89]   Will of Sarah Bolesworth, Spinster, 1819/20, L.R.O.

[90]   Will of Sarah Hurst, Spinster, 1809/107, L.R.O.

[91]   Evidence compiled from trades directories for the last fifty years of the nineteenth century shows that in some areas middlemen were well entrenched whilst in others they were apparently non-existent. Hoskins and McKinley, *The Victoria County History of*

wills out of a need to thank and acknowledge small favours, out of a sense of personal attachment to material goods, in order to help out family and friends in need and from a sense of personal integrity'.[92] However, relatives and 'friends' had a more important role in that they linked women to the wider economy, and in this sense, they were not 'small favours'.

Conclusions

The evidence delineated in this chapter has shown that women's experiences of property-holding could be diverse. Whilst some historians have seen the characteristics of women's property rights in the eighteenth and early nineteenth centuries as promoting a marginalisation in women's position, this study has shown that a host of imperatives arising from inheritance strategies ensured women's continued economic participation. This was especially true for those in the lower ranks of the middle class. The majority of spinsters or widows were unlikely to be as wealthy as men, and financial security would be less easy to obtain. Women, therefore, spread financial risks by engaging in a variety of income-earning and wealth-creating activities. Whether, for example, caring or supporting family members, preserving businesses for themselves or starting new ones and investing in real estate, women did far more than the 'hidden investment' concept implies. The role of women, it can be argued, could be as much about gaining the trappings of status by the accumulation of wealth, as it was through the pretence of economic inactivity. Clearly, some women actively sought to engage in business and extend their interests. Moreover, their reasons for doing so appear to have changed little over the period. Can we really say that these women did not aspire beyond self-support, as some historians have suggested was the aim of the middle-class widow with no other financial provision?[93] Women were, nevertheless, dependent on the economy of the region, the commercial foundations of the towns in which they lived and the social circles they inhabited. However, far from placing constraints on women, industrial development in the East Midlands created 'great prosperity and expansion' in the hosiery industry in the second half of the eighteenth century. This gave women, especially widows and spinsters, in the industrial towns additional opportunities to generate income and increase their levels of wealth.

Leicestershire, pp. 20–23.
    [92]   Erickson, *Women and Property*, p. 209.
    [93]   Davidoff and Hall, *Family Fortunes*, p. 287.

Chapter 9

Independent women, wealth and wills in nineteenth-century London

David R. Green[*]

Introduction

In 1851 the Registrar General noted with some concern that 42 per cent of women aged between twenty and forty were unmarried and that two-thirds of all women were self-supporting.[1] These figures, 'quite disproportionate and quite abnormal', according to William Greg, particularly amongst the middle class, drew attention not only to the 'spinster problem' but also to the large number of widows in Victorian society, many of whom had few prospects of remarriage.[2] The 'redundancy of women', it was argued, was responsible for perverting women's roles in the private sphere of the home and for impelling them into the public world of work. In turn, this posed questions about the domestic role of women as wives and mothers and raised issues about middle-class female education and the incompatibility of genteel status with the necessity of having to work.[3]

Just as contemporaries recognised the growing numbers of single women at one end of the age spectrum so, too, should we recognise their significance at the other. In 1851 spinsters and widows comprised over 42 per cent of women aged above forty-five years, rising to over 67 per cent of those above sixty-five years of age. At one end of the social spectrum, workhouses and outdoor relief lists were filled with working-class widows and elderly women no longer able to cope on their own. In 1841, for example, nearly half the recipients of outdoor relief in England and Wales were widows, rising to 55 per cent in 1846.[4] Even middle-class widows were often left in financial difficulties as a

[*] I would like to thank the Nuffield Foundation for their generous grant in support of some of this research (SOC/100/748).

[1] Poovey, M., *Uneven Developments: The Ideological Work of Gender in Mid-Victorian England* (London: Virago, 1989), p. 6.

[2] Greg, W., 'Why Are Women Redundant?', *National Review* 14 (April 1862), pp. 434–60.

[3] These issues are dealt with more fully elsewhere. See Hall, C., *White, Male and Middle-Class* (Cambridge: Polity, 1992), pp. 189–90.

[4] *Poor Law Commission*, eighth annual report (1841), Table A, pp. 622–3; Table B,

result of the death of their husband, particularly when the household income was dependent mainly on wages as opposed to rental or other sources of investment.[5] Charities, such as the Society for the Relief of Distressed Widows, founded in 1823, sprang up to provide for these distressed gentlewomen. Literary narratives of bourgeois life also made frequent mention of spinsters and widows in a variety of circumstances: as devoted single daughters caring for ageing mothers, as rich maiden aunts or as vindictive and cold-hearted spinsters forever cursing their misfortune at remaining unmarried. In *Emma*, for example, the kind but unexciting Miss Bates, who 'had never boasted either beauty or cleverness', spent her middle life 'devoted to the care of a failing mother, and the endeavour to make a small income go as far as possible'.[6] Dickens's view of spinsters was frequently less charitable: the narrow-minded Miss Murdstone, for example, made the young David Copperfield's life a misery, whilst Miss Havisham in *Great Expectations* plotted revenge on male society and despised her relatives who surrounded her in the expectation of receiving a legacy. Widows also appeared frequently in contemporary novels. In *Middlemarch*, Dorothea was in some ways fortunate at the early death of her husband, both in the sense of being released from having to endure a loveless marriage but also by the fact that with her financial position secure she was subsequently able to remarry according to her own desires. Her situation, however, was perhaps untypical: low rates of remarriage meant that after the death of their husband, most women remained single for the rest of their lives.[7]

These ageing but independent women are the central characters in this paper. As characters, however, they did more than just inhabit an imaginary literary landscape. Indeed, the very frequency with which they appeared in contemporary novels hints at their importance in nineteenth-century society. Moreover, in a legal sense their role as independent actors in relation to the ownership and disposal of wealth makes their position ambiguous in the debate about the separation of gender roles. Gentlemanly capitalism may, indeed, have driven the British economy forward, but the wealth so generated frequently ended up in women's hands. What they did with that wealth and how they distributed it after death are questions that have remained largely unanswered. Independent in both a legal and a financial sense, these women deserve greater attention than they have hitherto received.

This paper addresses three main issues. Firstly, it examines the quantitative significance of independent women as wealth holders in London, based on

---

pp. 630–31; *idem*, 13th annual report (1846), table A, p. 234; table B, p. 240.

    [5] Curran, C., 'Private Women, Public Needs: Middle-Class Widows in Victorian England', *Albion* 25 (1993), p. 225.

    [6] Austen, J., *Emma* (London: Wordsworth Edition, 1992), p. 31.

    [7] Rates of remarriage fell from about 30 per cent in the mid-sixteenth century to 11.27 per cent by 1851. See Curran, 'Private Women, Public Needs', p. 225.

evidence drawn largely from the census and the Probate Act books of the various ecclesiastical courts responsible for proving wills prior to 1858. It is argued that the metropolitan context is particularly important given the disproportionate number of widows and spinsters in London and the relative size of the city's middle class. Secondly, it examines the types of wealth bequeathed by middle-class women at the time of their death, distinguishing between cash, investments in stocks, public funds and other possessions, including leasehold property. Finally, it tries to unravel the bequesting strategies of women and the implications that such practices had for understanding the relationships between kinship, gender and wealth.

Wills and probates

Before answering these questions it is important to be aware of the nature of the data and the problems associated with their interpretation. The main sources of evidence used here relate to probate valuation records derived from the proving of wills in the ecclesiastical courts, as well as the individual wills made by Londoners themselves.[8] The data include an enumeration of all probate valuations of under £100,000 proved in London for 1800, 1830 and 1850, together with a more detailed analysis of women's wills for 1830 where the estate was valued at less than £10,000.[9] In total, 288 such wills have been examined, representing nearly 11 per cent of all wills proved in the capital and 35 per cent of women's wills. The first set of data provides a broad overview of wealth-holding in the capital, whilst the second allows more detailed analysis of the composition of women's wealth and the manner in which it was disposed of after death.[10]

In relation to valuation for probate, the main problems in assessing a testator's wealth concern the ownership of freehold property and the level of debt: leasehold property was included in the valuation for probate, but freehold

---

[8] There were three main ecclesiastical courts in London: the Consistory Court of London, the Commissary Court of London and the Prerogative Court of Canterbury. In terms of the numbers of wills proved, the last-named was of overwhelming importance.

[9] According to the probate data for 1800 there were no more than seventy-five 'upper value' estates of £10,000 or more, comprising a very small proportion of the total recorded for that year. Professor Rubinstein's research for the period from 1809 to 1839 shows that there were 409 London estates valued at above £100,000, an average of less than fourteen per annum. In terms of numbers, upper-value estates comprised a very small number of the total that passed through the remit of the courts. See Rubinstein, W. D., 'The Structure of Wealth-Holding in Britain 1809–39: a Preliminary Anatomy', *Historical Research* 65 (1992), p. 86.

[10] These sources are discussed more fully in Green, D. R. and Owens, A., 'Metropolitan Estates of the Middle Class 1800–50: Probates and Death Duties Revisited', *Historical Research* 70 (1997), pp. 294–311.

real estate was not.[11] Whilst not wishing to deny the problems raised by the exclusion of freehold land, it can be argued on two grounds that it was probably of relatively little consequence in assessing the value of estates in nineteenth-century London. First, much of the city, especially in the west, was owned by large aristocratic estates but housing was held on leasehold.[12] In such cases the value of the leasehold would have been included in the valuation for probate. Secondly, since landownership was correlated with wealth, the omission of land from valuations was probably of lesser importance for estates lower down the economic scale. For eighteenth-century London, Peter Earle has shown that less than 20 per cent of testators with estates worth at least £2000 possessed any real estate. Whilst, at the other end of the spectrum, Rubinstein notes that less than half of those who died between 1873 and 1875 with estates worth more than £100,000 owned land.[13] Since over 80 per cent of London probates in 1800 and 70 per cent in 1830 and 1850 were valued at below £2000, and 90 per cent below £10,000, it is unlikely, therefore, that land ownership would seriously distort the findings discussed here.

By contrast, the question of debt is more intractable since valuation was made on the gross rather than the net value of an estate. Any outstanding debts were therefore excluded from the valuation. This means that in theory an estate with a positive valuation could have been wholly consumed by the burden of debt, and there were instances when this situation undoubtedly arose.[14] More research is needed before we can arrive at a definitive answer to this problem and until that time it is wise to remain cautious about the evidence. However, without denying the significance of the problem, there are some grounds to question the significance of debt in relation to middle-class estates.

First, the disgrace of insolvency perhaps loomed larger in the middle-class conscience than it did for those higher up the social hierarchy. Personal property, in contrast to real estate, was liable to distraint for ordinary or

---

[11] See Holcombe, L., *Wives and Property* (Toronto: University of Toronto Press, 1983), pp. 9–10. Because feudal law tied landownership to the crown, it was legally impossible to dispose of land and for that reason a distinction was made between the two types of property. Strictly speaking, the testament dealt only with moveable property, which over time came to include other types of wealth including stock-in-trade, machinery, stocks, shares, bank deposit and leasehold property, whilst the will referred to real estate. In practice the will and testament were one and the same document.

[12] Summerson, J., *Georgian London* (London: Pleiades, 1945), pp. 23–4. Summerson noted that this system 'brought half London into being'.

[13] Earle, P., *The Making of the English Middle Class* (London: Methuen, 1989), pp. 155–6; Rubinstein, W. D., 'Cutting up Rich: a Reply to F. M. L. Thompson', *Economic History Review*, 2nd series XLV (1992), p. 357. The importance of personal assets compared to real estate for large businessmen has been confirmed by Nicholas, T., 'Businessmen and Land Ownership in the Late Nineteenth Century', *Economic History Review*, 2nd series LII (1999), pp. 27–44.

[14] English, B., 'Probate Valuations and Death Duty registers', *Historical Research* LVII (1984), pp. 83–4.

contract debts and therefore, unlike landed proprietors who could accrue large debts without fear of a forced sale of their estate, non-landed wealth holders could be obliged to sell their assets or face bankruptcy proceedings and possible imprisonment for debt.[15] Fear of bankruptcy was one of the recurring master-narratives of middling culture, as Charles Dickens knew only too well, and in times of need a range of social and family contacts could usually be called on to stave off the ignominy of the debtor's prison.[16]

Furthermore, as R. J. Morris has suggested, individuals were most likely to have accrued debts at certain stages of their life cycle, notably in early adulthood when raising a young family or when starting up in business.[17] Not infrequently, the terms of a will specified sums of money lent to children or younger relatives. Sophia Cracklow, for example, recorded how she had previously lent £1000 to her two nephews and that on her death this sum was to be deemed a bequest.[18] When she died in 1830, Elizabeth Adams was owed £3000 by her son-in-law, which sum was also bequeathed to him in her will.[19] Similarly, 'weighty and delicately balanced structures of credit and debt' characterised most trades, as Margaret Hunt notes, and few individuals could have avoided incurring trading debts in the course of their business.[20] Arthur Tegart, an apothecary from Pall Mall who died in 1839, is a good example. Near the time of his death he recorded in his will that he owed £6639 8s 6d, including a mortgage of £2000 to his brother Edward. His assets, however, far exceeded his liabilities and included real estate valued at £4600 and personal property amounting to £12,260, including monies owing to him of about £3000 and £7310 invested in the Equitable Assurance Company.[21]

Whilst those in trade and commerce were perhaps more likely to have accrued debts than others, it remained the case that most testators were probably at later stages of the family life cycle, when income generally exceeded household expenditure. It would have been less likely for persons at this stage of the life cycle, having accumulated assets over the course of their

---

[15] Staves, S., *Married Women's Separate Property in England 1660–1833* (Cambridge Mass.: Harvard University Press, 1990), p. 92.

[16] Hunt, M., *The Middling Sort: Commerce, Gender and the Family in England 1680–1780* (London: University of California Press, 1996), p. 34. In 1824 Charles Dickens's father was briefly imprisoned in the Marshalsea debtor's prison. This experience formed the backdrop for *Little Dorrit*, published in 1857.

[17] Morris, R. J., 'The Middle Class and the Property Cycle during the Industrial Revolution', in T. C. Smout (ed.), *The Search for Wealth and Stability* (London: Macmillan, 1979), pp. 91–113.

[18] Will of Sophia Cracklow, Public Record Office, PROB 11, film 1772, quire 364. The PROB 11 series contain copies of registered wills proved in the Prerogative Court of Canterbury. Microfilms of the registered wills are held in the Family Records Centre, London.

[19] Will of Elizabeth Adams, PROB 11, film 1766, quire 66.

[20] Hunt, *The Middling Sort*, p. 31.

[21] Will of Arthur Tegart , PROB 11, film 1766, quire 59.

lifetime, to have been burdened with large debts. This fits in well with the life-cycle theory of saving.[22] As Kotlikoff notes in relation to modelling inheritance and the life cycle, 'people save to prepare for their retirement when they must dissave and consume'.[23] During retirement the balance shifts from earnings to expenditure as savings are used to support individuals in their old age. In the absence of adequate pension provision, at some point such individuals may theoretically fall into debt as consumption exceeds earnings. However, in view of lower life-expectancy during the nineteenth century and the likelihood for most people that the period for retirement, or more precisely of incapacity for work because of old age, was relatively short, it is reasonable to assume that at the time of death, most middle-class testators still had a surplus of savings over debt.[24]

The other main issue concerning interpretation of the wills relates to the nature of bequests. As a means of transferring wealth, wills need to be set in the context of the family life cycle as a whole, for death is but one of several occasions at which significant proportions of wealth can be transferred from one generation to another. *Inter vivos* gifts were important aspects of bourgeois life. Marriage, for example, was often the occasion for such transfers, especially in relation to the provision of a dowry for daughters. Under these circumstances, married daughters might only have received token settlements in a will, although in practice they might have been given their share at the time of their marriage. Sons, too, might also have benefited at various points in their life cycle: in addition to marriage, for example, coming of age also frequently entailed the receipt of gifts from parents. Sons were also more likely than daughters to be given a share of the family business whilst their parents were still alive. For these reasons it is important not to see the will as the only mechanism for the inter-generational transfer of wealth but to set it in the broader context of the family life cycle. To do so, however, lies beyond the scope of this chapter, although awareness of the issue must colour interpretation of the evidence.

---

[22] For discussions of this see Modigliani, F., 'Measuring the Contribution of Intergenerational Transfers of Total Wealth: Conceptual Issues and Empirical Findings', in D. Kessler and A. Masson (eds), *Modelling the Accumulation and Distribution of Wealth* (Oxford: Clarendon, 1988), pp. 21–52; *idem*, 'The Role of Intergenerational Transfers and Life Cycle Saving in the Accumulation of Wealth', *Journal of Economic Perspectives* 2 (1988), pp. 15–40; Kotlikoff, L., 'Intergenerational Transfers and Savings', *Journal of Economic Perspectives* 2 (1988), pp. 41–58.

[23] Kotlikoff, 'Intergenerational Transfers and Savings', p. 52.

[24] The question of retirement is dealt with by Nenadic, S., 'Businessmen, the Urban Middle Classes and the "Dominance" of Manufactures in Nineteenth-Century Britain', *Economic History Review*, 2nd series XLIV (1991), p. 68; Davidoff, L. and Hall, C., *Family Fortunes: Men and Women of the English Middle Class 1780–1850*, (London: Hutchinson, 1987), pp. 225–7.

Independent women

In the first half of the nineteenth century single and widowed women outnumbered their adult male counterparts, a fact largely accounted for by the lower age at which women married compared to men, higher rates of male mortality, higher male migration and low rates of remarriage. The excess of women was particularly noticeable in cities such as London, where high demand for domestic servants attracted large numbers of young female migrants.[25] In London in 1851 women aged twenty-five and above outnumbered men by more than 104,000. In turn, this excess meant that many women living in the city inevitably remained single. Of course, lack of opportunity was not the only reason why women remained single. Though for many women marriage was a moral duty as well as a financial necessity, it was also a source of romantic love and personal happiness. Nevertheless, they could and did choose not to marry for a variety of reasons.[26] At the same time, for the reasons already mentioned, those who did marry faced the likelihood that they would become widows prematurely. Since both widows and spinsters were, in the legal sense, independent women, the outcome of these two sets of processes was that in London this group was of particular importance, especially amongst the older population.

Table 9.1
Status of London population aged 25 and above, 1851

	Single		Married		Widowed	
	No.	Per cent	No.	Per cent	No.	Per cent
Female	153,250	13.3	366,631	31.8	109,217	9.5
Male	111,267	9.6	376,424	32.6	36,773	3.2
Total	2,644,517	22.9	743,055	64.4	145,990	12.7

Source: 1851 census.

In 1851, for the first time, the census provided information about the proportion of the population that was married, single or widowed. In Britain as a whole, Michael Anderson notes that spinsters and widows accounted for

---

[25] Schwarz, L., *London in the Age of Industrialization* (Cambridge: Cambridge University Press, 1992), pp. 15–16, 46. Schwarz notes that in 1851 more than half the female labour force was engaged in domestic service and London accounted for more than one in five female domestic servants recorded in the census for England and Wales.

[26] From mid-century, debates about spinsterhood were linked to changes in the legal and economic status of women. See Freeman R. and Klaus, P., 'Blessed or Not? The New Spinster in England and the United States in the Late Nineteenth and Early Twentieth Centuries', *Journal of Family History* 9 (1984), pp. 394–414.

nearly 10 per cent of the population aged twenty-five and above.[27] In London, however, the proportion was nearly 23 per cent for women compared to only 13 per cent for men (Table 9.1). In other words, nearly one in four adult women in the city was single. Furthermore, as a result of the early onset of widowhood this proportion increased with age. Figure 9.1 shows that nearly half the women aged twenty and above were married, rising to nearly 70 per cent of those aged thirty or more. Women who had not married by the age of thirty were likely to have remained spinsters for the rest of their lives, and this group comprised a steady 20 per cent of the female population above that age. By the time women reached their sixties, nearly two-thirds were single, either because they had never married or, more likely, because they were widows.[28]

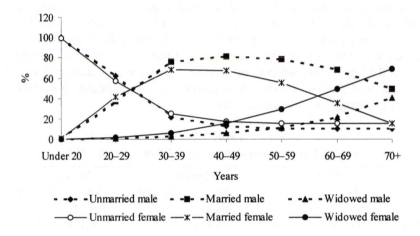

Figure 9.1: 'Conjugal condition' of the population, London 1851

Further evidence of the significance of independent women is provided in the 1851 census by the inclusion of information, albeit flawed, on the occupational status of women. In that year married women, widows and women of independent means were included under separate occupational categories as 'gentlewomen' and 'annuitants'. Though the terms themselves are ambiguous, the sense in which they were used implies that women recorded under these categories had no need to support themselves through paid

---

[27] Anderson, M., 'The Social Position of Spinsters in mid-Victorian Britain', *Journal of Family History* 9 (1984), p. 378.

[28] Of those aged 50–59 years, 15.3 per cent were single and 29.5 per cent widowed. For those aged 60–69 years, the figures were 15.5 per cent and 48.8 per cent respectively.

employment. This is evident when considering the age structure of women classified in this manner. Over 25,000 women were recorded under these categories, comprising a little over 3.3 per cent of the total adult female population. In terms of women's estates, however, what is more revealing is the proportion of different age groups accounted for by these categories. As Figure 9.2 shows, the older age groups were singularly over-represented, especially those aged between sixty and seventy-four years. Age alone would have precluded many of these women from entry to the labour market and it is far more likely that they were in fact widows and spinsters living independently from unearned income. In London over 40 per cent of women described as living off independent means were aged 60 and above. Similarly, in Birmingham and Essex two-thirds of independent women were aged over fifty-five.[29] The evidence of the census, coupled with the significance of such characters in narratives of middle-class life, suggests that they were a common feature of Victorian urban society.

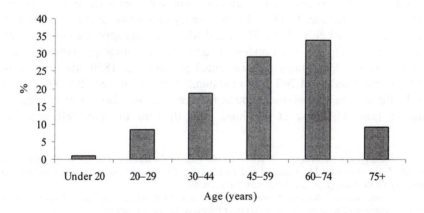

Figure 9.2: Age structure of gentlewomen and annuitants, London 1851

Women as testators

The demographic and social significance of independent women was mirrored by their importance as testators. For married women, the transition in a legal sense from dependence to independence occurred with the death of their husband. Upon marriage women 'died a kind of civil death' since, according to Blackstone, husband and wife were considered to be one person and that

---

[29] Davidoff and Hall, *Family Fortunes*, p. 314.

person was the husband.[30] Apart from property specified by making a separate legal settlement before or after marriage, or by consent of their husbands, married women had few legal rights to the ownership of personal property. Other than this separate settled wealth, wives had no right to dispose of their property through the mechanism of a will. Indeed, it was not until the Married Women's Property Act of 1882 that they were finally able to dispose of their property as they wished.[31] Therefore, in a legal sense, women were reborn as independent actors only upon the death of their husband. In common with their spinster counterparts, widows regained some legal parity with men, including the right to run a business in their own name and to the disposal of property on their own death. For both widows and spinsters, as Anny Sadrin has remarked, 'financial autonomy was the prerogative of the unwedded, the sentimentally deprived'.[32]

To understand the significance of women's estates, it is important to set them in the wider context of will making as a whole. In London, persons who died with personal goods, or *bona notabilia*, valued at £10 or more were required to have their estates proved by an ecclesiastical court.[33] Administrators appointed by the probate courts dealt those whose estates reached these figures but who died intestate. In 1841 for the country as a whole about 13.4 per cent of adults who died either left wills or had administrators appointed to deal with their estates.[34] Figures for London suggest that a similar proportion of the population also left estates that warranted probate.[35] In 1850 adult deaths in London amounted to 24,706 whilst the number of wills under £100,000 proved in the three main ecclesiastical courts for that year was 2811, which suggests that at least 11 per cent of those who died in the city left wills. If

---

[30] Collyer, J., *A Practical Treatise on the Law of Partnership* (1832), p. 72, quoted in Davidoff, L., Doolittle, M., Fink, J., and Holden, K., *The Family Story: Blood, Contact and Intimacy 1830–1960* (London: Longman, 1999), p. 62.

[31] See Staves, *Married Women's Property* and Holcombe, *Wives and Property* for a fuller discussion of women's legal rights over property during this period.

[32] Sadrin, A., *Parentage and Inheritance in the Novels of Charles Dickens* (Cambridge: Cambridge University Press, 1994), p. 10.

[33] Falconer, T., *On Probate Courts* (London: Reynel and Weight, 1850), p. 5. Executors of estates that fell below the threshold could still seek probate but were not required by law to do so. The laws of *bona notabilia*, however, were complex and unclear even to contemporaries. See Parliamentary Paper (PP) 1833 XXII *Law of Real Property: Fourth Report (wills)*, pp. 45–7; The best general introduction to the legal aspects of will making in this period is Camp, A. J., *Wills and their Whereabouts* (published by the author, 1974), pp. ix–xi. See also the chapter by Alastair Owens in this volume.

[34] In 1841 for England and Wales as a whole, 16,701 wills and 6,297 administrations were submitted to the Legacy Duty Office. The total number of adult deaths (aged over twenty years) in England and Wales in 1841 was 171,234. See PP 1843 XXI *Fifth Annual Report of the Registrar General of Births, Deaths and Marriages*, pp. 422–3.

[35] The evidence presented here refers solely to wills and excludes administrations, known as 'admons', that dealt with those who died intestate.

administrations are included, this figure rises to about 13.3 per cent of those who died.[36] As noted above, the very small number of estates valued above £100,000 would raise this percentage only very slightly.

In comparison to other places, women formed a large proportion of those who left wills in London. As Table 9.2 illustrates, about a third of London testators were female.[37] Elsewhere the percentage of female testators was lower. In eighteenth-century Birmingham and Sheffield, Berg suggests figures of 22.8 per cent and 18.1 per cent respectively; Davidoff and Hall estimate a figure of 28 per cent for Birmingham and Essex between 1780 and 1850, and, in Stockport between 1800 and 1857, Owens suggests a figure of 21 per cent.[38] In view of the fact that the proportion of Londoners leaving wills was comparable to the country as a whole, this over-representation of female testators most likely reflects factors peculiar to the city itself. Easier access to the legal system and greater levels of financial autonomy may have been important but what was probably of most significance was the relatively high proportion of widows and spinsters in the metropolitan population as a whole, as noted previously. In keeping with their demographic importance, widows comprised the majority of female testators in London, as the figures in Table 9.3 demonstrate. Between 1800 and 1850, they accounted for over half of women's wills, with spinsters increasing their share from nearly 28 per cent to 32 per cent over the same period. The remainder included the small number of married women who made wills as well as those for whom no status was given.

Table 9.2
Wills below £100,000 proved in London, 1800, 1830 and 1850

	Total	Male		Female	
		No.	Per cent	No.	Per cent
1800	2086	1375	63.9	711	34.1
1830	2661	1790	67.3	870	32.7
1850	2811	1858	66.1	953	33.9

Source: Prerogative Court of Canterbury, Probate Act Books; Commissary Court of London, Register of Wills; Consistory Court of London Register of Wills.

[36] See Green and Owens, 'Metropolitan Estates of the Middle Class', p. 297.

[37] Women's greater longevity might suggest that they would form a larger proportion of those leaving wills, but the number of women testators was curtailed by their legal status and the restrictions imposed upon them by their husband's wills, as well as their economic marginality. See Davidoff and Hall, *Family Fortunes*, p. 276.

[38] Berg, M., 'Women's Property and the Industrial Revolution', *Journal of Interdisciplinary History* XXIV (1993), p. 237; Davidoff and Hall, *Family Fortunes*, p. 273; for Stockport see the chapter by Alastair Owens in this volume.

Table 9.3
Status of female testators

	Spinster		Widow		Not given/other	
	No.	Per cent	No.	Per cent	No.	Per cent
1800	196	27.6	377	53.0	138	19.4
1830	284	32.6	479	55.1	107	12.3
1850	301	31.6	557	58.4	95	10.0

Source: Prerogative Court of Canterbury, Probate Act Books; Commissary Court of London,
         Register of Wills; Consistory Court of London, Register of Wills.

Women as wealth holders

Our understanding of wealth holding in nineteenth-century Britain is based
largely on the fortunes accumulated by men, often derived from the pursuit of
gentlemanly capitalism in London itself.[39] Despite the fact that women
accounted for about a third of all testators in London, we know relatively little
about their role as wealth holders. This section, therefore, explores the
significance of their estates compared to men's and the nature of their wealth
holding.

London not only provided opportunities to amass vast amounts of wealth for
those at the upper ends of the social scale but it also opened up myriad ways
for those lower down the hierarchy to make more modest fortunes. Pierce Egan
in *Tom and Jerry: Life in London*, wrote how

> London is the looking glass for talent – it is the faithful emporium of
> the enterprising, the bold, the timid, the bashful individual ... In no
> other place can FORTUNE be so successfully wooed as in London;
> and in no other place does she distribute her favours with so liberal a
> hand.[40]

---

[39] This has been the subject of extensive research. See Nenadic, 'Businessmen', pp. 66–
85; Rubinstein, W. D., 'Wealth, Elites and the Class Structure of Modern Britain', *Past and
Present* 76 (1976), pp. 99–126; Rubinstein, W. D., 'The Victorian Middle Classes: Wealth,
Occupation and Geography', *Economic History Review*, XXX (1977), pp. 602–23; Rubinstein,
W. D., *Men of Property* (London: Croom Helm, 1981); Rubinstein, W. D., *Capitalism, Culture
and Decline in Britain 1750–1990* (London: Routledge, 1993), pp. 25–31. See also the chapter
by W. D. Rubinstein in this volume. Rubinstein's views have not gone unchallenged. See
Berghoff, H., 'British businessmen as wealth holders 1870–1914: a closer look', *Business
History* 33 (1991), pp. 222–40.

[40] Egan, P., *Tom and Jerry: Life in London* (London, 1869, first published 1821);
quoted in Morris, R. J., 'Civil Society and the Nature of Urbanism: Britain 1750–1850', *Urban
History* 25 (1998), p. 295.

Accordingly, what is so striking about the overall distribution of estates in London is not that the few were so large but rather that the many were so small. Opportunities for setting up in business were plentiful, especially in the finishing trades such as furniture-making or tailoring that required relatively little start-up capital. In clothing, for example, it was relatively easy to set up as a sweater, the only requirement being security of between £5 and £50, whilst in furniture-making £3 or £4 was sufficient to start work.[41] For many women, small-scale manufacturing, retailing and the provision of food, drink and lodgings provided a means of accumulating small amounts of wealth in their own right. Using fire insurance records, David Barnett has recently calculated that between 1819 and 1825 there were over 1000 firms in London owned by women, nearly 90 per cent of which were insured for less than £500.[42]

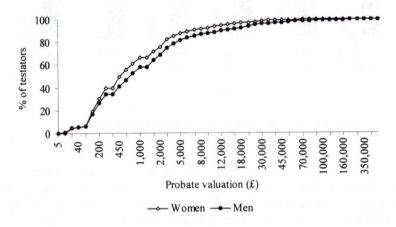

Figure 9.3: Probate valuations, London 1830

The significance of small-scale businesses was matched by the growing importance of commerce, the professions and white-collar work in the capital, all of which added to the opportunities to amass non-landed wealth. Not surprisingly, perhaps, the probate evidence reflects these myriad opportunities for accumulating wealth lower down the social hierarchy. Figure 9.3 shows

---

[41] Mayhew, H., *The Morning Chronicle Survey,* vol. 1, (Firle: Caliban, 1980; first published in 1849–50), pp. 115, 119; *idem,* vol. 5 (1982), pp. 194 and 200; *Northern Star,* 14 September 1844.

[42] Barnett, D., *London, Hub of the Industrial Revolution* (London: Tauris, 1998), p. 209.

that for all estates valued at £100,000 or less, 89 per cent of male estates and 93 per cent of female estates were valued at £10,000 or lower. What this suggests is that although London undoubtedly had more than its fair share of millionaires and half millionaires, what was perhaps of even greater significance was the mass of smaller middle-class wealth holders who fleshed out the social hierarchy. As suggested above, women were by no means an insignificant section of this body.

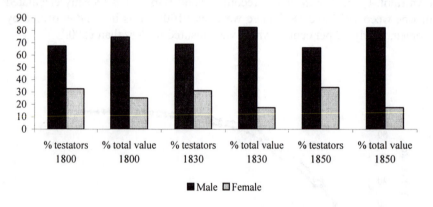

Figure 9.4: Testators and probate valuation, London 1800–1850

Throughout the period, evidence from the probate registers confirms that women were under-represented in terms of the total valuation of estates. As Figure 9.4 shows, whilst they formed about a third of all testators in 1800, 1830 and 1850, their share of the total value of estates fell from just over 25 per cent in 1800 to 17.5 per cent in 1850. We can do little more at this stage than speculate as to why this situation arose: the variation may reflect little more than anomalies in the data, although the pattern does suggest that the economic position of middle-class women was deteriorating in relation to men. This finding would echo the view of those who argue that increasing restrictions on middle-class women's ability to pursue their own livelihoods was a characteristic of the period, resulting from the evangelical emphasis on the strict separation of gender roles in nineteenth-century society.[43]

---

[43] The argument for a deterioration in the economic status of middle-class women is made by several authors including Davidoff and Hall, *Family Fortunes*, pp. 272–9, 305–8; Hall, *White, Male and Middle-Class*, pp. 75–93. This position has not gone unchallenged. See Hunt, *The Middling Sort*, pp. 125–46; Vickery, A., 'Golden Age to Separate Spheres', *Historical Journal* 36 (1993), pp. 383–414.

Interestingly, the reduction in the relative share of wealth accounted for by women's estates over the period parallels the findings of David Barnett in relation to the value of fire insurance policies also taken out by women between 1775 and 1825. According to this set of data, excluding the highly-capitalized firms of merchants, factors, brokers and wholesalers, women's share of capital value insured fell from 50 per cent in the 1770s to 32 per cent in the 1820s.[44] The evidence therefore suggests that in relative terms at least, women's share of wealth was falling in the first half of the nineteenth century.

The structure of women's wealth

A more detailed picture of women's wealth can be built up from the evidence contained in the wills themselves. Here, attention is focused on those women whose estates were valued at below £10,000 in 1830, partly because of the difficulties in collecting the data themselves but primarily because the vast majority of both female and male testators left estates sworn below this value. The process of inheritance was a complex business, entangled in the requirements of various labyrinthine legal systems, shrouded in the emotional bonds of love and affection, directed by moral duty and informed by the perceived economic needs of individuals within the family. Law, custom and family feeling, therefore, structured the pattern of inheritance and determined the nature of the last will and testament, the legal document by which inheritance was conducted. However, unlike the situation in France and Scotland, the reluctance of the English law to involve itself in dictating the terms of bequests allowed individuals free rein to dispose of their property as they wished, unencumbered by any legal requirements.[45] The contents of a will, therefore, can be used to tease out the complex interplay between moral duty, emotional attachment, individual character and family relationships.

---

[44] Barnett, *London*, p. 209.

[45] See Finch, J., Mason, J., Masson, J. Wallis, L., and Hayes, L., *Wills, Inheritance and Families* (Oxford: Clarendon Press, 1996), pp. 21–2; Staves, S., 'Resentment or Resignation? Dividing the Spoils Among Daughters and Younger Sons' in J. Brewer and S. Staves (eds), *Early Modern Conceptions of Property* (London: Routledge, 1995), pp. 199–200; Wedgwood, J., *The Economics of Inheritance* (Harmondsworth: Penguin, 1939), p. 90–100. For more detailed discussion of the inheritance practices in France see Diefendorf, B., 'Women and Property in Ancien Regime France: Theory and Practice in Dauphine and Paris', in Brewer and Staves, *Early Modern Conceptions of Property*, pp. 170–93; Hanlon, G., and Carruthers, E., 'Wills, Inheritance and the Moral Order in Seventeenth-Century Agenais', *Journal of Family History* 15 (1990), pp. 149–61; Laferrère, A., 'Inheritances and Gifts *Inter Vivos*: the Use of "Disposable Portion" for the Purpose of Unequal Division Between Siblings in France', *Continuity and Change* 7 (1992), pp. 377–404. For Scotland see the chapter by Ann McCrum in this volume.

Table 9.4
Bequests mentioned in women's wills, London 1830

	No. of wills	Per cent of wills
Cash	136	47.2
Stocks (consols, bank deposits)	84	29.2
Shares	5	1.7
Leasehold property	43	14.9
Real estate	13	4.5

Source: Sample of 288 wills proved in the Prerogative Court of Canterbury, 1830.
Note: Other forms of bequests, including personal possessions, valuables and household
         items were frequently mentioned but are not included in this table.

The main categories of wealth noted in women's wills are outlined in Table 9.4 and refer to the number of occasions on which specific categories of bequest were mentioned. Gifts of cash, ranging from £2 to £3000, were recorded in just under half the wills, and holdings of stocks, mainly in the form of consols and bank deposits, were noted in 29 per cent of estates.[46] Though cash bequests were mentioned more frequently, the average recorded amount was relatively small compared to the value of stocks: £146 in money compared to £811 in other investments. By contrast, the ownership of real estate, and to a lesser extent leasehold property, was recorded for only one in five estates. This figure contrasts sharply with work elsewhere: Berg found that 48 per cent of female testators in Birmingham and Sheffield owned real estate, whilst Owens's evidence for Stockport suggests a figure of 55 per cent.[47] This in itself is important because it lends weight to the earlier suggestion that in London the exclusion of real estate in the overall probate valuation is a relatively minor problem confined to a small proportion of wills. Nevertheless, when it was recorded, the ownership of leaseholds and real estate was not unimportant as a source of wealth. Mary North of Queen Street, Chelsea, for example, provided her son and daughter each with an annuity of £20 from the proceeds of three freehold messuages in Wandsworth.[48] Similarly, Hannah Waugh gave her married daughter, Jane Purvis, four leasehold houses for sale or separate use, free from the debts of her husband. Upon her death, the property was to be put in trust for her children and the proceeds divided equally.[49]

---

[46] The evidence of different types of wealth refers to the nature of the bequest. The assumption made here is that the nature of the bequest was a direct reflection of the type of wealth owned. Thus a gift of cash actually represented the ownership of money rather than a sum that could be raised by the sale of some other asset.

[47] Berg, 'Women's Property', p. 241; and the chapter by Alastair Owens in this volume.

[48] Will of Mary North, PROB 11, film 1767, quire 109.

[49] Will of Hannah Waugh, PROB 11, film 1766, quire 64.

Taking this analysis a stage further, and somewhat more tentatively, where types of property were specified as individual bequests in wills, it is possible to estimate the broad structure of wealth-holding. The assumption here is that specific bequests made in the will represent real holdings that belonged to the testator prior to their death. Of the total sample of wills, ninety-eight (34 per cent) included information about specific amounts of either stocks or cash and twenty (6.9 per cent) mentioned both. In a small number of additional cases the amounts mentioned in the will exceeded the probate valuation and in the absence of any additional evidence that the valuation was re-sworn at a higher value; these have been excluded from the analysis. Since the valuation of each will is known through probate, and assuming that estates were valued at the upper limit of their valuation banding, it is theoretically possible to estimate the relative share accounted for by stocks, cash and other forms of property such as household items and personal possessions.[50] In order to do so, it is necessary to subtract the various amounts in cash and stocks from the total valuation, leaving a residuary amount which was the value of all other property. For example, Ann Lott's estate was valued at £3000 on her death and consisted of £1200 in 4 per cent stocks bequeathed equally to her two sisters, a further £300 which was invested in 4 per cent stocks that were to be sold off and divided equally between six nieces and nephews, £70 in cash which was to be given to her remaining seven nieces and nephews, £90 to other named beneficiaries plus £12 to be spent on mourning rings. In addition, she owned four Waterloo Bridge annuities which were bequeathed to Jane Carpenter, one of her nieces and daughter of her executor. In her case, stocks accounted for at least 50 per cent of the estate, cash for nearly 6 per cent, leaving the remainder – a maximum of £1328 or 45 per cent of the estate – in the form of personal possessions left to one of her two sisters.[51]

Following this approach for the sample of 118 wills noted above we can estimate the average distribution of the different types of wealth. Bequests of stocks and shares accounted for 14 per cent, cash bequests for 21 per cent of probated wealth, leaving on average 65 per cent in the form of personal property, including furniture, clothing, bedding, china, plate and other valuables and personal possessions, in addition to leasehold property.[52] Using the same method, in the subset of twenty wills for which specific amounts of both stocks and cash were noted, the relative share of each type of property was 37 per cent, 19 per cent and 44 per cent respectively for stocks, cash and other property. Relatively few women owned stocks. Of those who did, this

---

[50] For discussion of the banding of valuations see Green and Owens, 'Metropolitan Estates of the Middle Class', pp. 300–301.

[51] Will of Ann Tempest Lott, PROB 11, film 1786, quire 186.

[52] For discussion of the significance of this type of property, see the chapters by Lorna Scammell and Geoffrey Crossick in this volume.

form of wealth was more likely to have formed a larger proportion of their estates. Table 9.5 illustrates this point by examining the proportion of an estate accounted for by these different forms of wealth. In general terms, cash tended to form a smaller proportion of estates than stocks. Approximately one in six women held cash equivalent to half the estate valuation compared to nearly half which held a similar proportion of their wealth in stocks. When amounts were specified, the average cash sum mentioned was £146, accounting for 23.8 per cent of an estate's value, compared to £811 in stocks, or 46.4 per cent of the valuation. These proportions, based on the sample of 118 wills, correspond broadly with the pattern noted in the subset of twenty wills that mentioned both stocks and cash, as discussed above. The results therefore lend further credence to the methodology adopted.

Table 9.5

Bequest of cash and stocks as a percentage of estate valuation

Per cent of estate valuation	No. of wills mentioning cash	No. of wills mentioning stocks
Under 10	47	1
10–29	35	13
30–49	15	7
Over 50	21	18
Total number	118	39

Source: See Table 9.3.

Clearly, the results outlined above rest on some general assumptions that need further qualification and should therefore be treated with some caution. However, they mirror the findings of research elsewhere. Davidoff and Hall, for example, note how women accounted for up to 20 per cent of loan capital in late eighteenth-century provincial towns whilst they also invested in a variety of joint-stock undertakings.[53] In London. the evidence suggests that women of even modest fortunes not infrequently held investments in a variety of stocks and shares, most notably in consols. Although returns were generally low, averaging around 3.6 per cent between 1820 and 1839, such investments provided safe, long-term annuities.[54] Many women would have inherited these from their husband's or father's estates, but equally there was nothing to prevent them investing in such funds in their own right. For spinsters, more

---

[53] Davidoff and Hall, *Family Fortunes*, pp. 211–12; and also the chapter by Penelope Lane in this volume.
[54] Mitchell, B. and Deane, P., *Abstract of British Historical Statistics* (Cambridge: Cambridge University Press, 1962), p. 455.

than widows – who could expect to rely on children to look after them in later life – annuities provided a means of ensuring that they could be cared for in their old age and, in that sense, they could be seen as an insurance policy against living too long.[55] In this respect women in London appeared to behave no differently to those elsewhere.[56]

Whilst the evidence suggests that about a third of middle-class women who left estates held investments in stocks and annuities, without further research the question of how they became involved in the financial sector is more difficult to answer. In part, the growing importance of the financial sector in the late eighteenth and nineteenth centuries provided more opportunities for middle-class investors as a whole, and as such women's involvement merely paralleled that of their male counterparts. However, two further processes were also important. First, and perhaps of most significance, husbands and fathers frequently left property in trust for their surviving spouse and children, the conditions of which usually involved maintaining the capital and providing for surviving relatives from the interest. Under such circumstances, widows' and spinster children's estates would have included any capital investments left in trust for their use.[57] For this reason it is important not just to assume that women's wealth at the time of death reflected their own notion of value.

A second and contrasting explanation rests on the likelihood that women invested in stocks and shares in their own right, a situation which was probably more likely in London where access to financial information was easier than in the provinces. From the eighteenth century, as Davidoff and Hall, Hunt and others have argued in relation to the middle class, growing separation of the public world of productive work from the private domestic realm of reproduction was paralleled by the gendered separation of male and female spheres of activity.[58] Middle-class women were increasingly excluded from conducting trade and therefore may have looked to alternative sources of making money, such as investment in the growing financial market, rentier income from the ownership of real estate or leasehold property, money-lending or letting lodgings.[59] For an earlier period, Peter Earle has noted the 'enormous importance of women, particularly widows, in the London investment market', and the evidence presented here suggests that this pattern continued or may even have intensified during the nineteenth century.[60] Whether women's

---

[55] Kessler, D. and Masson, P., 'Introduction' in *idem* (eds), *Modelling The Accumulation And Distribution Of Wealth*, p. 6; Menchik, P., 'Unequal Estate Division? Is it altruism, reverse bequests or simply noise?', in Kessler and Masson, *Modelling The Accumulation And Distribution Of Wealth*, p. 108.

[56] Davidoff and Hall, *Family Fortunes*, p. 211.

[57] This topic is the subject of further research by the author.

[58] See n. 40.

[59] Hunt, *The Middling Sort*, p. 146; see also the chapter by Lane in this volume.

[60] Earle, *Making of the English Middle Class*, pp. 171–4.

investments in the financial markets came through inheritance or choice, or a mixture of both, requires further research. However, it is likely that many women were active participants in the financial markets and made clear choices in relation to the nature of their investments.

Women's wills and social networks

In addition to recording the ownership of wealth, wills can also be used to shed light on the social relationships that existed between the testator and their family and friends.[61] What is at issue here is the role of gender in structuring social relations concerning bequesting strategies. Under English law, the relative freedom to dispose of one's property as one wished meant that the terms of the will could be used to recognise not only the traditional bonds of familial duty but also those of a more emotional nature. The terms of bequests and the choice of executors, in particular, allow us to explore the broader social implications embodied in wills and enable us to link individuals into broader networks of family and friends.

Executors

In relation to administering estates, executors were placed in a public position of trust, not only to administer the terms and conditions of the will itself but also to gather the estate for the purposes of probate valuation, arrange for the will to be proved and distribute any legacies.[62] In the majority of cases, testators appointed either one or two executors to carry out their wishes after death.[63] Of the sample of wills examined here 84 per cent of testators (N=242) appointed one or more executors to administer their estate. Although the norm was to have either one or two, in a small number of cases three were appointed. The remainder failed to appoint an executor, often because the will was hastily drawn up shortly before death and there was probably insufficient time to enquire about executors. As the figures in Table 9.6 show, it was more common to appoint male executors, either singly or as a pair, than it was to appoint other women, reflecting the importance of male relatives and friends, as well as the fact that many single women lived with their sibling brothers and chose them to administer their estate. However, in over a third of the cases

---

[61] Nearly 90 per cent of wills examined here were proved in the same year that they were written, confirming the fact that most people made their will when death was near.

[62] See the chapter by Alastair Owens in this volume.

[63] Wills without executors were known as 'admons with wills annexed'. Since many wills were made close to death, it may not always have been possible for female testators, many of whom were widows, to appoint executors.

female testators appointed other women to act as executors and in nearly a quarter of the wills women took on the duties of executors alone.

Table 9.6
Executor's gender, London 1830

Executor	No. of wills	Per cent of wills
Male	85	35.1
Male + Male	66	27.3
Male + Male + Male	5	2.1
Male + Male + Female	1	0.4
Female	48	19.8
Female + Female	9	3.7
Female + Male	27	11.2
Female + Female + Female	1	0.4
Total	242	100.0

Source: See Table 9.3.

Table 9.7
Widows and spinsters: gender of executors, London 1830

Testator's status	Female		Male		Total
	No.	Per cent	No.	Per cent	No.
Spinster	41	37.3	69	62.7	110
Widow	49	22.4	170	77.6	219
Total	90	27.4	239	72.6	329

Source: See Table 9.3.

The likelihood of appointing a female executor varied according to the marital status of the testator. Table 9.7 shows that spinsters were more likely than widows to prefer other women as executors, possibly as a result of the frequency with which single women shared accommodation. Over one in three spinsters appointed at least one female executor compared to one in five widows. For example, Ann Lanchester, a bookseller residing in Leman Street, Whitechapel, appointed her sister Martha, with whom she lived, as her sole executor and left her the entire estate.[64] Matilda Eccles, who also lived with her unmarried sister, did likewise, also leaving her the entire estate valued at

---

[64] Will of Ann Lanchester, PROB 1776, film 561, quire 281.

£100.[65] Affection as well as proximity could also influence the choice of executor. Elizabeth Curby, for example, appointed her friend Elizabeth Wilford, who lived in a neighbouring street, as sole executor and beneficiary of her will, whilst Ann Gunnell left her 'faithful attendant' Sarah Pettygrove the bulk of her estate, including £4600 in consols together with gold plate, linen and various personal effects.[66]

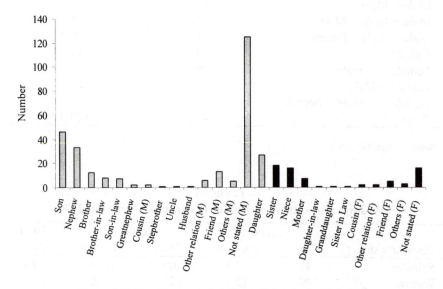

Figure 9.5: Executor's relationship to testators, London 1830

In view of the importance of executors, and the need to have a detailed knowledge of the testator's financial as well as familial affairs, it is hardly surprising that most were likely to have been relations of the deceased. When the executor's relationship to the testator was stated, or when it was possible to establish the relationship by reference to the links with beneficiaries, it appears that three-quarters of executors were close relations, the remainder being made up by other relations and friends in equal measure.[67] One has to be somewhat cautious of these figures, however, especially in relation to male executors since it is often impossible to infer a family connection by surname alone. Leaving aside this problem, Figure 9.5 shows that sons were most frequently

---

[65] Will of Matilda Eccles, PROB 11, film 1766, quire 84.

[66] Will of Ann Gunnell, PROB 11, film 1766, quire 89.

[67] But see the chapter by Jon Stobart in this volume.

appointed, followed by nephews, daughters, sisters and nieces. Not surprisingly, older family members were rarely appointed although it was not uncommon for mothers to act as executors for their daughters – a task that must have been tinged with considerable sadness at the loss of a child and a reminder that mortality was not solely the fate of the elderly.

Heirs

Davidoff and Hall argue that differences in inheritance practices were an important distinction between the middle classes and their social superiors. Whilst the aristocracy and large landed proprietors tended to practice primogeniture, the middle class practised partible inheritance, disposing of wealth to various family members rather than bequesting it to one.[68] In their study of 622 Birmingham and Essex wills from the middle class, they noted that the absence of primogeniture was 'striking' with evidence of partible inheritance appearing in 79 per cent of their sample.[69] The inheritance practices of women in London, outlined in Table 9.8, mirror closely those described by Davidoff and Hall with just under 73 per cent practising some form of partible inheritance. Also in keeping with their findings, the evidence here suggests that behaviour was influenced by wealth, since testators with smaller fortunes were far more likely than those with greater wealth to leave their property to one beneficiary. Table 9.8 shows that those with estates valued at less than £500 more frequently had three or fewer heirs than those with estates worth more than £2000. Clearly, the greater the fortune, the more scope there was to include a larger number of beneficiaries. This reminds us that whilst gender was an important factor structuring the ways in which inheritance was practiced so, too, was wealth, and these must be considered together.

Table 9.8
Inheritance practices, London 1830

Value of estate	No. of heirs			
	1	2–3	4–5	Over 5
Under £500	57	55	24	25
£500–1999	12	20	12	29
Over £2000	6	4	10	23
Total	75	79	46	77
Per cent of wills	27	29	17	28

Source: See Table 9.3.

---

[68] Wedgwood, *Economics of Inheritance*, pp. 164–5.
[69] Davidoff and Hall, *Family Fortunes*, p. 206.

Gender was certainly a strong influence on the ways in which wealth was passed down from women to sons, daughters and other relatives and friends. The clear delimitation of separate and gendered spheres amongst the bourgeoisie meant that whilst sons were expected to earn their own living, daughters were confined largely to domestic roles as wives and mothers. In terms of the gendered transmission of wealth through inheritance, the implications of this are twofold: on the one hand sons were more likely to have been provided with *inter vivos* gifts during the lifetime of the testator as a means of setting up in business, whilst, on the other, their ability to make their own way in life meant that there was less economic need to provide for them through inheritance. Perhaps for these reasons, when it came to appointing a universal heir, or residual legatee (who would normally expect to receive the bulk of the estate after all legacies and debts had been settled), the tendency was to favour women over men.[70] Sarah Sharpe, for example, left each of her two unmarried daughters, Anne and Catherine, £1117 in South Sea annuities and consols, half of the leasehold on her house in Nelson Terrace, Stoke Newington and half the residual property. She also prayed 'that there will be no dissent between my children after my death. And I trust and feel assured that my dear sons will render every assistance and comfort to their sisters who not having it in their power to increase their fortune as their brothers have by their own industry'.[71] Indeed, given the lack of opportunities for middle-class women to earn their own living, daughters and nieces relied heavily on their family to make provision for them, without which they were in a vulnerable economic position, especially in relation to securing a 'good' marriage.[72]

Whilst it was not necessarily the case that the residual legatee received the bulk of an estate, the evidence here suggests that in most cases they could expect a sizeable bequest. In terms of those estates in which at least two beneficiaries were named, the residual legatee, if such existed, could expect on average to receive approximately 84 per cent of the total probated worth of the estate.[73] This figure varied depending on the total number of beneficiaries named in the will, not surprisingly being higher when the number of beneficiaries was small.[74] This estimate is derived by subtracting the total stated money's worth of bequests to other beneficiaries from the total probate

---

[70] Wedgwood, *Economic of Inheritance*, p. 165.

[71] Will of Sarah Sharpe, PROB 11, film 1767, quire 121.

[72] This was a common theme in literary works of the period. See, for example, *Sense and Sensibility* (1811) by Jane Austen; *Shirley* (1849) and *Villette* (1853) by Charlotte Bronte. See also Staves, 'Resentment or resignation?', p. 197; Hunt, *The Middling Sort*, p. 153; Vickery, A., *The Gentleman's Daughter* (Boston: Yale University Press, 1998), pp. 21–2.

[73] There was a total of seventy-nine such estates.

[74] For example, residual legatees in estates with only two beneficiaries named on average received 90 per cent of the total probated wealth whilst those with five or more received about 80 per cent.

value, leaving a residual figure which represented the sum left to the residual legatee. This figure, however, is a rough approximation and needs to be treated with some caution. It is impossible, for example, to estimate the value of material bequests, such as clothes, plate, cutlery or jewellery, which were often left to other beneficiaries, and as a result these have not been taken into account when estimating the amount of the residual legacy. It is also likely to be an overestimate since it assumes that the real value of the estate was the upper value stated for probate, a problem noted earlier in the paper. Even making allowances for this, however, the evidence suggests that whoever was named as the residual legatee could reasonably expect to receive a significant proportion of the estate which, in all but a few instances, was larger than that of other beneficiaries named in the will.

In terms of the residual legatee, gender was an important consideration when appointing heirs. Figure 9.6 shows that sisters, daughters and nieces tended to be favoured to a greater extent than brothers, sons and nephews. Closer inspection by marital status of the testator, however, reveals that spinsters tended to favour female heirs to a greater extent than did widows. Not surprisingly, as far as widows were concerned children, especially daughters, were the most important beneficiaries. For spinsters, the main beneficiaries were siblings, notably sisters, and their children, especially nieces. The relationship between maiden aunt and niece, which repeats itself in many novels of the period, is certainly one that is strongly hinted at by the evidence discussed here. More generally, the pattern of inheritance confirms the significance of kinship networks and points to the close relationships that single women often had with their brothers and sisters. As they aged, middle-class spinsters increasingly resided with their siblings whilst, by contrast, their working-class counterparts found themselves increasingly dependent on institutional relief. In London suburbs, such as Brompton, co-residence with single brothers or sisters was fairly common for middle-class spinsters whilst more generally Michael Anderson has noted that at mid-century at least a quarter of spinsters aged fifty-five to sixty-four years lived with their siblings.[75] Co-residence with sisters, in particular, is suggested by the frequency with which they were the residual legatees of unmarried women, hinting at what Hufton has termed 'spinster clustering' – the grouping together of women in twos or threes to rent accommodation and share costs.[76] Sarah Bayley, for example, left her entire estate to her sister Elizabeth, with whom she lived in

[75] Freeman and Klaus, 'The New Spinster in England and the United States', pp. 406–7; Anderson, 'The Social Position of Spinsters', p. 389.

[76] Hufton, O., 'Women without Men: Widows and Spinsters in Britain and France in the Eighteenth Century', *Journal of Family History* 9 (1984), p. 362. For good examples of this in provincial society see Davidoff and Hall, *Family Fortunes*, p. 314; Vickery, *The Gentleman's Daughter*, p. 22.

Lambeth Walk, whilst Jane Byerley, a retired servant in the royal household, left the bulk of her estate to her widowed sister Ann Jennings who was living with her in Vauxhall Road.[77]

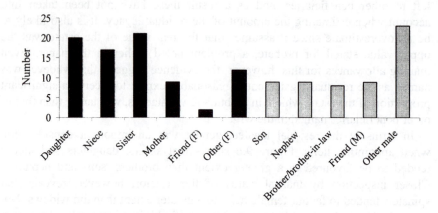

Figure 9.6: Residual legatee, London 1830

Such clustering of single women, however, also reflected the importance of unrelated female companions and servants. The close bonds that could be developed in such circumstance were illustrated by the terms of Sophia Johnson's will which left Catherine Hitchcock, her 'faithful and affectionate servant', £400 together with silver cutlery, furniture, linen, clothes and kitchen utensils. Her lodgings were also to be kept up for a few weeks and 12 shillings were to be paid if Catherine wished to stay there.[78] In terms of inheritance practices, therefore, the evidence suggests that bonds of affection and kinship links, especially those concerning other women, were both recognised and reinforced through bequesting strategies. In this context, such strategies need to be interpreted not only in terms of the transfer of wealth itself but also in relation to the production and reproduction of gendered social relations.

Conclusion

This paper has argued, in line with feminist historians, that gender plays a crucial role in structuring social relationships. However, whilst there is broad

---

[77] Will of Sarah Bayley, PROB 11, film 1774, quire 483; will of Jane Byerley, PROB 11, film 1772, quire 232.
[78] Will of Sophia Johnson, PROB 11, film 1766, quire 76.

agreement that gender was a key dimension in understanding social relations, debate exists about the timing and extent to which separate gendered spheres of action functioned in eighteenth- and nineteenth-century society.[79] In the context of wealth holding, with a few exceptions historians have argued that just as middle-class women were increasingly marginalised from the realm of productive work, so they were divorced from the ownership of wealth. Their weak economic position was apparently reflected in terms of their absence from the upper echelons of wealth holders in Britain, which was dominated above all by commercial, monied men from the metropolis.[80] However, this argument ignores the fact that lower down the social hierarchy, middle-class women not only outlived and therefore outnumbered men, but also that as widows they frequently inherited their husband's property. Wealth may have been accumulated primarily by men, but it frequently ended up in women's hands. Though the terms of inheritance may in some cases have hindered their freedom of action, widows and spinsters were in a very real sense independent women capable of making choices about how best to provide for themselves and how to dispose of their wealth. That they made such choices is evident from the various forms in which they held wealth, the strategies they adopted to dispose of it and the persons they asked to administer their estates. In these respects, at least, the stereotype of female passivity and the strict delimitation of gendered spheres of action fit uneasily with the active role of these women.

In the context of women's wealth holding in late eighteenth- and early nineteenth-century urban society, it appears that London was exceptional by virtue of the quantitative significance of female testators. The importance of women in the demographic structure of the city partly accounts for this situation but so too do the opportunities for making an independent living, easier access to financial services and advice, and higher overall levels of wealth. In that spinsters and widows were free to dispose of their wealth as and how they wished, it would not be an exaggeration to say that London was the mecca for independent women. As this chapter has demonstrated, their role in the overall ownership of wealth and involvement in the financial markets is something that deserves greater attention than it has hitherto received.

Though women's freedom to dispose of property may have been circumscribed by limitations imposed by husbands and fathers, notably in relation to the use of trusts, nevertheless female testators tended to behave in ways that clearly favoured other women.[81] The significance of bequests to

---

[79] See Hall, *White, Male and Middle-Class*, pp. 95–107. For critical discussion of the separate spheres argument see Vickery, 'Golden Age to Separate Spheres', pp. 383–414; *idem*, *The Gentleman's Daughter*, pp. 1–10.

[80] See the chapter by W. D. Rubinstein in this volume.

[81] The use of trusts is discussed more fully in Davidoff and Hall, *Family Fortunes*, pp. 209–10; Hunt, *The Middling Sort*, 159.

daughters and nieces in particular can be interpreted partly as a way of providing a portion sufficient to secure unmarried women an advantageous match, and partly as an attempt to provide for their independence. In this sense it can be argued that through inheritance practices women were actively seeking to promote a gendered notion of female independence and freedom of action. However, to gauge the implications of these bequesting strategies, further work is needed on the ways that inheritance differed between male and female beneficiaries. The suggestion that men tended to inherit property with which they could work whilst women were left property in the form of annuities or trusts, which would provide an income whilst still leaving them dependent, needs more research than space allows for here.[82] In general, the ways in which inheritance was structured and the active role of women in the administration of estates points to the existence of a distinctive set of social networks in which relationships of trust, duty and emotion were strongly influenced by considerations of gender.

At the same time, however, it is important not to overemphasise the role of gender or the existence of separate spheres to the exclusion of other dimensions of social life. Definitions of masculinity and femininity, the one implying the possession of dependants and the other emphasising the status of dependence, fit uneasily with the status of independent women discussed here. Other dimensions of social life, notably in relation to marital status, have been shown to have been important and in this respect the distinction in behaviour between widows and spinsters is a timely reminder that even gender was cross-cut by other and perhaps more subtle forms of social relationships.

---

[82] This suggestion is made in Hall *White, Male and Middle-Class*, p. 177.

Bibliography

A'Beckett, T. T., *Law Reforming Difficulties Exemplified in a Letter to Lord Brougham and Vaux Accompanied by an Analysis of a Bill for the Improvement of the Law Relating to the Administration of Deceased Persons' Estates* (London: Henry Butterworth, 1842).

Addy, J., *Death, Money and the Vultures: Inheritance and Avarice, 1660–1750* (London: Routledge, 1992).

Anderson, M., 'The Social Position of Spinsters in mid-Victorian Britain', *Journal of Family History* 9 (1984), pp. 337–93.

Anderson, M., *Family Structure in Nineteenth Century Lancashire* (Cambridge: Cambridge University Press, 1971).

Angleraud, B., 'Les boulangers lyonnais aux XIXe–XXe siècles (1836 à 1914). Une étude sur la petite bourgeoisie boutiquière', Doctoral thesis, University of Lyon 2, 1993.

Austen, J., *Emma* (London: Wordsworth Edition, 1992).

Ayçoberry, P., 'Histoire sociale de la ville de Cologne (1815–1875)', Doctoral thesis, University of Paris 1, 1977.

Bagley, J. J., 'Matthew Markland, a Wigan Mercer', *Transactions, Lancashire and Cheshire Antiquarian Society* 68 (1959), pp. 45–68.

Barker, H., 'Women, Work and the Industrial Revolution: Female Involvement in the English Printing Trades, c. 1700–1840', in H. Barker and E. Chalus (eds), *Gender in the Eighteenth Century* (London: Longman, 1997), pp. 81–100.

Barker-Benfield, G., *The Culture of Sensibility: Sex and Society in Eighteenth-Century England* (Chicago: Chicago University Press, 1992).

Barlee, E., *A Visit to Lancashire in December 1862* (London: Sheeley, Jackson and Halliday, 1863).

Barnett, D., *London, Hub of the Industrial Revolution* (London: Tauris, 1998).

Bechhofer, F. and Elliott, B., 'A Progress Report on Small Shopkeepers and The Class Structure', SSRC Research Report, 1975.

Bechhofer, F. and Elliott, B., 'Petty Property: the Survival of a Moral Economy', in F. Bechhofer and B. Elliott (eds), *The Petite Bourgeoisie. Comparative Studies of the Uneasy Stratum* (London: Macmillan, 1981), pp. 188–200.

Bedale, C., 'Property Relations and Housing Policy: Oldham in the Late-nineteenth and Early-twentieth Centuries', in J. Melling (ed.), *Housing, Social Policy and the State* (London: Croom Helm, 1980), pp. 37–72.

Behagg, C., *Politics and Production in the Early Nineteenth Century* (London: Routledge, 1990).

Bell's Principles of the Law of Scotland, 4th edn (Edinburgh: T. and T. Clark, 1839).

Berg, M., 'Small Producer Capitalism in Eighteenth-century England', *Business History* 35 (1993), pp. 17–39.

Berg, M., 'Women's Property and the Industrial Revolution', *Journal of Interdisciplinary History* 24 (1993), pp. 233–50.

Berghoff, H., 'British Businessmen as Wealth Holders 1870–1914: A Closer Look', *Business History* 33 (1991), pp. 222–40.

Bernt. W., *The Netherlandish Painters of the Seventeenth Century*, 3 vols (London: Phaidon, 1970).

Bettey, J. H. and Wilde, D. S., 'The Probate Inventories of Dorset Farmers', *Local Historian* 12 (1977), pp. 228–34.

Bird, J. B., *The Laws Respecting Wills, Testaments and Codicils*, 6th edn (London: W. Clarke and Sons, 1817).

Blackstone, W., *Commentaries on the Laws of England* (London: T. Tegg, 1850).

Bocock, R. *Consumption* (London: Routledge, 1993).

Boltanski, L., *Les Cadres. La formation d'un groupe social* (Paris: Les Éditions de Minuit, 1982).

Bonfield, L., *Marriage Settlements, 1601–1740: The Adoption of the Strict Settlement* (Cambridge: Cambridge University Press 1983).

Borsay, P., *The English Urban Renaissance: Culture and Society in the Provincial Town, 1660–1770* (Oxford: Clarendon Press, 1989).

Bourdieu, P., Boltanski, L. and de Saint-Martin, M., 'Les stratégies de recon-version. Les classes sociales et le système d'enseignement', *Information sur les Sciences Sociales* 12 (1973), pp. 61–113.

Bourillon, F., 'Etude de la sociabilité dans un milieu pré- et post-Haussmannien. Le quartier des Arts et Métiers à Paris entre 1850 et 1880', Thesis (3ème cycle), University of Paris X, Nanterre, 1985.

Boyer, M., 'Les métiers de la viande à Lyon de 1860 à 1914', Thesis (3ème cycle), University of Lyon 2, 1985.

Brants, V., *La lutte pour le pain quotidien. Précis des leçons d'économie politique* (Paris: H. Champion, 1885).

Brewer, J., 'English Radicalism in the Age of George III', in J. G. A. Pocock (ed.), *Three British Revolutions. 1641, 1688, 1776* (Princeton: Princeton University Press, 1980), pp. 323–67.

Brewer, J. and Porter, R. (eds), *Consumption and the World of Goods* (London: Routledge, 1993).

Brewer, J. and Staves, S. 'Introduction', in J. Brewer and S. Staves (eds), *Early Modern Conceptions of Property* (London: Routledge, 1995), pp. 1–18.

Broad, J., 'Alternate Husbandry and Permanent Pasture in the Midlands, 1650–1800', *Agricultural History Review* 28 (1980), pp. 77–89.

Bücher, K., 'Eigentumsverhältnisse der Leipziger Handwerker', in Schriften des Vereins für Socialpolitik, 67, *Unterschungen über die Lage des Handwerks* vol. 6 (1897), pp. 699–705.

Bullock, N., 'Berlin', in M. Daunton (ed.), *Housing the Workers, 1850–1914. A Comparative Perspective* (Leicester: Leicester University Press, 1990), pp. 182–248.

Bushman, R., *The Refinement of America: People, Houses, Cities* (New York: Knopf, 1992).

Cain, P. J. and Hopkins, A. G., *British Imperialism: Crisis and Deconstruction: 1914–1990* (London: Longman, 1993).

Cain, P. J. and Hopkins, A. G., *British Imperialism: Innovation and Expansion 1688–1914* (London: Longman, 1993).

Camp, A. J., *Wills and Their Whereabouts* (London: published by the author, 1974).

Campbell, C., 'Understanding Traditional and Modern Patterns of Consumption in Eighteenth-Century England: a Character-Action Approach', in J. Brewer and R. Porter (eds), *Consumption and the World of Goods* (London: Routledge, 1993), pp. 40–57.

Campbell, C., *The Romantic Ethic and the Spirit of Modern Consumption* (Oxford: Blackwell, 1987).

Capdevielle, J., *Le fétichisme du patrimoine. Essai sur un fondement de la classe moyenne* (Paris: Presses de la Fondation nationale des Sciences politiques, 1986).

Chaline, J.-P., *Les bourgeois de Rouen. Une élite urbaine au XIXe siècle* (Paris: Presses de la Fondation nationale des sciences politiques, 1982).

Chalklin, C. W., *The Provincial Towns of Georgian England: A Study in the Building Process, 1740–1820* (London: Edward Arnold, 1974).

Chapman, S. D., 'The Genesis of the British Hosiery Industry, 1600–1750', *Textile History* 3 (1972), pp. 7–49.

Chapman, S. D., 'Enterprise and Innovation in the British Hosiery Industry, 1750–1850', *Textile History* 5 (1974), pp. 14–37.

Chester Jordan, W., *Women and Credit in Pre-Industrial and Developing Societies* (Philadelphia: Princeton University Press, 1993).

Churches, C., 'Women and Property in Early Modern England: A Case Study', *Social History* 23 (1998), pp. 165–80.

Clark, A., *Working Life in the Seventeenth Century* (London, 1919, reprinted Routledge, 1992).

Clark, P., *The English Alehouse: A Social History, 1200–1830* (London: Longman, 1983).

Clark, P. (ed.), *The Transformation of English Provincial Towns, 1600–1800* (London: Hutchinson, 1984).

Clark, P., 'Small Towns in England 1550–1850: National and Regional Population Trends', in P. Clark (ed.), *Small Towns in Early Modern Europe* (Cambridge: Cambridge University Press, 1995), pp. 90–110.

Clark, P. and Corfield, P. (eds), *Industry and Urbanisation in Eighteenth Century England*, Centre for Urban History, University of Leicester, Working Paper 6 (Leicester, 1994).

Clark, P. and Slack, P., *English Towns in Transition* (Oxford: Oxford University Press, 1976).

Clive, E., *The Law of Husband and Wife* (Edinburgh: W. Green, 1982).

Codaccioni, F.-P., 'Les fortunes à Lille (1821–1908)', in Daumard (ed.), *Les Fortunes Françaises*, pp. 275–428.

Collyer, J., *A Practical Treatise on the Law of Partnership* (1832).

Cooper, J. C., 'Patterns of Inheritance and Settlement by Great Landowners From the Fifteenth to the Eighteenth centuries', in J. Goody, E. P. Thompson and J. Thirsk (eds), *Family and Inheritance in Western Europe, 1200–1800* (Cambridge: Cambridge University Press, 1976), pp. 192–327.

Corfield, P., *The Impact of English Towns, 1700–1800* (Oxford: Oxford University Press, 1982).

Corfield, P., 'Walking the City Streets: Social Role and Social Identification in the Towns of Eighteenth-Century England', *Journal of Urban History* 16 (1990), pp. 132–74.

Cox, J., Wills, *Inventories and Death Duties* (London: Public Record Office, 1988).

Cressy, D., 'Kinship and Kin Interaction in Early Modern England', *Past and Present* 113 (1986), pp. 38–69.

Crossick, G., 'Metaphors of the Middle: The Discovery of the Petite Bourgeoisie 1880–1914', *Transactions of the Royal Historical Society* 6th series, 4 (1994), pp. 251–79.

Crossick, G., 'Formation ou invention des classes moyennes? Une analyse comparée: Belgique-France–Grande-Bretagne 1880–1914', *Revue belge d'histoire Contemporaine* 26 (1996), pp. 105–38.

Crossick, G., 'Past Masters: in Search of the Artisan in European History', in G. Crossick (ed.), *The Artisan and the European Town, 1500–1900* (Scolar Press: Aldershot, 1997), pp. 1–40.

Crossick, G., 'La bourgeoisie britannique au 19e siècle: recherches, approches, problematiques', *Annales. Histoire, Sciences Sociales*, 6 (1998), pp. 1089–130.

Crossick, G. and Haupt, H.-G., *The Petite Bourgeoisie in Europe 1780–1914. Enterprise, Family and Independence* (London: Routledge, 1995).

Crossick, G. and Jaumain, S. (eds), *Cathedrals of Consumption: The European Department Store, 1850–1939* (Aldershot: Ashgate, 1999).

Curle, A. O., 'A Roxburghshire House and its Contents in 1729', *Scottish Historical Review* 5 (1968), pp. 265–72.

Curran, C., 'Private Women, Public Needs: Middle-Class Widows in Victorian England', *Albion* 25 (1993), pp. 217–36.

D'Cruze, S., 'The Middling Sort in Eighteenth-Century Colchester: Independence, Social Relations and the Community Broker', in J. Barry and C. Brooks (eds), *The Middling Sort of People: Culture, Society and Politics in England, 1550–1800* (London: Macmillan, 1994), pp. 181–207.

Darrow, M. H., *Revolution in the House: Family, Class and Inheritance in Southern France, 1775–1825* (Princeton: Princeton University Press, 1989).

Daumard, A. (ed.), *Les fortunes françaises au XIXᵉ siècle* (Paris: Mouton, 1973).

Daumard, A., *La bourgeoisie parisienne de 1815 à 1848* (Paris: École Pratique des Hautes Études, 1963)

Daunton, M. J., '"Gentlemanly capitalism" and British industry, 1820–1914', *Past and Present* 122 (1989), pp. 119–58.

Daunton, M. J., *Coal Metropolis: Cardiff 1870–1914* (Leicester: Leicester University Press, 1977).

Davidoff, L. and Hall, C., *Family Fortunes: Men and Women of the English Middle Class 1780–1850* (London: Hutchinson, 1987).

Davidoff, L., Doolittle, M., Fink, J., and Holden, K., *The Family Story: Blood, Contact and Intimacy 1830–1960* (London: Longman, 1999).

Davidson, C., *'A Woman's Work is Never Done': A History of House-work in the British Isles, 1650–1950* (London: Chatto and Windus, 1982).

De Grazia, V. and Furlough, E. (eds), *The Sex of Things. Gender and Consumption in Historical Perspective* (Berkeley: University of California Press, 1996).

De Vries, B., 'Amsterdamse Vermogens en Vermogensbezitters, 1855–1875', in *AAG Bijdragen*, 28, *Dertig Jaar Afdeling Agrarische Geschiedenis*, Wageningen 1986.

De Vries, J., 'Between Purchasing Power and the World of Goods: Understanding the Household Economy in Early Modern Europe', in J. Brewer and R. Porter (eds), *Consumption and the World of Goods* (London: Routledge, 1993), pp. 85–132.

De Vries, J., 'The Industrial Revolution and the Industrious Revolution', *Journal of Economic History* 54 (1994), pp. 249–271.

Defaudon, B., 'Bourg-en-Bresse: aperçu d'une société urbaine au debut du XIXᵉ siècle 1815–1848', Mémoire de maitrise, University of Lyon 2, 1976.

Defoe, D., *A Tour Through the Whole Island of Great Britain* (London: Everyman, 1962).

Dennis, R. and Daniels, S., '"Community" in the Social Geography of Victorian Cities', *Urban History Yearbook* (1981), pp. 7–23.

Dennis, R., *English Industrial Cities of the Nineteenth Century: A Social Geography* (Cambridge: Cambridge University Press, 1984).

Désert, G., 'Immigration et ségrégation à Caen', in M. Garden and Y. Lequin (eds), *Habiter la Ville. XVe-XXe Siècle* (Lyon: Presses Universitaires de Lyon, 1984), pp. 175–91.

Devine, T. M. and Mitchinson, R. (eds), *People and Society in Scotland*, vol. 1 (Edinburgh: John Donald, 1988).

Deyon, P., 'Roubaix dans la première moitié du XIXe siècle', in M. Garden and Y. Lequin (eds), *Construire la Ville XVIIIe–XXe siècles* (Lyon: Presses Universitaires de Lyon, 1983), pp. 117–29.

Dickinson, H. T., *Liberty and Property. Political Ideology in Eighteenth-Century Britain* (London: Methuen, 1977).

Dickinson, J. and Russell, R. (eds) *Family, Economy and State: The Social Reproduction Process Under Capitalism* (London: Croom Helm, 1986).

Dickson, R., *A Practical Exposition of the Law of Wills* (London: Sherwood, Gilbert and Piper, 1830).

Diefendorf, B. B., 'Women and Property in *Ancien Regime* France: Theory and Practice in Dauphine and Paris', in J. Brewer and S. Staves (eds), *Early Modern Conceptions of Property* (London: Routledge, 1995), pp. 170–93.

Ditz, T., *Property and Kinship: Inheritance in Early Connecticut, 1750–1820* (Princeton: Princeton University Press, 1986).

Douglas, M., *Implicit Meanings: Essays in Anthropology* (London: Routledge and Paul, 1975).

Douglas, M. and Isherwood, B., *The World of Goods: Towards an Anthropology of Consumption* (New York: W. W. Norton and Co., 1978 and London: Routledge, 1996).

Duff, A., *Treatise on Deeds Chiefly Affecting Moveables* (Edinburgh: Bell and Bradfute, 1840).

Dupeux. G. and Herpin, J., 'Les fortunes bordelaises', in A. Daumard (ed.), *Les fortunes françaises au XIXe siècle* (Paris: Mouton, 1973), pp. 431–551.

Duplat, G., *La classe moyenne. Son rôle social. Son action politique. Sa situation économique. Les réformes urgentes* (Brussels, 1914).

Earle, P., *The Making of the English Middle Class: Business, Society and Family Life in London, 1660–1730* (London: Methuen, 1989).

Edgren, L., *Lärling Gesäll Mästare. Hantverk och hantverkare i Malmö 1750–1847* (Lund: Universitetsförlaget Dialogos, 1987).

Edwards, R., 'The Conversation Pictures of Joseph Van Aken', *Appollo* 132 (February 1936), pp. 79–85.

Egan, P., *Tom and Jerry: Life in London* (London, 1869, first published 1821).

Ehmer, J., 'The Artisan Family in Nineteenth-Century Austria: Embourgeoisement of the Petite Bourgeoisie?', in G. Crossick and H.-G. Haupt (eds), *Shopkeepers and Master Artisans in Nineteenth-Century Europe* (London: Methuen, 1984), pp. 195–218.

Elliott, B. and McCrone, D., 'Landlords in Edinburgh: Some Preliminary Findings', *Sociological Review* 23 (1975), pp. 539–62.

Engels, F., *The Condition of the Working Class in England* (London: Granada Publishing, 1969, originally published in English in 1892).

Englander, D., *Landlord and Tenant in Urban Britain 1838–1918* (Oxford: Clarendon Press, 1983).

English, B., 'Probate Valuations and Death Duty registers', *Historical Research* 57 (1984), pp. 80–91.

Erickson, A. L., *Women and Property in Early Modern England* (London: Routledge, 1997).

Ernaux, A., *La place* (Gallimard: Paris, 1983).

Falconer, T., *On Probate Courts* (London: Reynel and Weight, 1850).

Faure, A., 'The Grocery Trade in Nineteenth-century Paris: a Fragmented Corporation', in G. Crossick and H.-G. Haupt (eds), *Shopkeepers and Master Artisans in Nineteenth-Century Europe* (London: Methuen, 1984), pp. 155–74.

Felkin, W., *History of the Machine-Wrought Hosiery and Lace Manufacturers* (1867, reprinted Newton Abbot: David and Charles, 1967).

Field, J., 'Wealth, Styles of Life and Social Tone Amongst Portsmouth's Middle Class', in R. J. Morris (ed.), *Class, Power and the Social Structure of British Nineteenth-Century Towns* (Leicester: Leicester University Press, 1986), pp. 67–106.

Finch, J., Mason, J., Masson, J., Wallis, L., and Hayes, L., *Wills, Inheritance and Families* (Oxford: Clarendon Press, 1996).

Finch, J. and Wallis, L., 'Death, Inheritance and the Life Course', in D. Clark (ed.) *The Sociology of Death* (Oxford: Blackwell, 1993), pp. 50–68.

Fine, B. and Leopold, E. *The World of Consumption* (London: Routledge, 1993).

Foster, J., *Class Struggle and the Industrial Revolution: Early Industrial Capitalism in Three English Towns* (London: Methuen, 1973).

Francis, H. J., *A History of Hinckley* (Hinckley: W. Pickering and Sons, 1930).

Fraser, P., *Treatise on Husband and Wife According to the Law of Scotland* (Edinburgh: T. and T. Clark, 1840).

Freeman R. and Klaus, P., 'Blessed or Not? The New Spinster in England and the United States in the Late Nineteenth and Early Twentieth Centuries', *Journal of Family History* 9 (1984), pp. 394–414.

Fukuyama, F., *The End of History and the Last Man* (New York: Free Press, 1992).

Gaillard, J., *Paris, la Ville (1852–1870),* (Lille, 1976).

Glennie, P. and Thrift, N. 'Modern Consumption: Theorising Commodities and Consumers', *Environment and Planning D* 11 (1993), pp. 603–6.

Glennie, P. and Thrift, N., 'Consumers, Identities, and Consumption Spaces in Early-Modern England', *Environment and Planning A* 28 (1996), pp. 25–45.

Glennie, P., 'Consumption Within Historical Studies', in D. Miller (ed.), *Acknowledging Consumption: a review of new studies* (London: Routledge, 1995), pp. 164–203.

Goffman, E., *The Presentation of Self in Everyday Life* (Harmondsworth: Penguin, 1969).

Goody, J., Thirsk, J., and Thompson, E. P. (eds), *Family and Inheritance: Rural Society in Western Europe, 1200–1800* (Cambridge: Cambridge University Press, 1976).

Green, D. R. and Owens, A., 'Metropolitan Estates of the Middle Class 1800–50: Probates and Death Duties Revisited', *Historical Research* 70 (1997), pp. 294–311.

Greg, W., 'Why Are Women Redundant?', *National Review* 14 (April 1862), pp. 434–60.

Gresle, F., *L'univers de la boutique. Les petits patrons du Nord (1920–1975)* (Lille: Presses Universitaires de Lille, 1981).

Grundy, J. E., 'The Origins of the Liverpool Cowkeepers', Mlitt thesis, University of Lancaster, 1982.

Gunn, S., 'The Failure of the Victorian Middle Class: A Critique', in J. Seed and J. Wolff (eds), *The Culture of Capital: Art, Power and the Nineteenth-Century Middle Class* (Manchester: Manchester University Press, 1988), pp. 17–44.

Gunn, S., 'The Manchester Middle Class 1850–80', unpublished University of Manchester PhD thesis (1992).

Habakkuk, J., 'English Land Ownership, 1680–1740', *Economic History Review* 2nd Series, 10 (1939–40), pp. 2–17.

Habakkuk, J., 'Marriage Settlements in the Eighteenth Century', *Transactions of the Royal Historical Society* 4th Series, 32 (1950), pp. 15–30.

Habakkuk, J., 'The Rise and Fall of English Landed Families, 1600–1800', *Transactions of the Royal Historical Society* 5th Series, 29 (1979), pp. 187–207.

Habakkuk, J., *Marriage, Debt and the Estates System: English Landownership* (Oxford: Clarendon Press, 1994).

Hadfield, C., *The Canals of the East Midlands* (Newton Abbot: David and Charles, 1976).

Hall, C., *White, Male and Middle-Class* (Cambridge: Polity, 1992).

Hamnett, C., Harmer, M. and Williams, P., *Safe as Houses: Housing Inheritance in Britain* (London: Paul Chapman Publishing, 1991).

Hanlon, G., and Carruthers, E., 'Wills, Inheritance and the Moral Order in Seventeenth-Century Agenais', *Journal of Family History* 15 (1990), pp. 149–61.

Hann, C. M., 'Introduction: The Embeddedness of Property', in C. M. Hann (ed.), *Property Relations. Renewing the Anthropological Tradition* (Cambridge: Cambridge University Press, 1998), pp. 1–47.

Harris, J., *Private Lives, Public Spirit: A Social History of Britain, 1870–1914* (Oxford: Oxford University Press, 1993).

Harvey, D., *Social Justice and the City* (London: Edward Arnold, 1973).

Heginbotham, H., *Stockport: Ancient and Modern*, vol. II (London: publisher unknown, 1892).

Hickox, M. S. 'The English Middle-Class Debate', *British Journal of Sociology* 45 (1995), pp. 311–423.

Hill, B., *Women, Work and Sexual Politics in Eighteenth Century England* (Oxford: Basil Blackwell, 1994).

Hillier, D., *The Story of Ashby de la Zouch* (Buckingham, Barracuda, 1984).

Hobhouse, E. (ed.), *Diary of a West Country Physican, AD 1684–1726. Extracts from Dr. Claver Morris' Diary* (London: Simpkin Marshall, 1934).

Holcombe, L., *Wives and Property: The Reform of Married Women's Property Law* (Oxford: Martin Robinson, 1974).

Holderness, B. A., 'Credit in a Rural Community, 1660–1800: Some Neglected Aspects of Probate Inventories', *Midland History* 3 (1975), pp. 94–115.

Holderness, B. A., 'Widows in Pre-Industrial Society: An Essay Upon Their Economic Functions', in R. M. Smith (ed.), *Land, Kinship and Lifecycle* (Cambridge, Cambridge University Press, 1984), pp. 423–42.

Holme, R., 'The Academy of Armory and Blazon' (London, published for the Roxburgh Club, 1905).

Houlbrooke, R., 'Death, Church and the Family in England Between the Late Fifteenth and Early Eighteenth Centuries' in R. Houlbrooke (ed.) *Death, Ritual and Bereavement* (London: Routledge, 1989), pp. 25–42

Houlbrooke, R., *Death, Religion and the Family in England, 1480–1750* (Oxford: Clarendon Press, 1998).

Hudson, J. C., *Plain Directions for Making Wills in Conformity with the Law* (London: Longman and Co., 1838).

Hudson, P. (ed.), *Regions and Industries: A Perspective on the Industrial Revolution* (Cambridge, Cambridge University Press, 1989).

Hudson, P., *The Industrial Revolution* (London: Edward Arnold, 1992).

Hufton, O., 'Women without Men: Widows and Spinsters in Britain and France in the Eighteenth Century', *Journal of Family History* 9 (1984), pp. 355–76.

Hunt, M., *The Middling Sort: Commerce, Gender and the Family in England 1680–1780* (London and Berkeley: University of California Press, 1996).

Jackson, C. (ed.), 'A Family History Begun by James Fretwell', *Surtees Society* 65 (1875), pp. 163–244.

Jacquemet, G., *Belleville au XIXᵉ siècle. Du faubourg à la ville* (Paris: Éditions de l'ÉHSS, 1984).

Jalland, P., *Death in the Victorian Family* (Oxford: Oxford University Press, 1996).

Jenkins, D., *The Agricultural Community in South-West Wales at the turn of the Twentieth Century* (Cardiff: University of Wales Press, 1971).

Johnston, J., 'Family, Kin and Community in Eight Lincolnshire Parishes, 1567–1800', *Rural History* 6 (1995), pp. 179–92.

Joyce, P., *Visions of the People: Industrial England and the Question of Class, 1848–1914* (Cambridge: Cambridge University Press, 1991).

Joyce, P., *Democratic Subjects: The Self and the Social in Nineteenth-Century England* (Cambridge: Cambridge University Press, 1994).

Joyce, P., 'The End of Social History?', *Social History* 20 (1995), pp. 73–92.

Joyce, P., *Class: A Reader* (Oxford, Oxford University Press, 1995).

Kessler, D. and Masson, P., 'Introduction', in D. Kessler and A. Masson (eds) *Modelling the Accumulation and Distribution of Wealth* (Oxford: Clarendon, 1988), pp. 1–18.

Kidd, A. and Nicholls, D., 'Introduction: The Making of the British Middle Class', in A. Kidd and D. Nicholls (eds), *The Making of the British Middle Class? Studies of Regional and Cultural Diversity since the Eighteenth Century* (Stroud: Sutton, 1998), pp. xv–xxiii.

King, G., 'An ESTIMATE of the Yearly Consumption of FLESH in the Nation', reproduced in P. Laslett (ed.), *The Earliest Classics* (Farnborough: Gregg International, 1973).

King, S., 'Migrants on the Margin? Mobility, Integration and Occupations in the West Riding, 1650–1820', *Journal of Historical Geography* 23 (1997), pp. 284–303.

Kirk, N., (ed.) *Social Class and Marxism: Defences and Challenges* (Aldershot: Scolar Press, 1996).

Kirk, N., *The Growth of Working Class Reformism in Mid-Victorian England* (Beckenham: Croom Helm, 1984).

Koditscheck, T., *Class Formation and Urban Industrial Society: Bradford, 1750–1850* (Cambridge: Cambridge University Press, 1990).

Kotlikoff, L., 'Intergenerational Transfers and Savings', *Journal of Economic Perspectives* 2 (1988), pp. 41–58.

Kusamitsu, T. 'Novelty, Give us Novelty: London Agents and Northern Manufacturers', in M. Berg (ed.), *Markets and Manufacturers in Early Industrial Europe* (London: Routledge, 1991), pp. 114–37.

Laferrère, A., 'Inheritances and Gifts *Inter Vivos*: the Use of "Disposable Portion" for the Purpose of Unequal Division Between Siblings in France', *Continuity and Change* 7 (1992), pp. 377–404.

Lamar, M., '"Choosing" Partible Inheritance Strategies: Chilean Merchant Families, 1795–1825', *Journal of Social History* 28 (1994), pp. 125–46.

Lane, P. 'An Industrialising Town: Social and Business Networks in Hinckley, Leicestershire c. 1750-1835', in J. Stobart and P. Lane (eds), *Trade, Towns and Regions* (forthcoming).

Langton, J., 'Residential Patterns in Pre-industrial Cities: Some Case Studies from Seventeenth-century Britain', *Transactions, Institute of British Geographers* 65 (1975), pp. 8–23.

Langton, J., 'The Continuity of Regional Culture: Lancashire Catholicism from the Late-sixteenth to the Early-nineteenth Century', in E. Royle (ed.), *Issues of Regional Identity* (Manchester: Manchester University Press, 1997), pp. 82–101.

Laslett, P., 'Size and Structure of the Household in England over Three Centuries', *Population Studies* 23 (1969), pp. 199–223.

Laslett, P., *The World We Have Lost – Further Explored* (London: Methuen, 1983).

Latham, R. and Matthews, W. (eds), *The Diary of Samuel Pepys: A New and Complete Transcription*, 11 vols (London: G. Bell, 1970–83).

Le Yaouanq, J., 'Aspects de l'immigration departementale à Paris au xixe siècle: les commerçants et artisans ligeriens', *Cahiers de l'Institut d'Histoire de la Presse et de l'Opinion* 3 (1974–75), pp. 7–39.

Le Yaouanq, J., 'Trajéctoires sociales à Paris au XIXe Siècle: le monde de la boutique', *Bulletin du Centre Pierre Léon d'Histoire Économique et Sociale* 4 (1993), pp. 25–40.

Leach, W., 'Transformations in a Culture of Consumption: Women and Department Stores, 1890–1925', *Journal of American History* 71 (1984), pp. 319–42.

Léon, P., *Géographie de la fortune et structures sociales à Lyon au XIXe Siècle (1815–1914)* (Lyon: Presses Universitaires de Lyon, 1974).

Levine, D. and Wrightson, K., *The Making of an Industrial Society: Whickham 1560–1765* (Oxford: Oxford University Press, 1991).

Litzenberger, C., 'Computer-Based Analysis of Early-Modern English Wills', *History and Computing* 7 (1995), pp. 143–51.

Longhofer, J., 'Toward a Political Economy of Inheritance: Community and Household among the Mennonites' *Theory and Society* 22 (1993), pp. 337–62.

Macfarlane, A., *The Family Life of Ralph Josselin* (Cambridge: Cambridge University Press, 1970).

MacFarlane, A., *The Origins of English Individualism. The Family, Property and Social Transition* (Oxford: Blackwell, 1978).

Macpherson, C. (ed.) *Property: Mainstream and Critical Positions* (Toronto: University of Toronto Press, 1978)

Macpherson, C. B., *The Political Theory of Possessive Individualism: Hobbes to Locke* (Oxford: Clarendon Press, 1962).

Manchester, A. H., 'The Reform of the Ecclesiastical Courts' *American Journal of Legal History* 10 (1966), pp. 51–75.

Marcelin, P., 'Souvenirs d'un passé artisanal', *Les cahiers rationalistes* 253 (1968), pp. 35–72.

Markham, G., *The English Housewife* (London, 1683).

Marshall, J. D. (ed.), 'The Autobiography of William Stout of Lancaster', *Chetham Society*, 3rd series, 14 (1967).

Marshall, J. D. and Walton, J. K., *The Lake Counties from 1830 to the Mid-Twentieth Century* (Manchester: Manchester University Press, 1981).

Mascuch, M., 'Social Mobility and the Middling Self-identity: the Ethos of British Autobiographers, 1600–1750', *Social History* 20 (1995), pp. 45–61.

Mass Observation, *Browns and Chester: Portrait of a Shop* (London: Lindsay Drummond Ltd., 1947).

Mathias, P., *Retailing Revolution. A History of Multiple Retailing in the Food Trades based upon the Allied Suppliers Group of Companies* (London: Longman, 1967).

Mayhew, H., *The Morning Chronicle Survey*, vol. 1 (Firle: Caliban, 1980; first published in 1849–50).

McCracken, G., *Culture and Consumption: New Approaches to the Symbolic Character of Consumer Goods and Activities* (Bloomington: Indiana University Press, 1988).

McCrone, D. and Elliott, B., 'The Decline of Landlordism: Property Rights and Relationships in Edinburgh', in R. Rodger (ed.), *Scottish Housing in the Twentieth Century* (Leicester: Leicester University Press, 1989), pp. 214–37.

McKendrick, N., Brewer, J. and Plumb, J., *The Birth of a Consumer Society: The Commercialization of Eighteenth-Century England* (London: Hutchinson, 1982).

McLaren, J., *The Law of Scotland in Relation to Wills and Succession*, vol. 1 (Edinburgh: Bell and Bradfute, 1868).

Menchik, P., 'Unequal Estate Division? Is it Altruism, Reverse Bequests or Simply Noise?', in D. Kessler and A. Masson (eds), *Modelling the Accumulation and Distribution of Wealth* (Oxford: Clarendon, 1988), pp. 105–16.

Michie, R. C., *Money, Mania and Markets* (Edinburgh: John Donald, 1981).

Mill, J. S., *Principles of Political Economy with Some of Their Applications to Social Philosophy*, Book II (London: George Routledge and Sons, 1891).

Miller, D., 'Consumption as the Vanguard of History', in Miller, D. (ed.), *Acknowledging Consumption: a review of new studies* (London: Routledge, 1995), pp. 1–40.

Mills, D., 'Rural Industries and Social Structure: Framework Knitters in Leicestershire, 1670–1851', *Textile History* 13 (1982), pp. 183–203.

Misson, H., *Memoirs and Observations in his Travels over England* (translated Mr Ozell, London, 1719).

Mitchell B. and Deane, P., *Abstract of British Historical Statistics* (Cambridge: Cambridge University Press, 1962).

Modigliani, F., 'Measuring the Contribution of Intergenerational Transfers of Total Wealth: Conceptual Issues and Empirical Findings', in D. Kessler and A. Masson (eds) *Modelling the Accumulation and Distribution of Wealth* (Oxford: Clarendon, 1988), pp. 21–52.

Modigliani, F., 'The Role of Intergenerational Transfers and Life Cycle Saving in the Accumulation of Wealth', *Journal of Economic Perspectives* 2 (1988), pp. 15–40.

Morgan, A. N., *David Morgan. 1833–1919. The Life and Times of a Master Draper in South Wales* (Risca: Starling Press, 1977).

Morris, C. (ed.), *The Journeys of Celia Fiennes* (London: Futura, 1983).

Morris, R. J., 'The Middle Class and the Property Cycle During the Industrial Revolution', in T. C. Smout (ed.), *The Search for Wealth and Stability: Essays in Social and Economic History Presented to M. W. Flinn* (London: Macmillan, 1979), pp. 91–113.

Morris, R. J., *Class, Sect and Party: The Making of the British Middle Class, Leeds, 1820–50* (Manchester: Manchester University Press, 1990).

Morris, R. J., 'Civil Society and the Nature of Urbanism: Britain 1750–1850', *Urban History* 25 (1998), pp. 289–301.

Morris, R. J., 'Reading the Will: Cash Economy, Capitalists and Urban Peasants in the 1830s', in A. Kidd and D. Nicholls (eds), *The Making of the British Middle Class? Studies of Regional and Cultural Diversity since the Eighteenth Century* (Stroud: Sutton, 1998), pp. 113–29.

Morris, R. J. and McCrum, A., 'Wills, Inventories and the Computer', *History and Computing*, 7 (1995), Special Issue.

Morris, R. J. and Nenadic, S., 'The Family and the Small Firm: Edinburgh 1861–1891', ESRC End of Award Report, 1992.

Mrs Hannah Glasse, *The ART of COOKERY made Plain and Easy* (1st edn, London, publisher unknown, 1747).

Muldrew, C., *The Economy of Obligation: The Culture of Credit and Social Relations in Early Modern England* (Basingstoke: Macmillan, 1998).

Nenadic, S., 'The Structure, Values and Influence of the Scottish Urban Middle Class: Glasgow 1800 to 1870', PhD thesis, University of Glasgow, 1986.

Nenadic, S., 'The Rise of the Urban Middle Class', in T. M. Devine and R. Mitchinson (eds), *People and Society in Scotland*, vol. 1 (Edinburgh: John Donald, 1988), pp. 109–26.

Nenadic, S., 'Businessmen, the Urban Middle Classes and the "Dominance" of Manufactures in Nineteenth-Century Britain', *Economic History Review* 44 (1991), pp. 66–85.

Nenadic, S., 'Middle-Rank Consumers and Domestic Culture in Edinburgh and Glasgow 1720–1840', *Past and Present* 145 (1994), pp. 122–56.

Nicholas, T., 'Businessmen and Land Ownership in the Late Nineteenth Century', *Economic History Review* 2nd Series, 52 (1999), pp. 27–44.

Nicholas, T., 'Wealth Making in Nineteenth- and Early Twentieth-Century Britain: Industry v. Commerce and Finance', *Business History* 41 (1999), pp. 16–36.

Nichols, J., *The History and Antiquities of Hinckley* (London, John Nichols, 1782).

Nichols, J., *The History and Antiquities of Leicester*, 4 vols (London, John Nichols, 1804-11).

Nord, P., 'Les mouvements de petits propriétaires et la politique (des années 1880 à la première guerre mondiale)', *Revue historique* 558 (1986), pp. 407–33.

Nord, P., *Paris Shopkeepers and the Politics of Resentment* (Princeton: Princeton University Press, 1986).

Offer, A., *Property and Politics* (Cambridge: Cambridge University Press, 1981).

Overton, M., *A Bibliography of British Probate Inventories* (Newcastle upon Tyne: University of Newcastle upon Tyne, Department of Geography, Occasional Paper, 1983).

Overton, M., *The Agricultural Revolution* (Cambridge: Cambridge University Press, 1996).

Owens, A., 'Inheritance and the Life-Cycle of Family Firms in Early Nineteenth-Century England', unpublished paper.

Penner, J. E., *The Idea of Property in Law* (Oxford: Oxford University Press, 1997).

Pinchbeck, I., *Women Workers and the Industrial Revolution* (London, 1930, reprinted Routledge, 1969).

Pontet, J., 'Craftsmen and Revolution in Bordeaux', in G. Crossick (ed.), *The Artisan and the European Town, 1500–1900* (Scolar Press: Aldershot, 1997), pp. 116–30.

Pooley, C. and D'Cruze, S., 'Migration and Urbanization in North-west England circa 1760–1830', *Social History* 19 (1994), pp. 339–58.

Pooley, C., 'Residential Differentiation in Victorian Cities: A Reassessment', *Transactions, Institute of British Geographers* 9 (1984), pp. 131–44.

Poovey, M., *Uneven Developments: The Ideological Work of Gender in Mid-Victorian England* (London: Virago, 1989).

Porter, R., 'The Gift Relation: Philanthropy and Provincial Hospitals in Eighteenth-Century England', in G. Lindsay and R. Porter (eds), *The Hospital in History* (London: Routledge, 1989), pp. 149–78.

Prior, M., 'Women and the Urban Economy of Oxford 1500–1800', in M. Prior (ed.), *Women in English Society 1500–1800* (London: Methuen, 1985).

Raison-Jourde, F., *La colonie auvergnate de Paris au XIXᵉ Siècle* (Paris: Ville de Paris, Commission des Travaux Historiques, 1976).

Rappaport, E., *Shopping for Pleasure: Gender, Commerce and Public Life in London's West End, 1860–1914* (Princeton: Princeton University Press, 1999).

Reed, M., 'The Peasantry of Nineteenth-Century England: A Neglected Case?', *History Workshop Journal* 18 (1984), pp. 53–71.

Reed, M., 'Nineteenth-Century Rural England: a Case for "Peasant studies"?', *Journal of Peasant Studies* 14 (1986–87), pp. 78–99.

Riden, P., *Probate Records and the Local Community* (Gloucester: Alan Sutton, 1985).

Riley, D. 'Wealth and Social Structure in North-Western Lancashire in the Later Seventeenth Century: A New Use for Probate Inventories', *Transactions, Historic Society of Lancashire and Cheshire* 141 (1992), pp. 77–100.

Rogers, N., 'Introduction – Making the English Middle Class, ca. 1700–1850', *Journal of British Studies* 32 (1993), pp. 299–304.

Royle, S., '"The Spiritual Destitution is Excessive – the Poverty Overwhelming": Hinckley in the Mid-Nineteenth Century', *Transactions of the Leicestershire Archaeological and Historical Society* (1978–79), pp. 51–60.

Royle, S., 'Functional Divergence: Urban Development in Eighteenth and Nineteenth Century Leicestershire', Leicester University Geography Department Occasional Paper, 3 (1981).

Rubinstein, W. D., 'Wealth, Elites and the Class Structure of Modern Britain', *Past and Present* 76 (1976), pp. 99–126.

Rubinstein, W. D., 'The Victorian Middle Classes: Wealth, Occupation and Geography', *Economic History Review* 2nd Series, 30 (1977), pp. 602–23.

Rubinstein, W. D., *Men of Property: The Very Wealthy in Britain Since the Industrial Revolution* (London: Croom Helm, 1981).

Rubinstein, W. D., *Elites and the Wealthy in Modern British History* (Brighton: Harvester, 1987).

Rubinstein, W. D., 'The Structure of Wealth-Holding in Britain 1809–39: a Preliminary Anatomy', *Historical Research* 65 (1992), pp. 74–89.

Rubinstein, W. D., 'Cutting up Rich: a Reply to F. M. L. Thompson', *Economic History Review* 45 (1992), pp. 350–61

Rubinstein, W. D., *Capitalism, Culture and Decline in Britain 1750–1990* (London: Routledge, 1993).

Rubinstein, W. D., 'Businessmen into Landowners: The Question Revisited', in N. Harte and R. Quinault (eds), *Land and Society in Britain, 1700–1914* (Manchester: Manchester University Press, 1996), pp. 90–118.

Rubinstein, W. D. and Duman, D., 'Probate Valuations: a Tool for the Historian' *Local Historian* XI (1974), pp. 68–71.

Rule, J., 'The Property of Skill in the Period of Manufacture', in P. Joyce (ed.), *The Historical Meanings of Work* (Cambridge: Cambridge University Press, 1987), pp. 99–118.

Sabean, D. *Property, Production and the Family in Neckarhausen, 1700–1870* (Cambridge: Cambridge University Press, 1990).

Sadrin, A., *Parentage and Inheritance in the Novels of Charles Dickens* (Cambridge: Cambridge University Press, 1994).

Savage, M., Barlow, J., Dickens, P., and Fielding, T., *Property, Bureaucracy and Culture: Middle Class Formation in Contemporary Britain* (London: Routledge, 1992).

Schwarz, L., *London in the Age of Industrialization* (Cambridge: Cambridge University Press, 1992).

Scott, W., *The Story of Ashby de la Zouch* (London: George Brown, 1907).

Sewell, W. H., *Work and Revolution in France. The Language of Labour From the Old Regime to 1848* (Cambridge: Cambridge University Press, 1980).

Shammas, C., *The Pre-industrial Consumer in England and America* (Oxford: Oxford University Press, 1990).

Sked, S., 'Women Teachers and the Expansion of Girls' Schooling in England, c. 1760–1820', in H. Barker and E. Chalus (eds), *Gender in the Eighteenth Century* (London: Longman, 1997), pp. 81–100.

Somers, M. R., 'The "Misteries" of Property. Rationality, Rural-Industrialization, and Community in Chartist Narratives of Political Rights', in J. Brewer and S. Staves (eds), *Early Modern Conceptions of Property* (London: Routledge, 1995), pp. 62–92.

Spring, E., *Law, Land and Family: Aristocratic Inheritance in England 1300–1800* (Chapel Hill: University of North Carolina Press, 1990).

Spufford, M., 'The Limitations of the Probate Inventory', in J. Chartres and D. Hey (eds), *English Rural Society, 1500–1800* (Cambridge: Cambridge University Press, 1990), pp. 139–74.

Staves, S., *Married Women's Separate Property in England 1660–1833* (Cambridge Mass.: Harvard University Press, 1990).

Staves, S., 'Resentment or Resignation? Dividing the Spoils Among Daughters and Younger Sons' in J. Brewer and S. Staves (eds), *Early Modern Conceptions of Property* (London: Routledge, 1995), pp. 194–218.

Steinberg, M. W., 'Culturally Speaking: Finding a Commons Between Post-Structuralism and the Thompsonian Perspective', *Social History* 21 (1996), pp. 193–214.

Stone, L. and Stone, J. C., *An Open Elite?* (Oxford: Clarendon Press, 1984).

Stone, L., *The Family, Sex and Marriage in England, 1500–1800* (New York: Harper and Row, 1977).

Styles, J., 'Manufacture, Consumption and Design in Eighteenth-Century England, in J. Brewer and R. Porter (eds), *Consumption and the World of Goods* (London: Routledge, 1993), pp. 527–54.

Summerson, J., *Georgian London* (London: Pleiades, 1945).

Sutton, P. C., *Masters of Seventeenth Century Dutch Genre Painting: Exhibition Catalogue* (Royal Academy of Arts and Philadelphia Museum of Art, 1984).

Tadmor, N., 'The Concept of the Household-Family in Eighteenth-century England', *Past and Present* 151 (1996), pp. 111–40.

Te Brake, W., *Regents and Rebels. The Revolutionary World of an Eighteenth-Century Dutch City* (Oxford: Basil Blackwell, 1989).

Thirsk, J., 'Agrarian History 1540–1950', in W. G. Hoskins and R. M. McKinley (eds), *The Victoria County History of Leicestershire*, II (Oxford: Oxford University Press, 1954), pp. 199–264.

Thompson, E. P., *The Making of the English Working Class* (Harmondsworth: Penguin, 1963)

Thompson, F. M. L., 'Business and Landed Elites in the Nineteenth Century', in *idem* (ed.), *Landowners, Capitalists and Entrepreneurs* (Oxford: Clarendon Press, 1994), pp. 139–170.

Thompson, F. M. L. (ed.), *Landowners, Capitalists and Entrepreneurs: Essays for Sir John Habakkuk* (Oxford: Clarendon Press, 1994).

Thrift, N. and Glennie, P., 'Historical Geographies of Urban Life and Modern Consumption', in G. Kearns and C. Philo (eds), *Selling Places: The City as Cultural Capital, Past and Present* (Oxford: Pergamon Press, 1993), pp. 33–48.

Tittler, R., 'Money-Lending in the West Midlands: the Activities of Joyce Jeffries 1638–49, *Historical Research* 67 (1994), pp. 249–63.

Turner, E. (ed.), 'The Marchant Diary, 1714–28', *Sussex Archaeological Collection* 25 (1873), pp. 1–11.

Van den Eeckhout, P., "Brussels", in M. Daunton (ed.), *Housing the Workers, 1850–1914. A Comparative Perspective* (Leicester: Leicester University Press, 1990), pp. 67–106.

Van Molle, L., *Chacun pour tous. Le Boerenbond belge 1890–1990* (Leuven: Universitaire pers Leuven, 1990).

Vann, R., 'Wills and the Family in an English Town: Banbury, 1550–1800, *Journal of Family History* 4 (1979), pp. 346–67.

Vickery, A., 'Golden Age to Separate Spheres: A Review of the Categories and Chronology of English Women's History', *Historical Journal* 36 (1993), pp. 383–414.

Vickery, A., 'Women and the World of Goods: a Lancashire Consumer and her Possessions, 1751–81', in J. Brewer and R. Porter (eds), *Consumption and the World of Goods* (London: Routledge, 1993), pp. 274–301.

Vickery, A., *The Gentleman's Daughter* (Boston: Yale University Press, 1998).

Volkov, S., *The Rise of Popular Antimodernism in Germany: The Urban Master Artisans 1873–1896* (Princeton: Princeton University Press, 1978).

Wadsworth, A. and Mann, J. de L., *The Cotton Trade in Lancashire, 1600–1780* (Manchester: Manchester University Press, 1931).

Wahrman, D., *Imagining the Middle Class: The Political Representation of Class in England, 1780–1840* (Cambridge: Cambridge University Press, 1995).

Walker, M., *German Home Towns. Community, State, and General Estate 1648–1871* (Ithaca: Cornell University Press, 1971).

Walkowitz, J., *City of Dreadful Delight* (London: Virago Press, 1992).

Walsh, A., *Statistics for the Social Sciences* (New York: Harper Row, 1990).

Watson, J., *A Treatise on the Law of Scotland Respecting Succession Depending on Deeds of Settlement* (Edinburgh: Bell and Bradfute, 1826).

Weatherill, L., 'A Possession of One's Own: Women and consumer behaviour 1660–1740', *Journal of British Studies* 25 (1986), pp. 132–56.

Weatherill, L., 'The Growth of the Pottery Industry in England, 1660 to 1815', unpublished PhD thesis, London School of Economics, University of London, 1982.

Weatherill, L., 'Consumer Behaviour and Social Status in England, 1660–1750', *Continuity and Change* 2 (1986), pp. 191–216.

Weatherill, L., 'The Business of Middleman in the English Pottery Trade before 1780', *Business History* 28 (1986), pp. 51–76.

Weatherill, L., *Consumer Behaviour and Material Culture, 1660–1760* (London: Routledge, 1988 and 1996).

Weatherill, L., 'The Meaning of Consumer Behaviour in Late Seventeenth- and Early Eighteenth-Century England', in J. Brewer and R. Porter (eds), *Consumption and the World of Goods* (London: Routledge, 1993), pp. 206–27.

Weatherill, L. (ed.), 'The Account Book of Richard Latham, 1724–1767', *British Academy Records of Social and Economic History*, NS 15 (1990).

Weber, M., 'Class, Status and Power', in H. Gerth and C. W. Mills (eds), *From Max Weber: Essays in Sociology* (London: Routledge, 1991), pp. 180–95.

Wedgwood, J., *The Economics of Inheritance* (Harmondsworth: Penguin, 1939).

Wells, F. W., *The British Hosiery and Knitwear Industry* (Newton Abbot: David and Charles, 1972).

Wilenski, R. H., *Flemish Painters, 1430–1830* (London: Faber and Faber, 1960).

Wilentz, S., *Chants Democratic. New York City and the Rise of the American Working Class, 1788–1850* (New York and Oxford: Oxford University Press, 1984).

Williams, P., 'Constituting Class and Gender: A Social History of the Home, 1700–1901', in N. Thrift and P. Williams (eds), *Class and Space: The Making of Urban Society* (London: Routledge and Keegan Paul, 1987), pp. 166–76.

Williams, R., *Dream Worlds: Mass Consumption in Late Nineteenth-Century France* (Berkeley: University of California Press, 1982).

Winstanley, M., 'Industrialization and the Small Farm: Family and Household Economy in Nineteenth-Century Lancashire', *Past and Present* 152 (1996), pp. 157–95.

Winstanley, M., 'Owners and Occupiers: Property, Politics and Middle-Class Formation in Early Industrial Lancashire', in A. Kidd and D. Nicholls (eds), *The Making of the British Middle Class? Studies of Regional and Cultural Diversity since the Eighteenth Century* (Stroud: Sutton, 1998), pp. 92–112.

Witte, E. and Craeybecks, J., *La Belgique politique de 1830 à nos jours* (Brussels: Editions Labor, 1987).

Wolloch, I., *The New Regime. Transformations of the French Civic Order, 1789–1820s* (New York: W. W. Norton, 1994).

Wright, S., 'Holding Up Half the Sky: Women and their Occupations in Eighteenth Ludlow', *Midland History* 14 (1989), pp. 53–74.

Wrightson, K. and Levine, D., *Poverty and Piety in an English Village: Terling 1525–1700* (2nd edn, Oxford: Oxford University Press, 1995).

Wykes, D., 'Sources for a Study of Leicester Trade and Industry, 1660–1835', *Business Archives* 45 (1979), pp. 7–17.

Young, C., 'Financing the Micro-scale Enterprise: Rural Craft Producers in Scotland, 1840–1914', *Business History Review* 69 (1995), pp. 398–421.

Index